STEED and Mrs PEEL

A VERY CIVIL ARMAGEDDON

BOOM! STUDIOS

ROSS RICHIE Chief Executive Officer • MATT GAGNON Editor-in-Chief • FILIP SABLIK VP-Publishing & Marketing • LANCE KREITER VP-Licensing & Merchandising • PHIL BARBARO Director of Finance • BRYCE CARLSON Managing Editor • DAFNA PLEBAN Editor • SHANNON WATTERS Editor • ERIC HARBURN Editor • CHRIS ROSA Assistant Editor • STEPHANIE GONZAGA Graphic Designer • JASMINE AMIRI Operations Coordinator • DEVIN FUNCHES E-Commerce & Inventory Coordinator • BRIANNA HART Executive Assistant

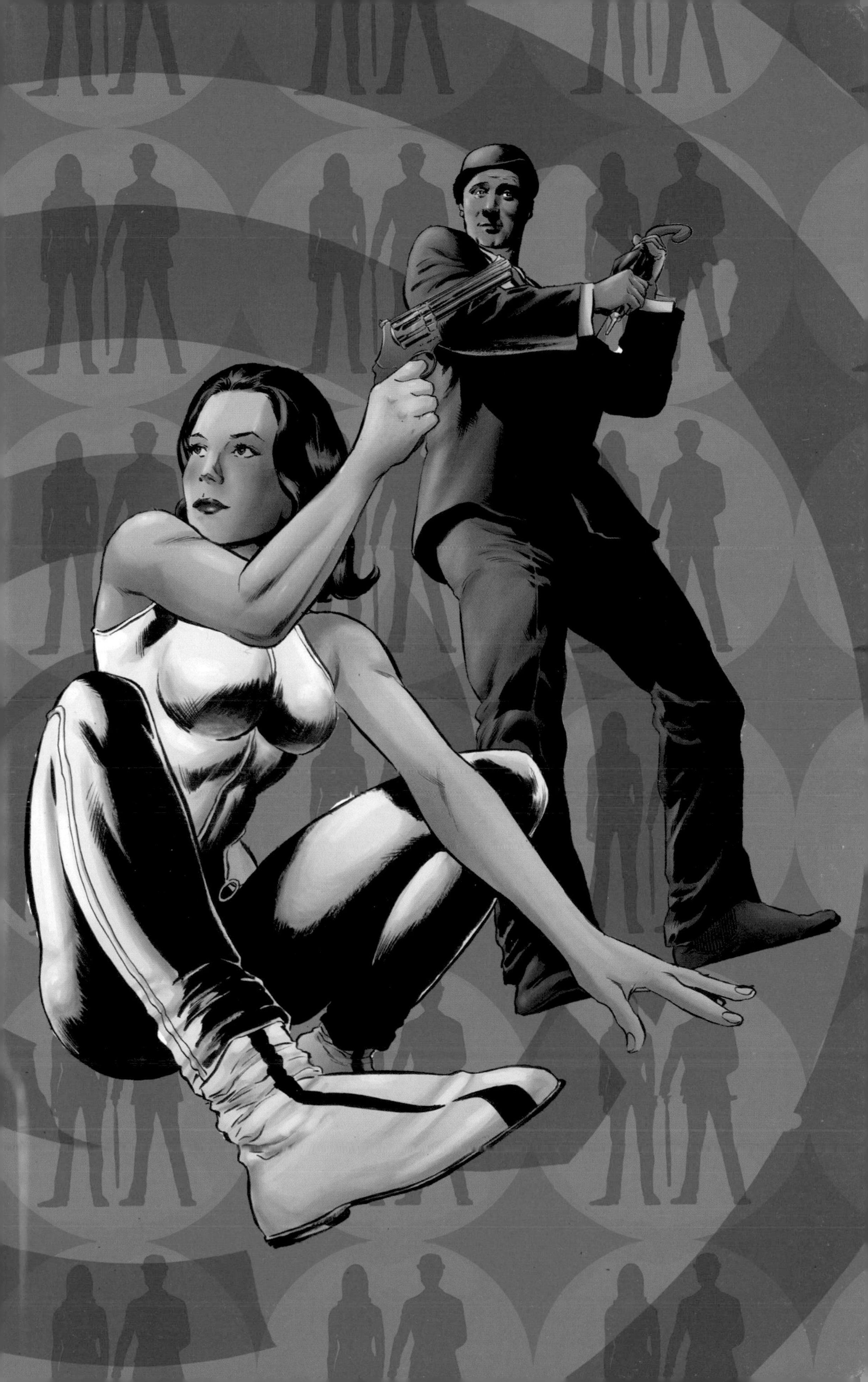

A VERY CIVIL ARMAGEDDON
PROLOGUE

Written by
MARK WAID

Art by
STEVE BRYANT

Colors by
RON RILEY

Letters by
STEVE WANDS

CHAPTERS 1-3

Story by
MARK WAID

Script by
CALEB MONROE

Art by
WILL SLINEY

Colors by
RON RILEY

Letters by
ED DUKESHIRE

Cover by
JOSEPH MICHAEL LINSNER

Assistant Editor
CHRIS ROSA

Editor
MATT GAGNON

Trade Design
KASSANDRA HELLER

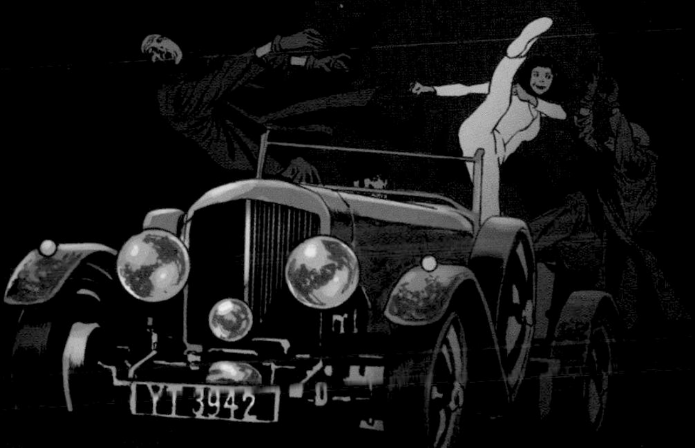

YT 3942

PROLOGUE

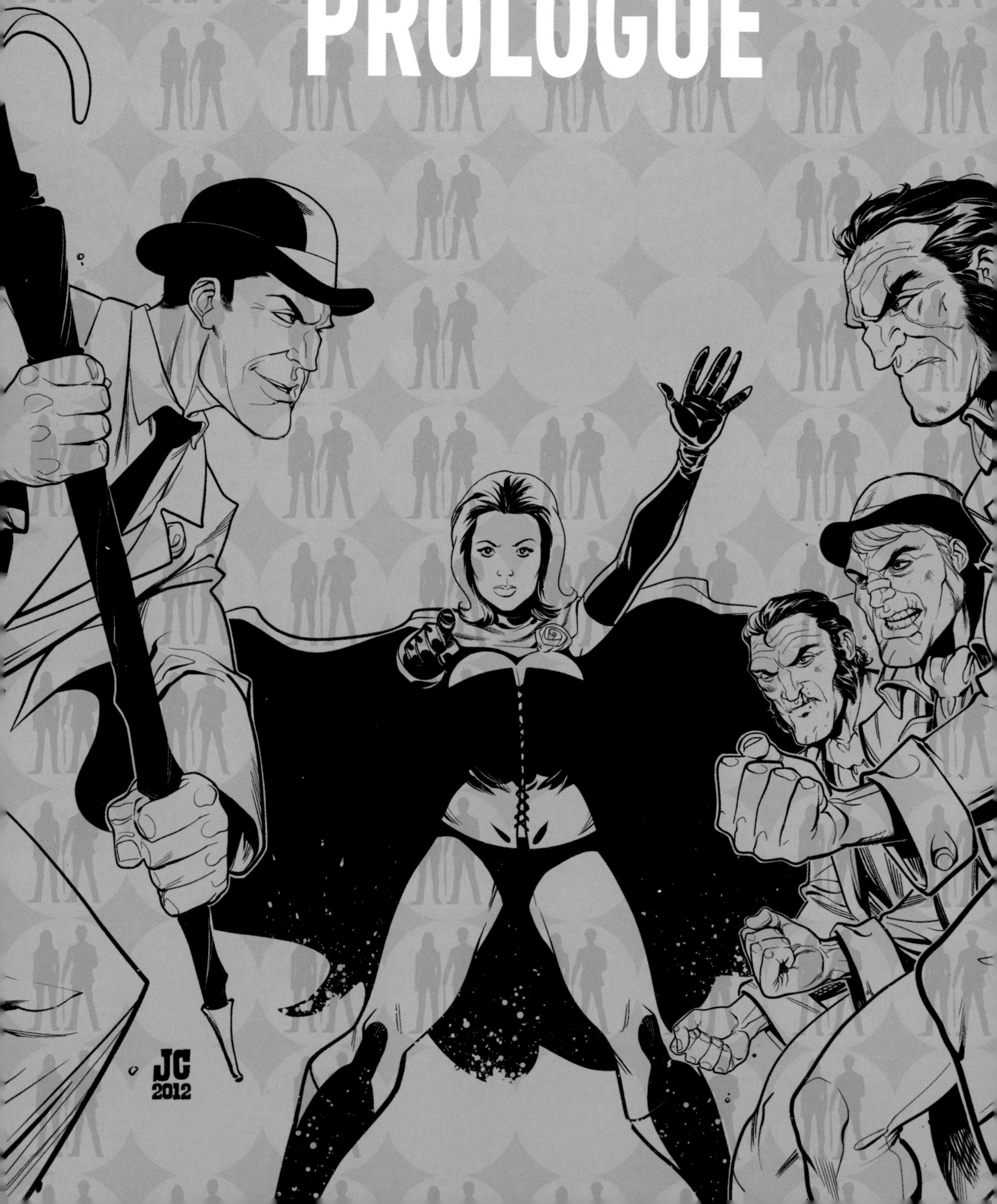
JC
2012

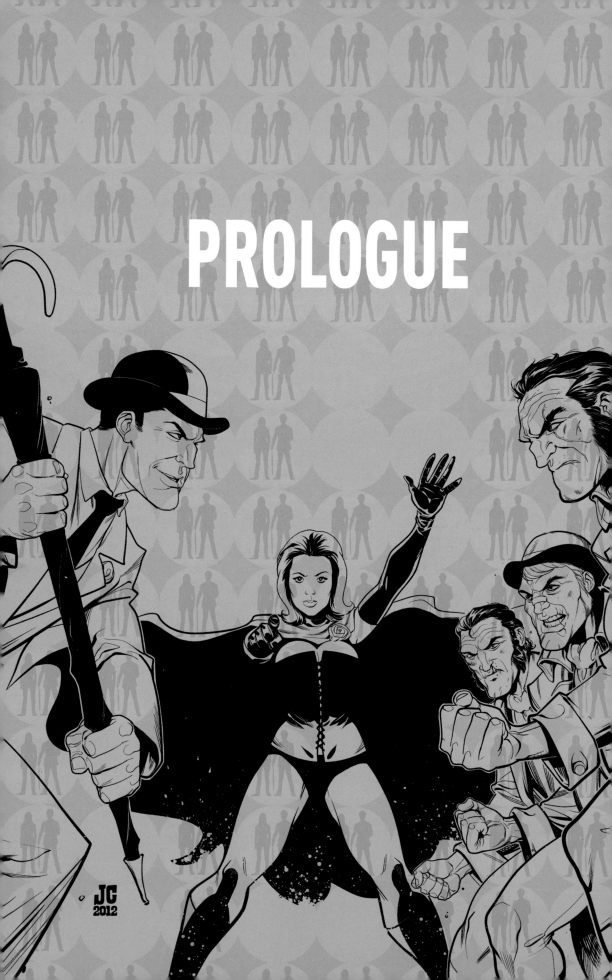

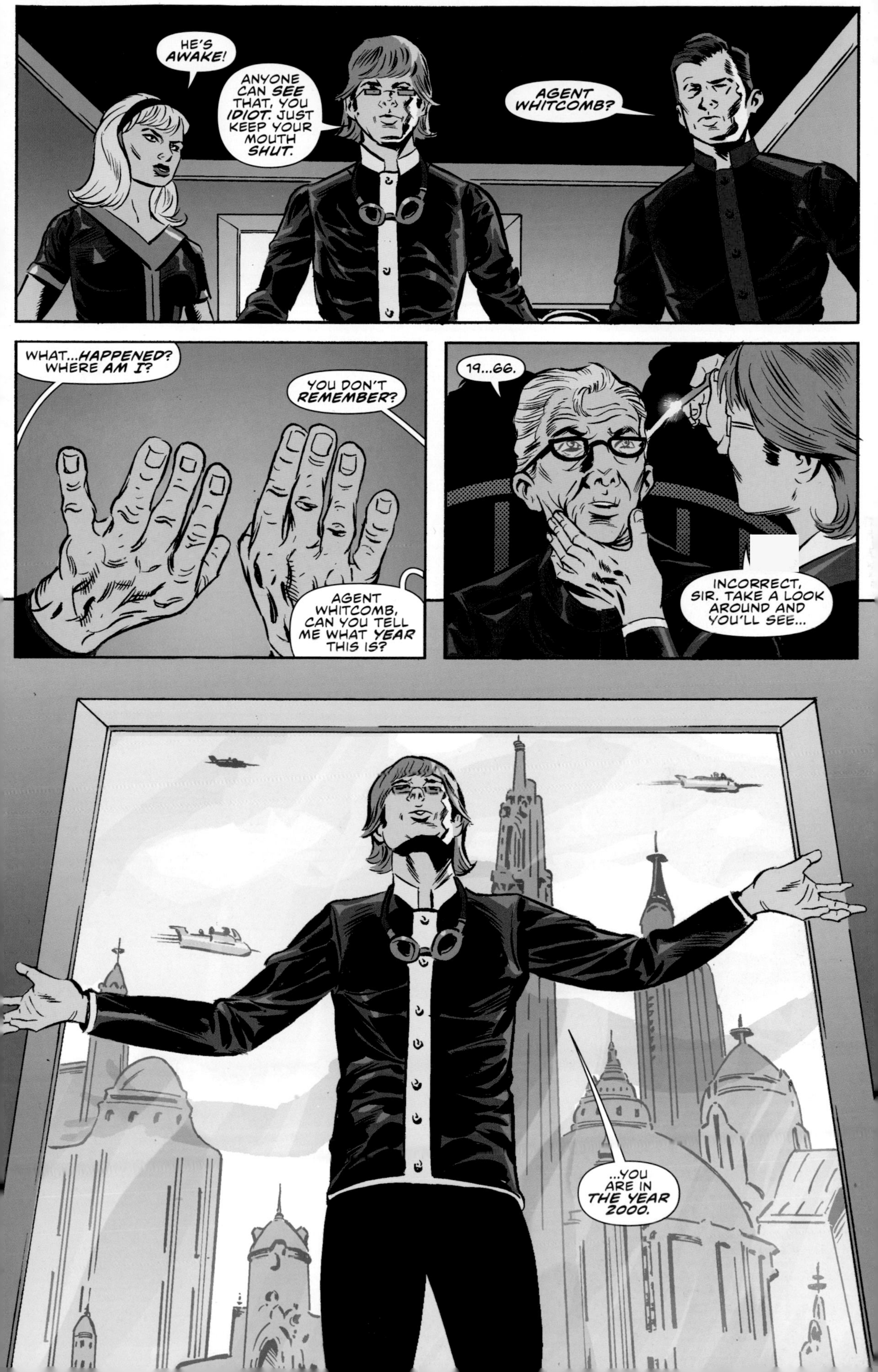
HE'S AWAKE!
ANYONE CAN SEE THAT, YOU IDIOT. JUST KEEP YOUR MOUTH SHUT.
AGENT WHITCOMB?
WHAT...HAPPENED? WHERE AM I?
YOU DON'T REMEMBER?
AGENT WHITCOMB, CAN YOU TELL ME WHAT YEAR THIS IS?
19...66.
INCORRECT, SIR. TAKE A LOOK AROUND AND YOU'LL SEE...
...YOU ARE IN THE YEAR 2000.

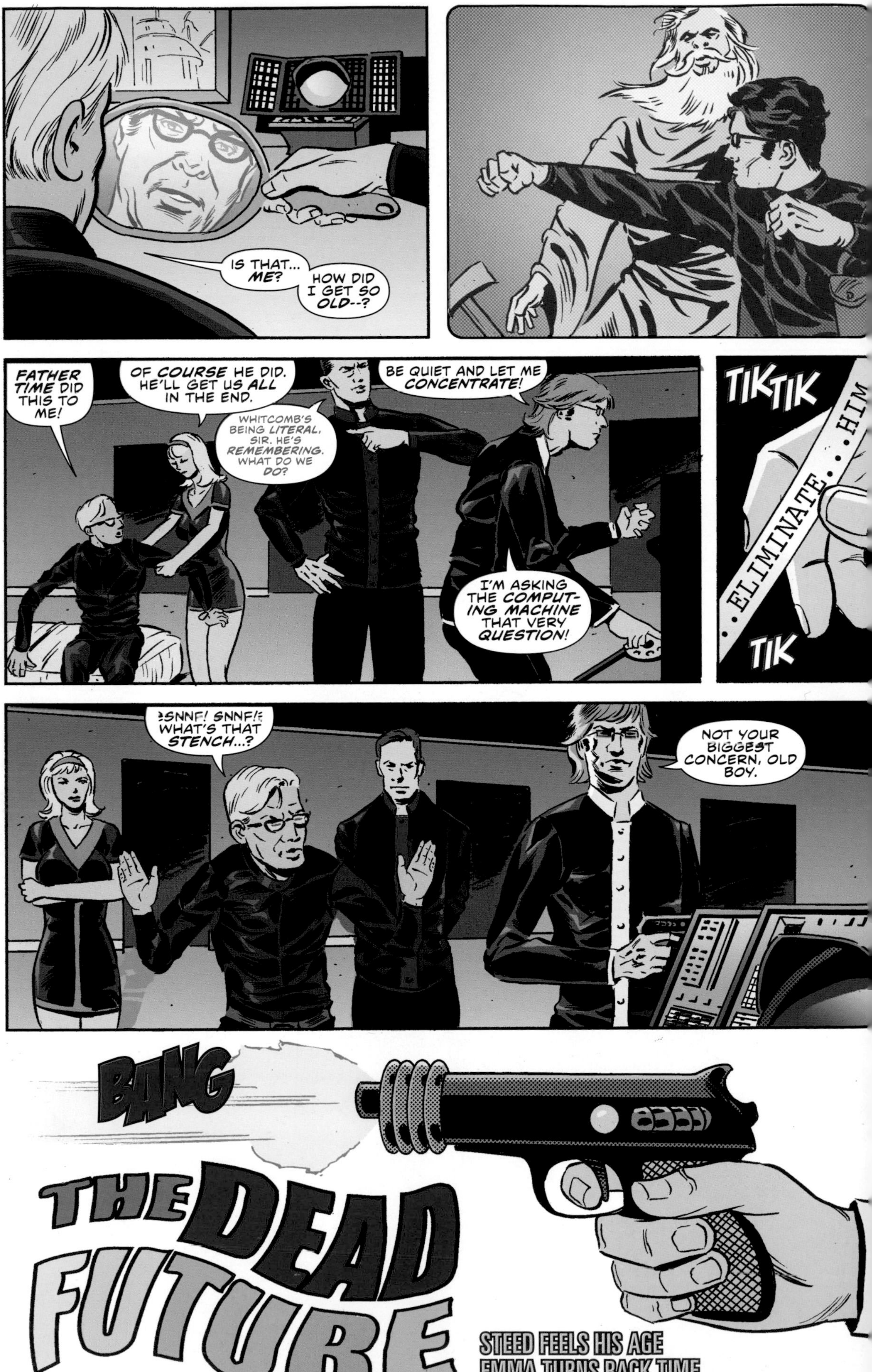

IS THAT... ME?
HOW DID I GET SO OLD--?
FATHER TIME DID THIS TO ME!
OF COURSE HE DID. HE'LL GET US ALL IN THE END.
WHITCOMB'S BEING LITERAL, SIR. HE'S REMEMBERING. WHAT DO WE DO?
BE QUIET AND LET ME CONCENTRATE!
I'M ASKING THE COMPUTING MACHINE THAT VERY QUESTION!
TIK TIK
. . ELIMINATE . . . HIM
TIK
SNNF! SNNF! WHAT'S THAT STENCH...?
NOT YOUR BIGGEST CONCERN, OLD BOY.
BANG
THE DEAD FUTURE
STEED FEELS HIS AGE
EMMA TURNS BACK TIME

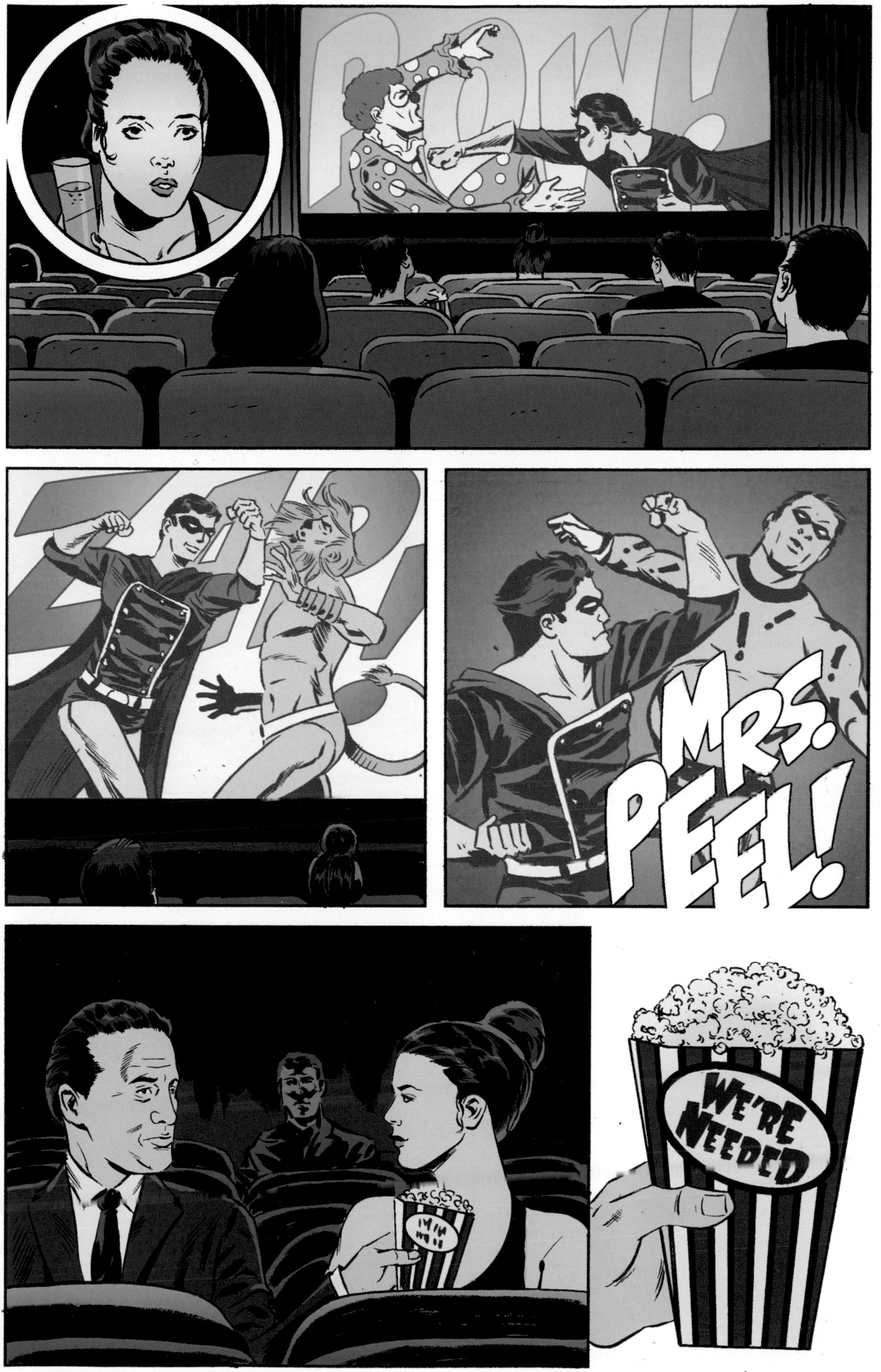
POW!
MRS. PEEL!
WE'RE NEEDED

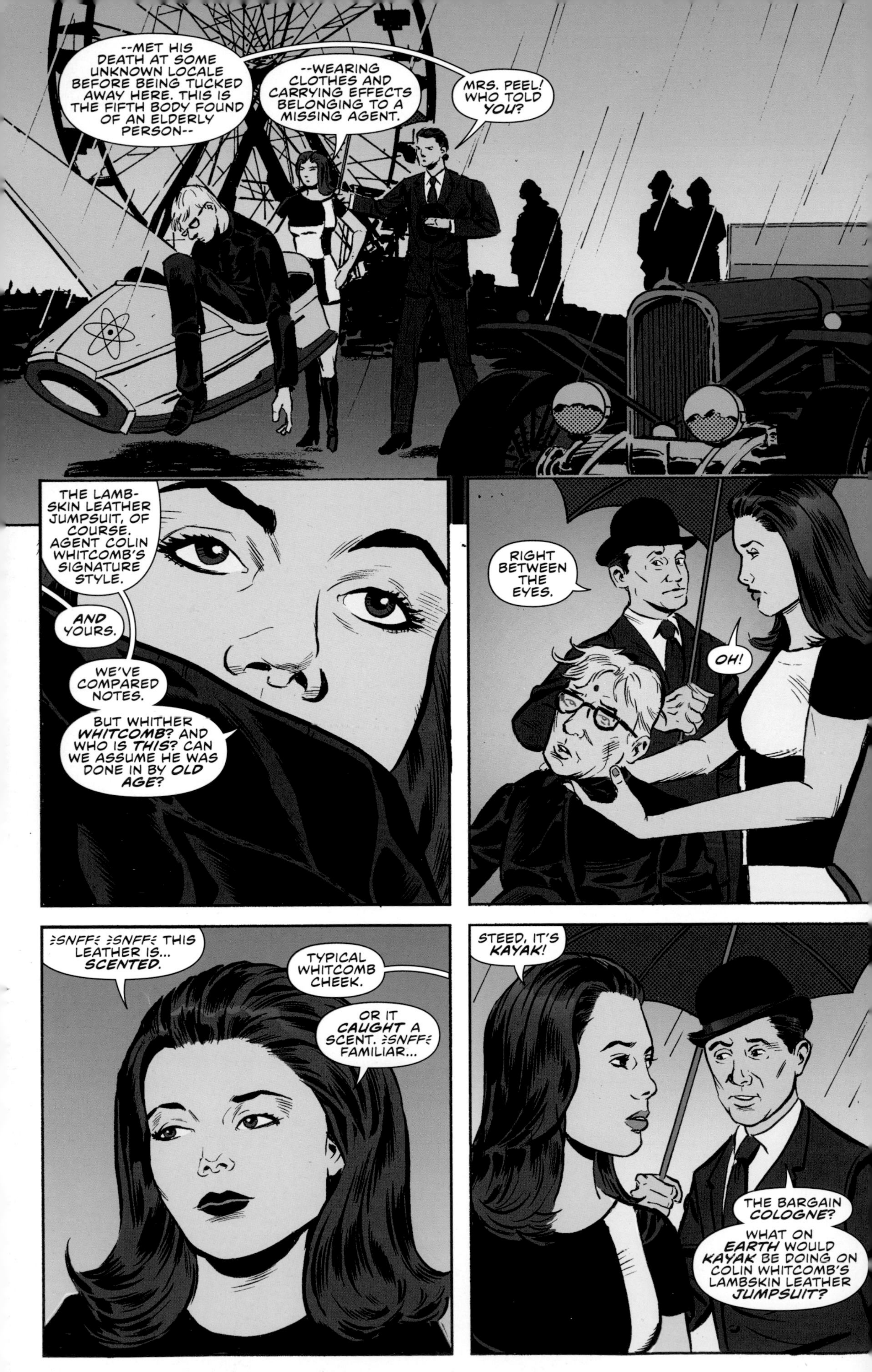
--MET HIS DEATH AT SOME UNKNOWN LOCALE BEFORE BEING TUCKED AWAY HERE. THIS IS THE FIFTH BODY FOUND OF AN ELDERLY PERSON--
--WEARING CLOTHES AND CARRYING EFFECTS BELONGING TO A MISSING AGENT.
MRS. PEEL! WHO TOLD YOU?
THE LAMB-SKIN LEATHER JUMPSUIT, OF COURSE. AGENT COLIN WHITCOMB'S SIGNATURE STYLE.
AND YOURS.
WE'VE COMPARED NOTES.
BUT WHITHER WHITCOMB? AND WHO IS THIS? CAN WE ASSUME HE WAS DONE IN BY OLD AGE?
RIGHT BETWEEN THE EYES.
OH!
SNFF SNFF THIS LEATHER IS... SCENTED.
TYPICAL WHITCOMB CHEEK.
OR IT CAUGHT A SCENT. SNFF FAMILIAR...
STEED, IT'S KAYAK!
THE BARGAIN COLOGNE?
WHAT ON EARTH WOULD KAYAK BE DOING ON COLIN WHITCOMB'S LAMBSKIN LEATHER JUMPSUIT?

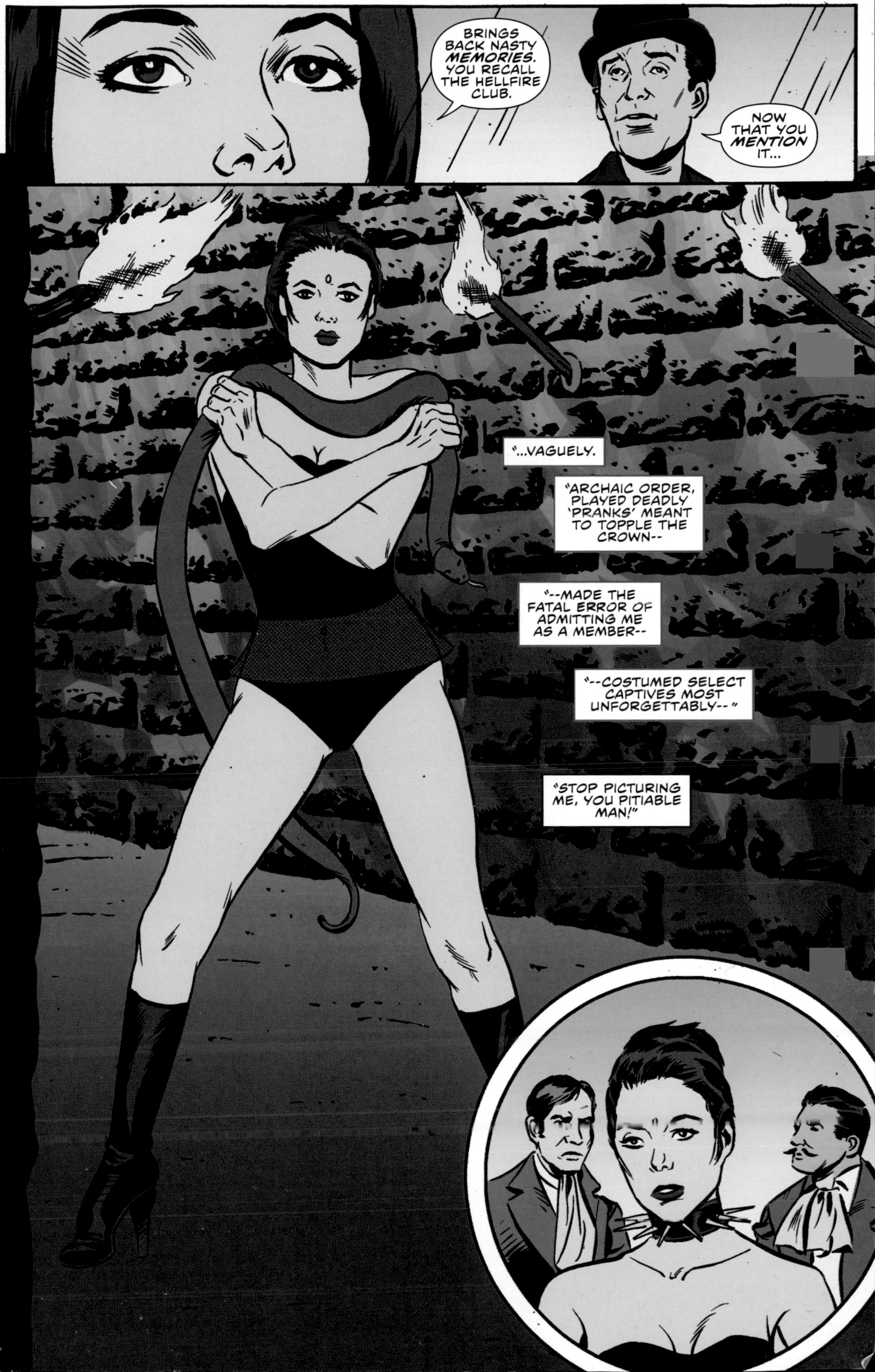
BRINGS BACK NASTY MEMORIES. YOU RECALL THE HELLFIRE CLUB.
NOW THAT YOU MENTION IT...
"...VAGUELY.
"ARCHAIC ORDER, PLAYED DEADLY 'PRANKS' MEANT TO TOPPLE THE CROWN--
"--MADE THE FATAL ERROR OF ADMITTING ME AS A MEMBER--
"--COSTUMED SELECT CAPTIVES MOST UNFORGETTABLY--"
"STOP PICTURING ME, YOU PITIABLE MAN!"

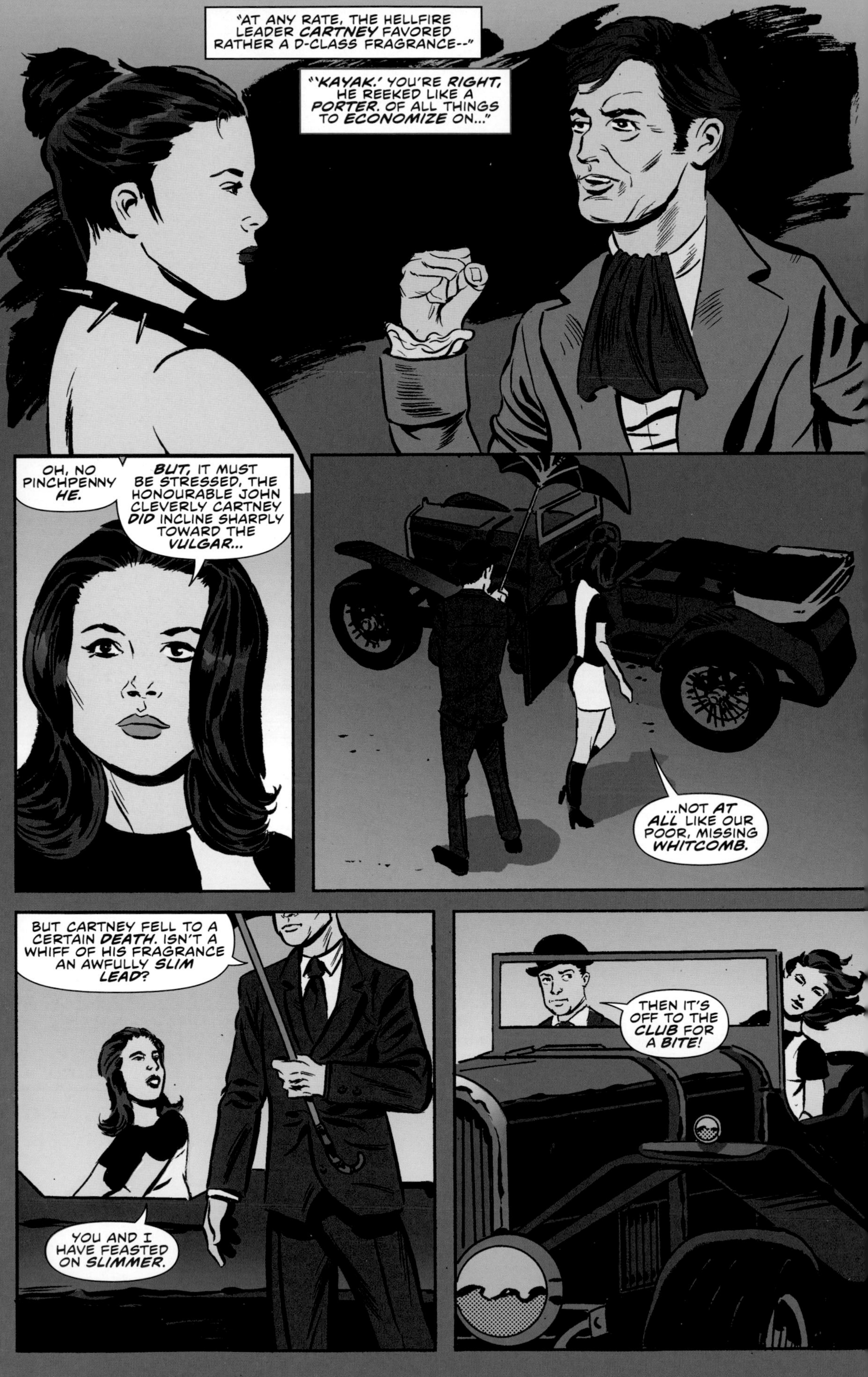
"AT ANY RATE, THE HELLFIRE LEADER CARTNEY FAVORED RATHER A D-CLASS FRAGRANCE--"
"'KAYAK.' YOU'RE RIGHT, HE REEKED LIKE A PORTER. OF ALL THINGS TO ECONOMIZE ON..."
OH, NO PINCHPENNY HE.
BUT, IT MUST BE STRESSED, THE HONOURABLE JOHN CLEVERLY CARTNEY DID INCLINE SHARPLY TOWARD THE VULGAR...
...NOT AT ALL LIKE OUR POOR, MISSING WHITCOMB.
BUT CARTNEY FELL TO A CERTAIN DEATH. ISN'T A WHIFF OF HIS FRAGRANCE AN AWFULLY SLIM LEAD?
YOU AND I HAVE FEASTED ON SLIMMER.
THEN IT'S OFF TO THE CLUB FOR A BITE!

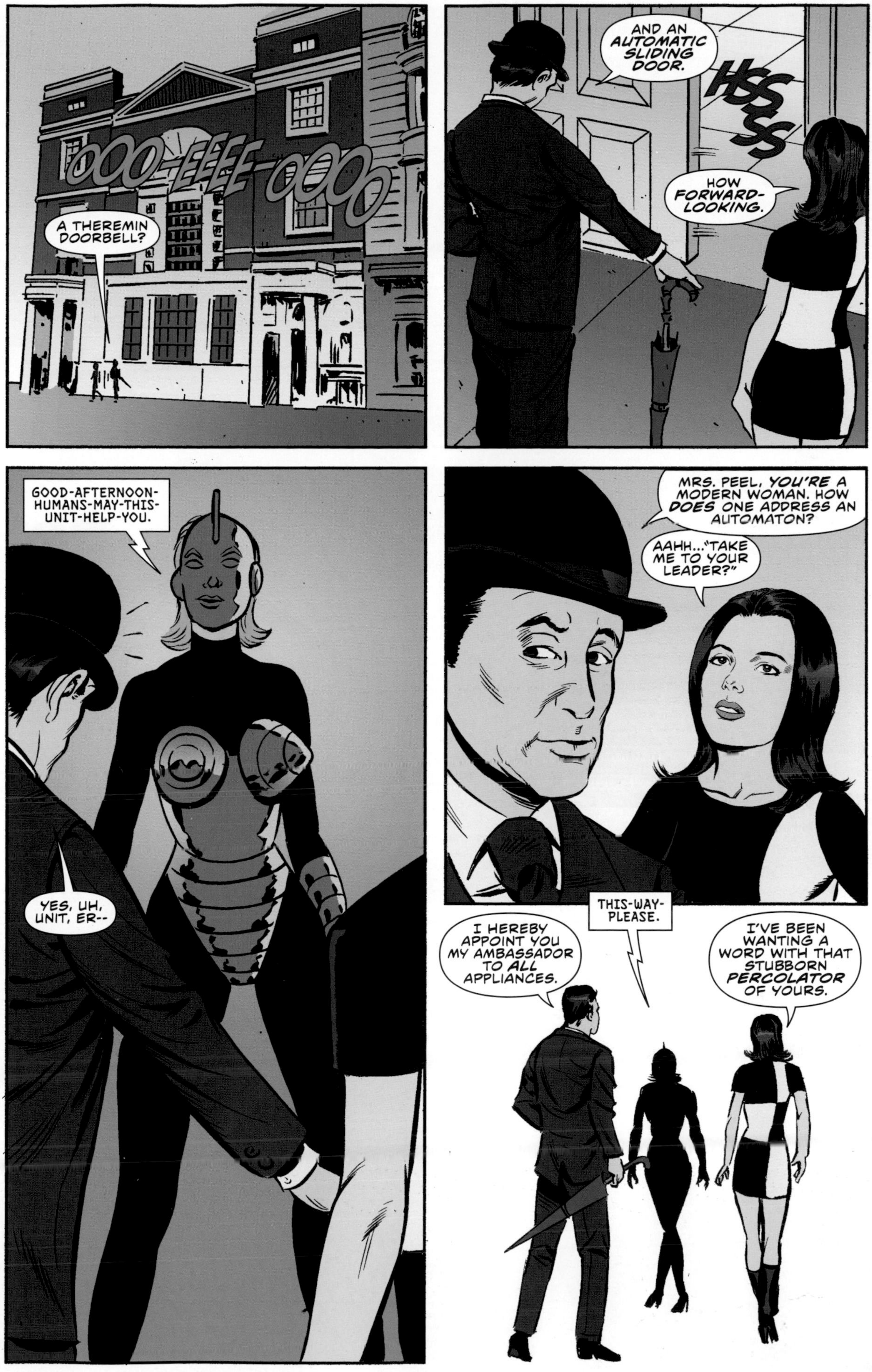
OOO-EEEE-OOOO
A THEREMIN DOORBELL?
AND AN AUTOMATIC SLIDING DOOR.
HSSSS
HOW FORWARD-LOOKING.
GOOD-AFTERNOON-HUMANS-MAY-THIS-UNIT-HELP-YOU.
YES, UH, UNIT, ER--
MRS. PEEL, YOU'RE A MODERN WOMAN. HOW DOES ONE ADDRESS AN AUTOMATON?
AAHH..."TAKE ME TO YOUR LEADER?"
I HEREBY APPOINT YOU MY AMBASSADOR TO ALL APPLIANCES.
THIS-WAY-PLEASE.
I'VE BEEN WANTING A WORD WITH THAT STUBBORN PERCOLATOR OF YOURS.

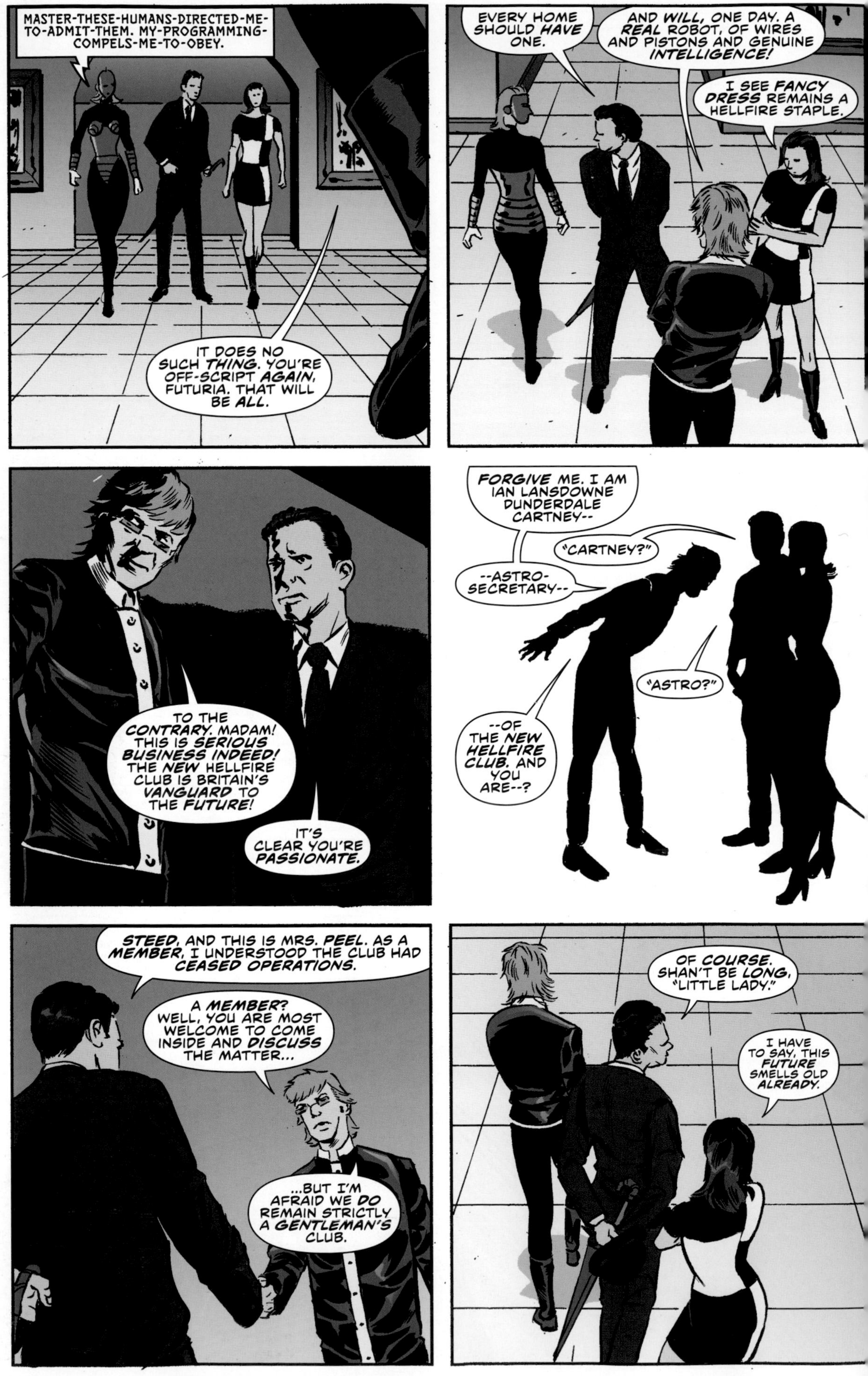
MASTER-THESE-HUMANS-DIRECTED-ME-TO-ADMIT-THEM. MY-PROGRAMMING-COMPELS-ME-TO-OBEY.
IT DOES NO SUCH THING. YOU'RE OFF-SCRIPT AGAIN, FUTURIA. THAT WILL BE ALL.
EVERY HOME SHOULD HAVE ONE.
AND WILL, ONE DAY. A REAL ROBOT, OF WIRES AND PISTONS AND GENUINE INTELLIGENCE!
I SEE FANCY DRESS REMAINS A HELLFIRE STAPLE.
TO THE CONTRARY, MADAM! THIS IS SERIOUS BUSINESS INDEED! THE NEW HELLFIRE CLUB IS BRITAIN'S VANGUARD TO THE FUTURE!
IT'S CLEAR YOU'RE PASSIONATE.
FORGIVE ME. I AM IAN LANSDOWNE DUNDERDALE CARTNEY--
"CARTNEY?"
--ASTRO-SECRETARY--
"ASTRO?"
--OF THE NEW HELLFIRE CLUB. AND YOU ARE--?
STEED, AND THIS IS MRS. PEEL. AS A MEMBER, I UNDERSTOOD THE CLUB HAD CEASED OPERATIONS.
A MEMBER? WELL, YOU ARE MOST WELCOME TO COME INSIDE AND DISCUSS THE MATTER...
...BUT I'M AFRAID WE DO REMAIN STRICTLY A GENTLEMAN'S CLUB.
OF COURSE. SHAN'T BE LONG, "LITTLE LADY."
I HAVE TO SAY, THIS FUTURE SMELLS OLD ALREADY.

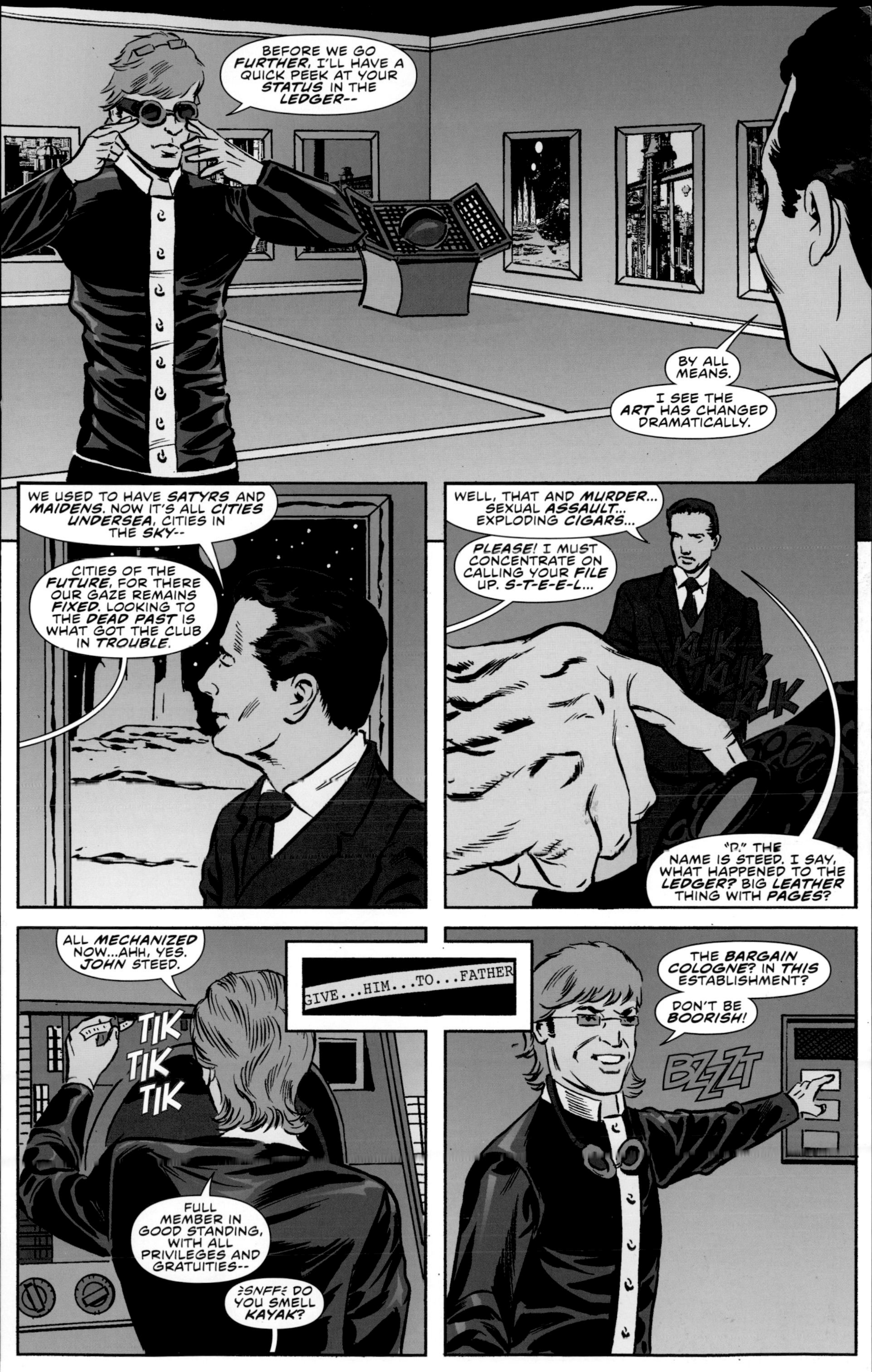

BEFORE WE GO FURTHER, I'LL HAVE A QUICK PEEK AT YOUR STATUS IN THE LEDGER--
BY ALL MEANS.
I SEE THE ART HAS CHANGED DRAMATICALLY.
WE USED TO HAVE SATYRS AND MAIDENS. NOW IT'S ALL CITIES UNDERSEA, CITIES IN THE SKY--
CITIES OF THE FUTURE, FOR THERE OUR GAZE REMAINS FIXED. LOOKING TO THE DEAD PAST IS WHAT GOT THE CLUB IN TROUBLE.
WELL, THAT AND MURDER... SEXUAL ASSAULT... EXPLODING CIGARS...
PLEASE! I MUST CONCENTRATE ON CALLING YOUR FILE UP. S-T-E-E-L...
KLIK KLIK KLIK
"D." THE NAME IS STEED. I SAY, WHAT HAPPENED TO THE LEDGER? BIG LEATHER THING WITH PAGES?
ALL MECHANIZED NOW...AHH, YES. JOHN STEED.
TIK TIK TIK
GIVE...HIM...TO...FATHER
FULL MEMBER IN GOOD STANDING, WITH ALL PRIVILEGES AND GRATUITIES--
SNFF DO YOU SMELL KAYAK?
THE BARGAIN COLOGNE? IN THIS ESTABLISHMENT?
DON'T BE BOORISH!
BZZZT

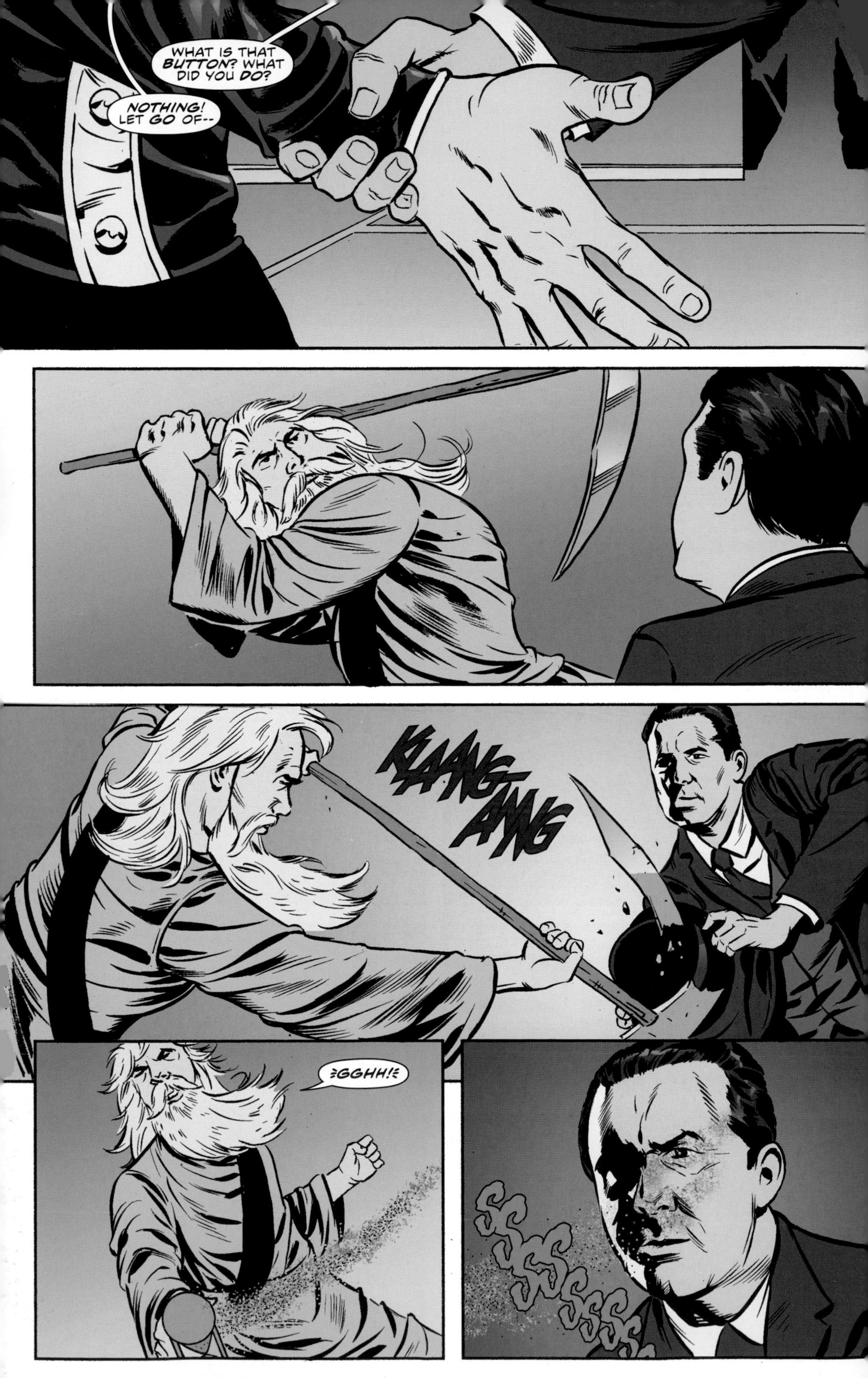
WHAT IS THAT BUTTON? WHAT DID YOU DO?
NOTHING! LET GO OF--
KLAANG-ANG
GGHH!
SSSSSSSSS

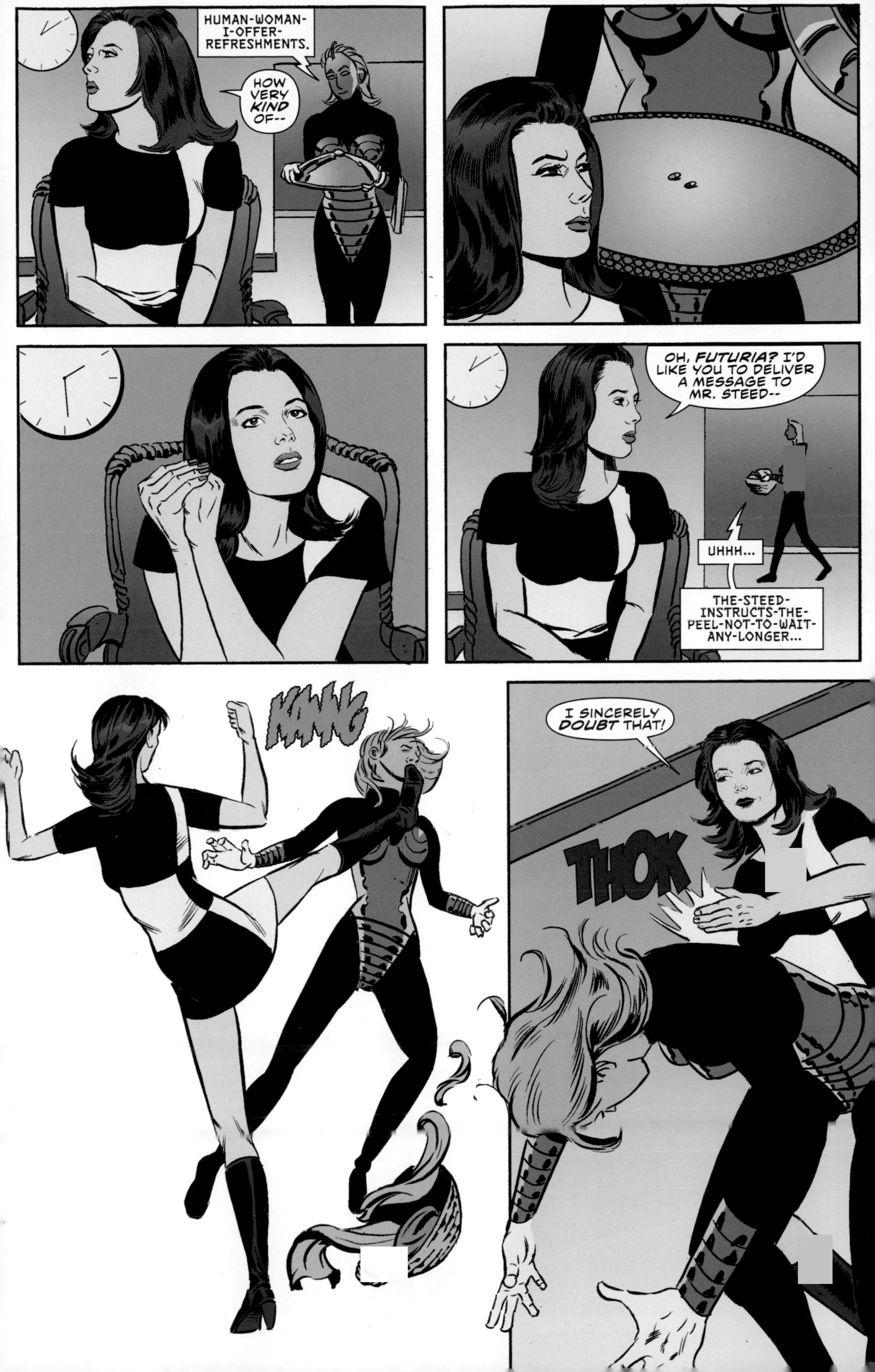
HUMAN-WOMAN-I-OFFER-REFRESHMENTS.
HOW VERY KIND OF--
OH, FUTURIA? I'D LIKE YOU TO DELIVER A MESSAGE TO MR. STEED--
UHHH...
THE-STEED-INSTRUCTS-THE-PEEL-NOT-TO-WAIT-ANY-LONGER...
KANG
I SINCERELY DOUBT THAT!
THOK

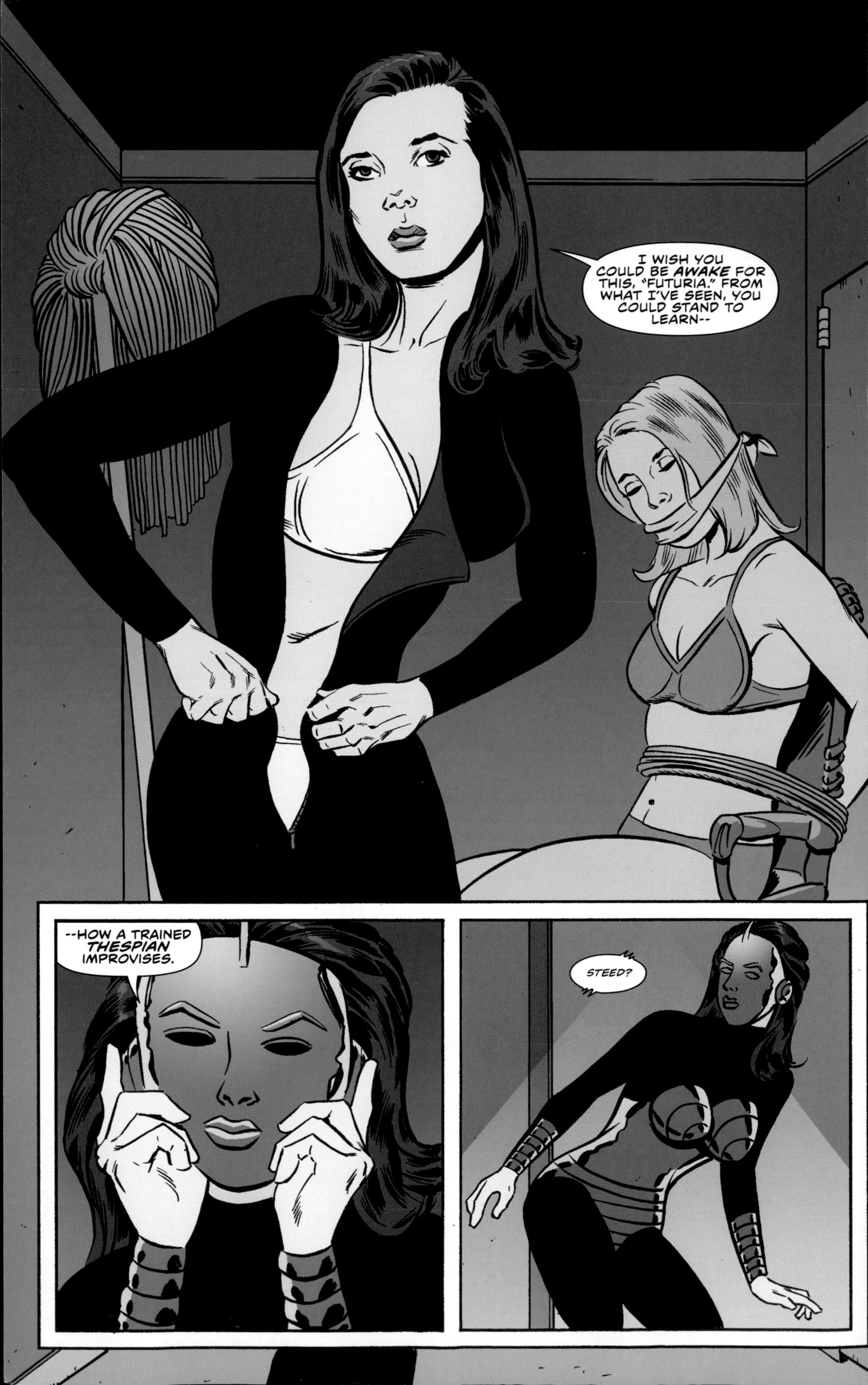
I WISH YOU COULD BE AWAKE FOR THIS, "FUTURIA." FROM WHAT I'VE SEEN, YOU COULD STAND TO LEARN--
--HOW A TRAINED THESPIAN IMPROVISES.
STEED?

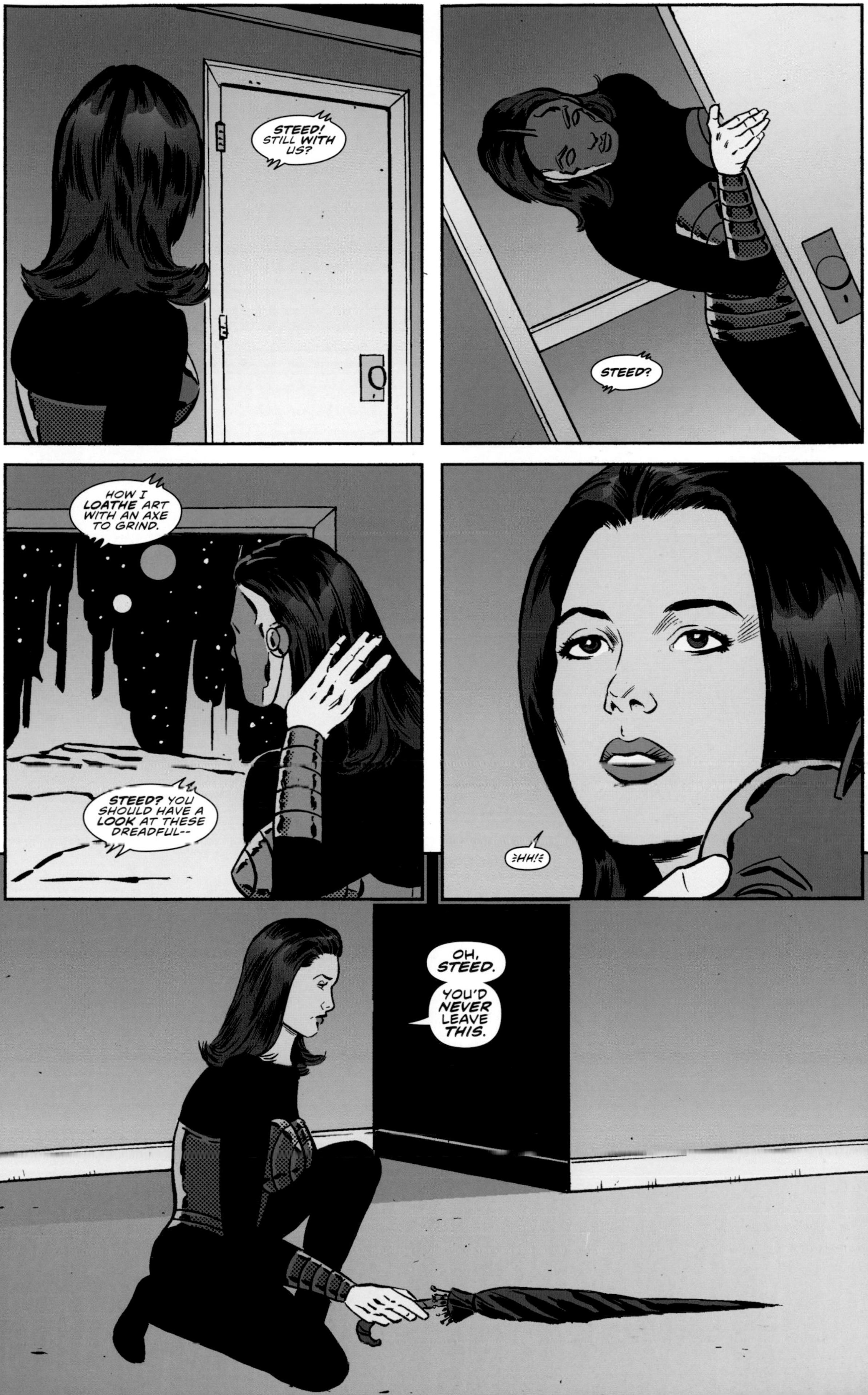
STEED! STILL WITH US?
STEED?
HOW I LOATHE ART WITH AN AXE TO GRIND.
STEED? YOU SHOULD HAVE A LOOK AT THESE DREADFUL--
HH!
OH, STEED.
YOU'D NEVER LEAVE THIS.

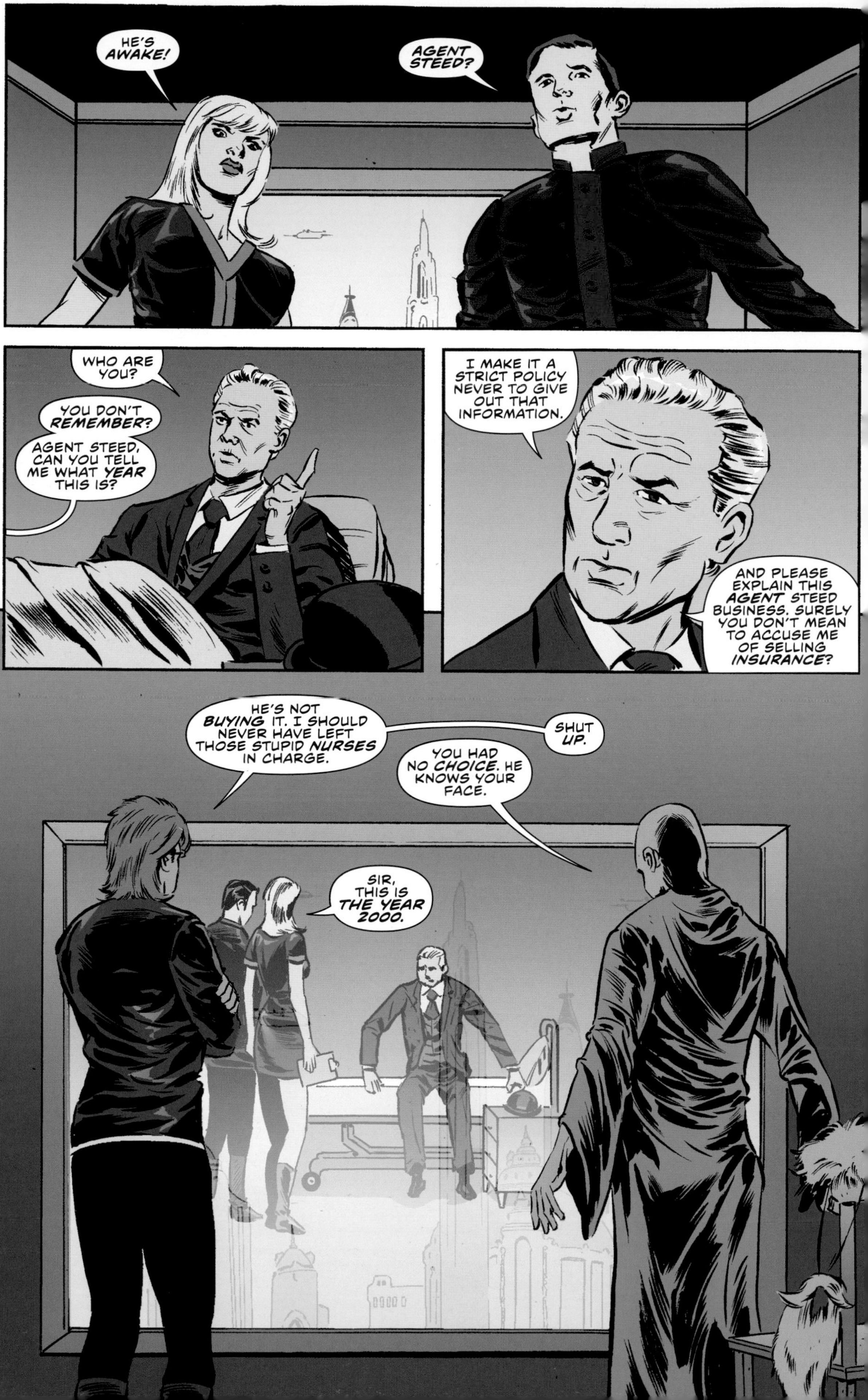
HE'S AWAKE!
AGENT STEED?
WHO ARE YOU?
YOU DON'T REMEMBER?
AGENT STEED, CAN YOU TELL ME WHAT YEAR THIS IS?
I MAKE IT A STRICT POLICY NEVER TO GIVE OUT THAT INFORMATION.
AND PLEASE EXPLAIN THIS AGENT STEED BUSINESS. SURELY YOU DON'T MEAN TO ACCUSE ME OF SELLING INSURANCE?
HE'S NOT BUYING IT. I SHOULD NEVER HAVE LEFT THOSE STUPID NURSES IN CHARGE.
SHUT UP.
YOU HAD NO CHOICE. HE KNOWS YOUR FACE.
SIR, THIS IS THE YEAR 2000.

IF IT'S THIRTY-FIVE YEARS LATER, WHY HAVEN'T I CHANGED INTO SOMETHING MORE *FASHIONABLE?*

WE PRESERVED YOUR OLD SUITS, SIR, AND IT'S A GOOD THING.

OF *COURSE.* HE WANTS TO FEEL LIKE *HIMSELF.* ANYONE WOULD.

YOU SEEM MORE *ALERT* IN THEM.

LOOK AT THE *MIRACLES* YOU AWOKE TO. FLYING AUTOMOBILES. MOVING SIDEWALKS. A TOWER FOR CONTROLLING *WEATHER.*

AND A DECENT *BRANDY,* I HOPE, OR ALL THAT EFFORT IS IN *VAIN.*

COOL ONE, THAT STEED. HE'S *TOYING* WITH THOSE TWO.

WHY SHOULD HE SUSPECT *ANYTHING,* WHEN HE LOOKS AND FEELS LIKE A MAN OF 80?

SNAP

TIK TIK TIK

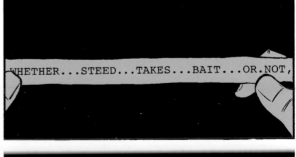

WHETHER...STEED...TAKES...BAIT...OR.NOT,

...HE...DIES...TONIGHT

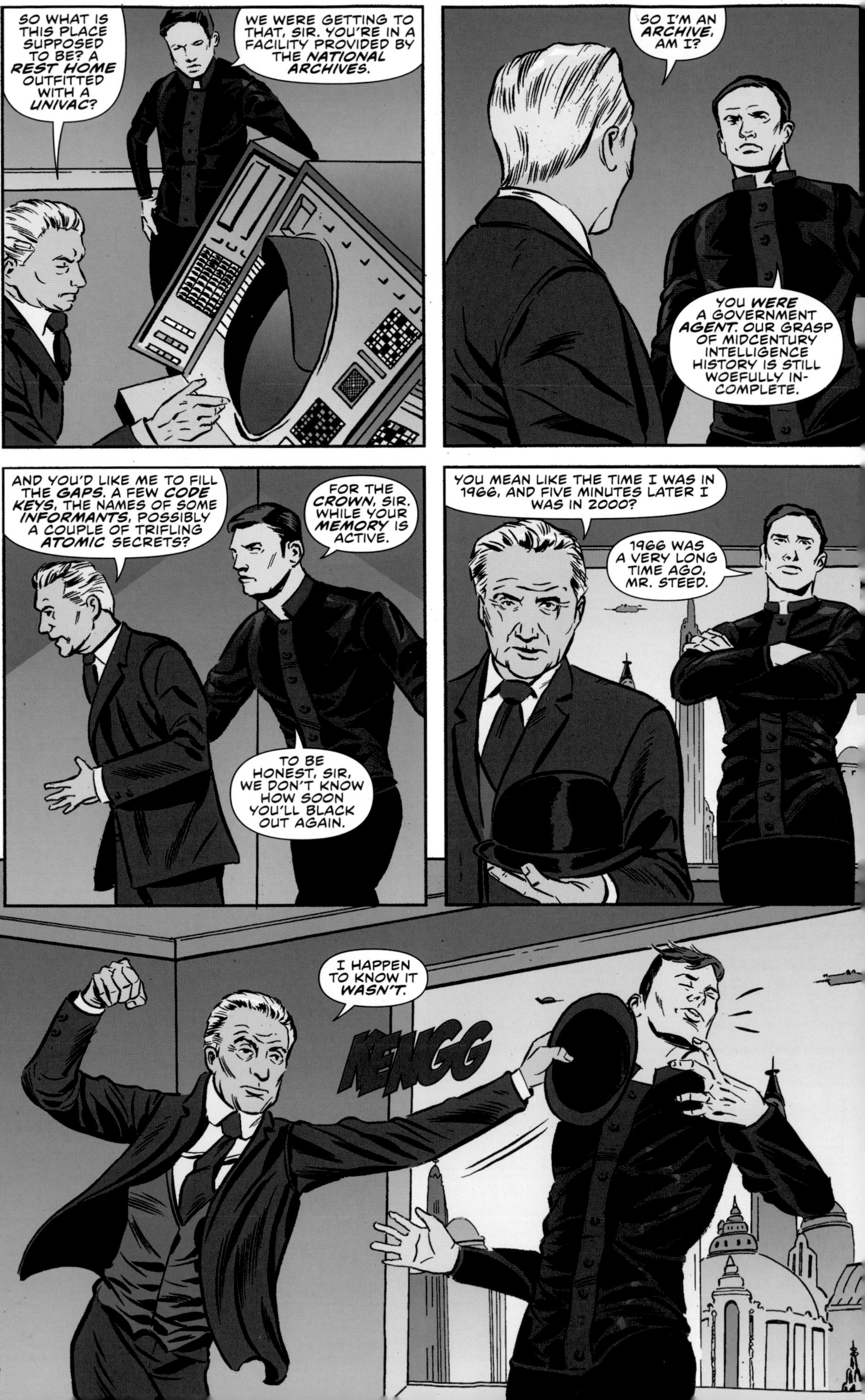
SO WHAT IS THIS PLACE SUPPOSED TO BE? A REST HOME OUTFITTED WITH A UNIVAC?
WE WERE GETTING TO THAT, SIR. YOU'RE IN A FACILITY PROVIDED BY THE NATIONAL ARCHIVES.
SO I'M AN ARCHIVE, AM I?
YOU WERE A GOVERNMENT AGENT. OUR GRASP OF MIDCENTURY INTELLIGENCE HISTORY IS STILL WOEFULLY IN-COMPLETE.
AND YOU'D LIKE ME TO FILL THE GAPS. A FEW CODE KEYS, THE NAMES OF SOME INFORMANTS, POSSIBLY A COUPLE OF TRIFLING ATOMIC SECRETS?
FOR THE CROWN, SIR. WHILE YOUR MEMORY IS ACTIVE.
TO BE HONEST, SIR, WE DON'T KNOW HOW SOON YOU'LL BLACK OUT AGAIN.
YOU MEAN LIKE THE TIME I WAS IN 1966, AND FIVE MINUTES LATER I WAS IN 2000?
1966 WAS A VERY LONG TIME AGO, MR. STEED.
I HAPPEN TO KNOW IT WASN'T.
KENGG

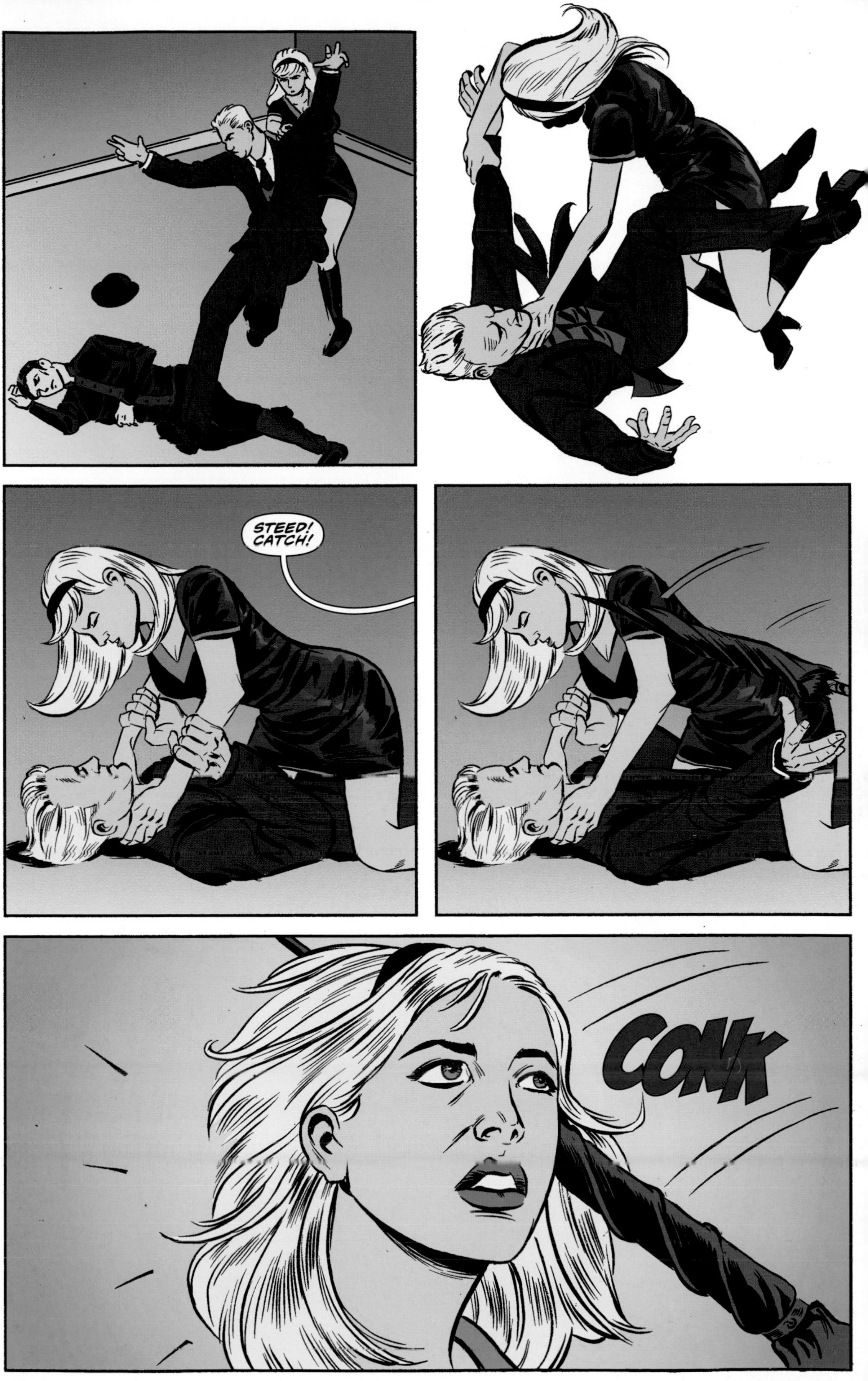
STEED! CATCH!
CONK

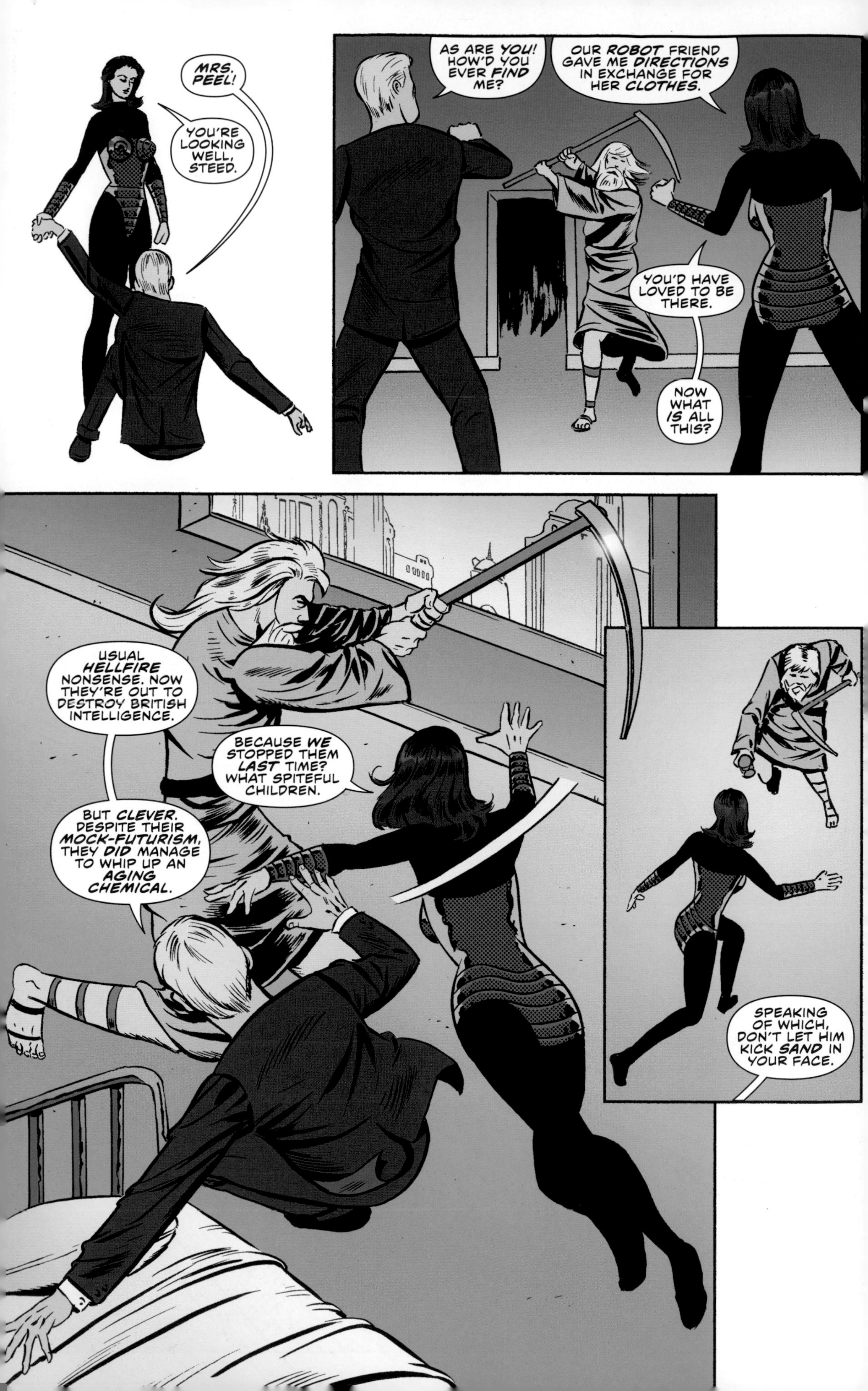
MRS. PEEL!
YOU'RE LOOKING WELL, STEED.
AS ARE YOU! HOW'D YOU EVER FIND ME?
OUR ROBOT FRIEND GAVE ME DIRECTIONS IN EXCHANGE FOR HER CLOTHES.
YOU'D HAVE LOVED TO BE THERE.
NOW WHAT IS ALL THIS?
USUAL HELLFIRE NONSENSE. NOW THEY'RE OUT TO DESTROY BRITISH INTELLIGENCE.
BECAUSE WE STOPPED THEM LAST TIME? WHAT SPITEFUL CHILDREN.
BUT CLEVER. DESPITE THEIR MOCK-FUTURISM, THEY DID MANAGE TO WHIP UP AN AGING CHEMICAL.
SPEAKING OF WHICH, DON'T LET HIM KICK SAND IN YOUR FACE.

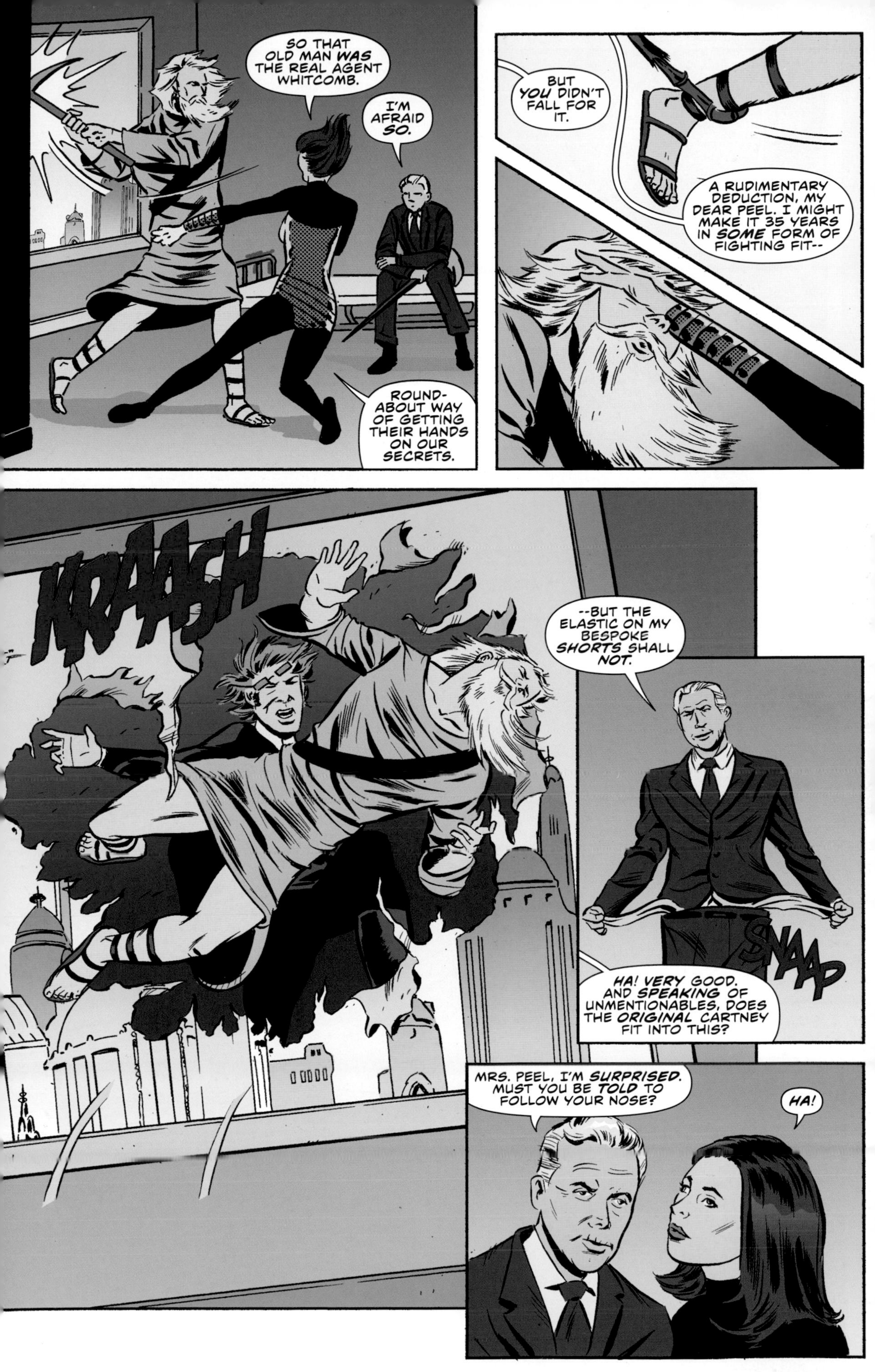
SO THAT OLD MAN WAS THE REAL AGENT WHITCOMB.
I'M AFRAID SO.
ROUND-ABOUT WAY OF GETTING THEIR HANDS ON OUR SECRETS.
BUT YOU DIDN'T FALL FOR IT.
A RUDIMENTARY DEDUCTION, MY DEAR PEEL. I MIGHT MAKE IT 35 YEARS IN SOME FORM OF FIGHTING FIT--
KRAASH
--BUT THE ELASTIC ON MY BESPOKE SHORTS SHALL NOT.
SNAAP
HA! VERY GOOD. AND SPEAKING OF UNMENTIONABLES, DOES THE ORIGINAL CARTNEY FIT INTO THIS?
MRS. PEEL, I'M SURPRISED. MUST YOU BE TOLD TO FOLLOW YOUR NOSE?
HA!

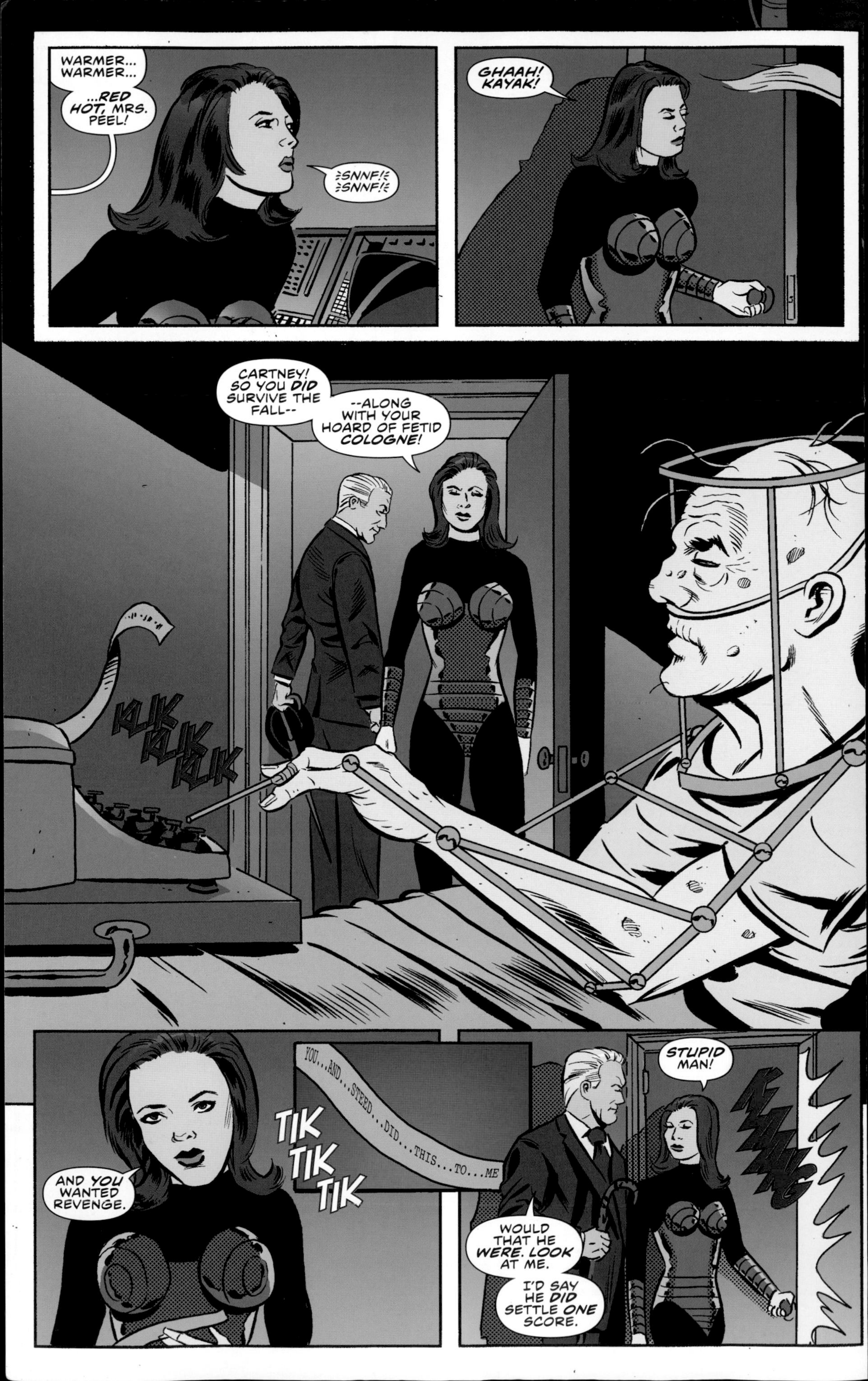
WARMER... WARMER...
...RED HOT, MRS. PEEL!
SNNF! SNNF!
GHAAH! KAYAK!
CARTNEY! SO YOU DID SURVIVE THE FALL--
--ALONG WITH YOUR HOARD OF FETID COLOGNE!
KLIK KLIK KLIK
AND YOU WANTED REVENGE.
YOU...AND...STEED...DID...THIS...TO...ME
TIK TIK TIK
STUPID MAN!
WOULD THAT HE WERE. LOOK AT ME.
I'D SAY HE DID SETTLE ONE SCORE.

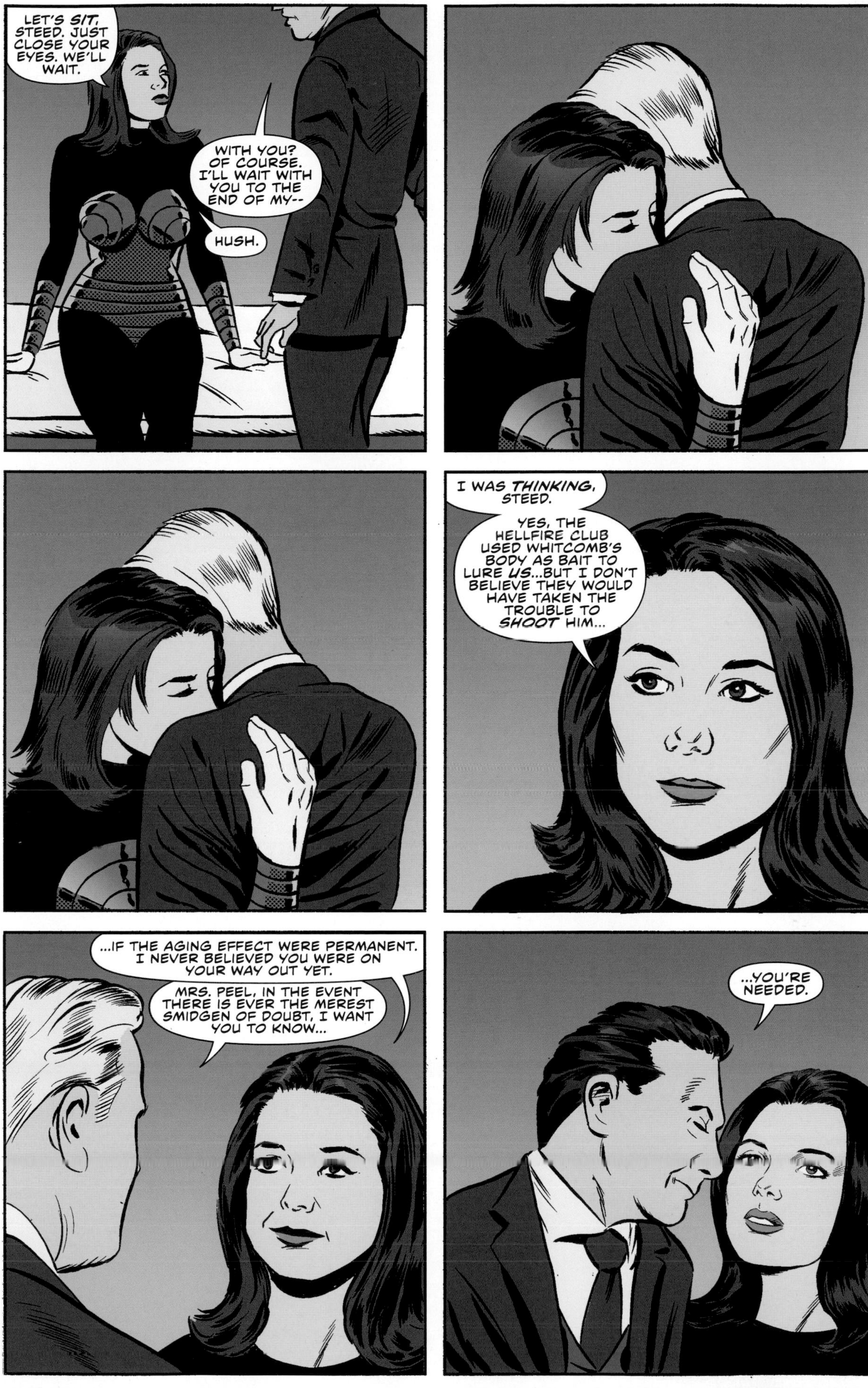
LET'S *SIT*, STEED. JUST CLOSE YOUR EYES. WE'LL WAIT.
WITH YOU? OF COURSE. I'LL WAIT WITH YOU TO THE END OF MY--
HUSH.
I WAS *THINKING*, STEED.
YES, THE HELLFIRE CLUB USED WHITCOMB'S BODY AS BAIT TO LURE *US*...BUT I DON'T BELIEVE THEY WOULD HAVE TAKEN THE TROUBLE TO *SHOOT* HIM...
...IF THE AGING EFFECT WERE PERMANENT. I NEVER BELIEVED YOU WERE ON YOUR WAY OUT YET.
MRS. PEEL, IN THE EVENT THERE IS EVER THE MEREST SMIDGEN OF DOUBT, I WANT YOU TO KNOW...
...YOU'RE NEEDED.

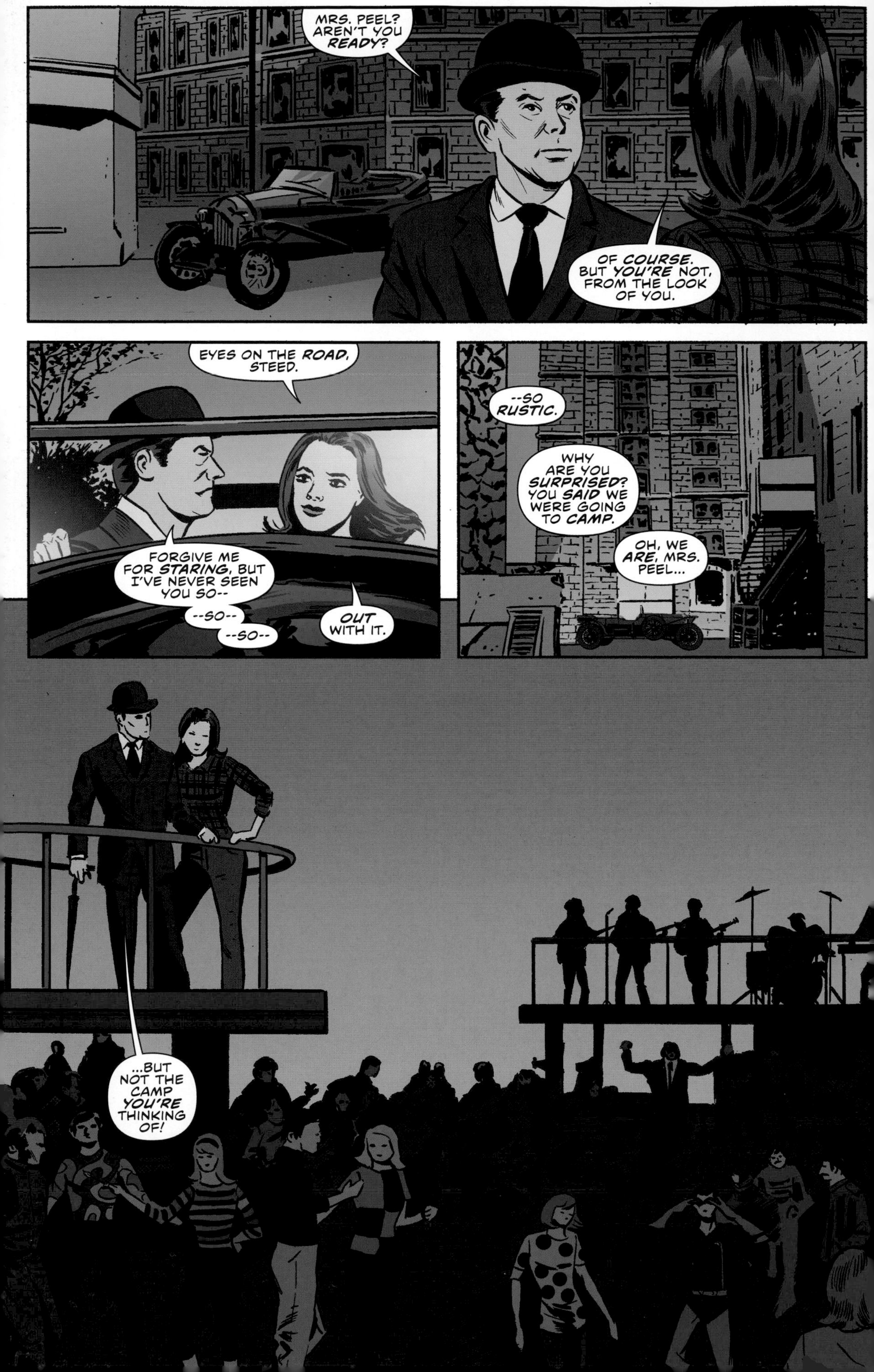
MRS. PEEL? AREN'T YOU READY?
OF COURSE. BUT YOU'RE NOT, FROM THE LOOK OF YOU.
EYES ON THE ROAD, STEED.
FORGIVE ME FOR STARING, BUT I'VE NEVER SEEN YOU SO--
--SO--
--SO--
OUT WITH IT.
--SO RUSTIC.
WHY ARE YOU SURPRISED? YOU SAID WE WERE GOING TO CAMP.
OH, WE ARE, MRS. PEEL...
...BUT NOT THE CAMP YOU'RE THINKING OF!

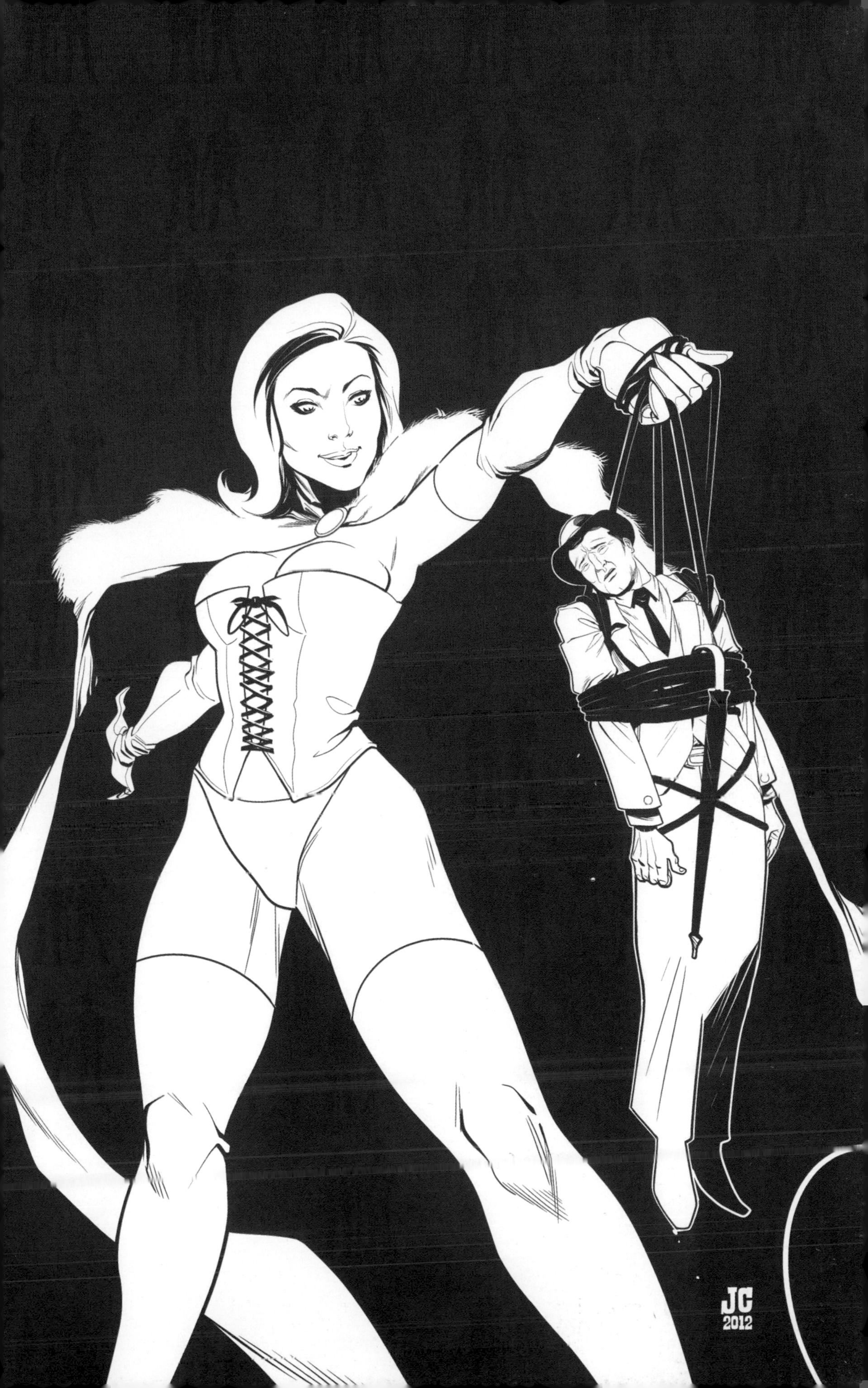
JC
2012

CHAPTER ONE

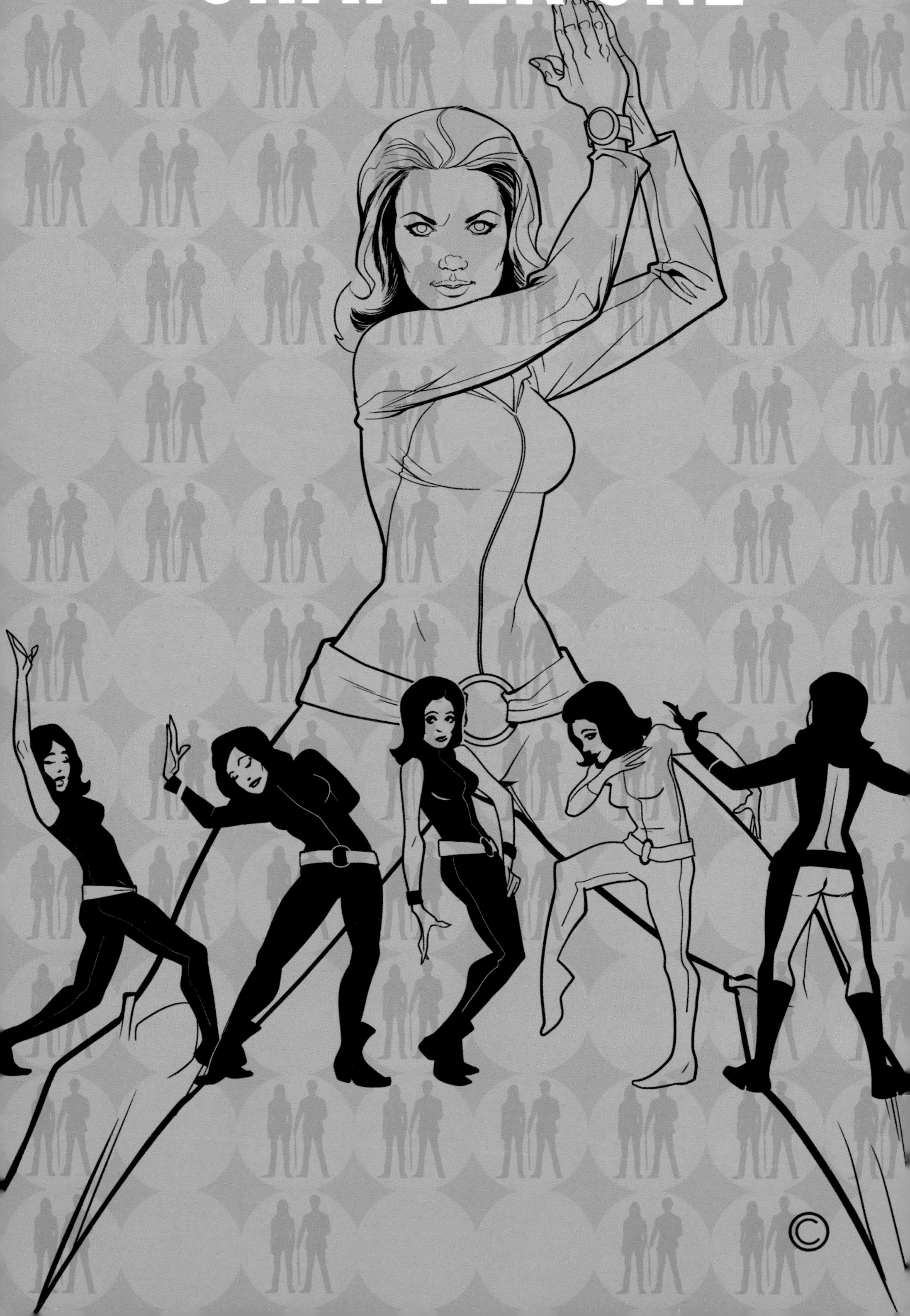

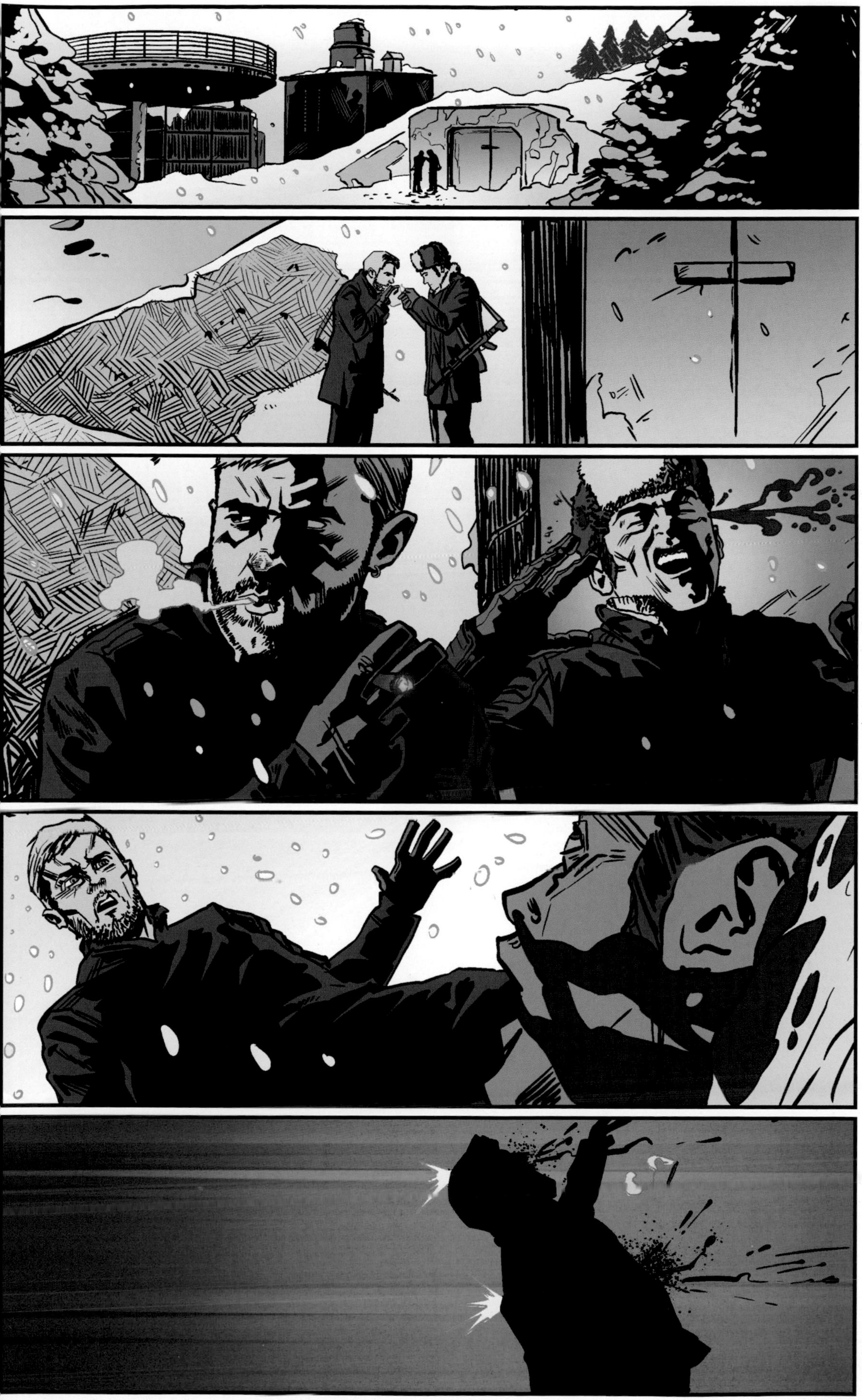

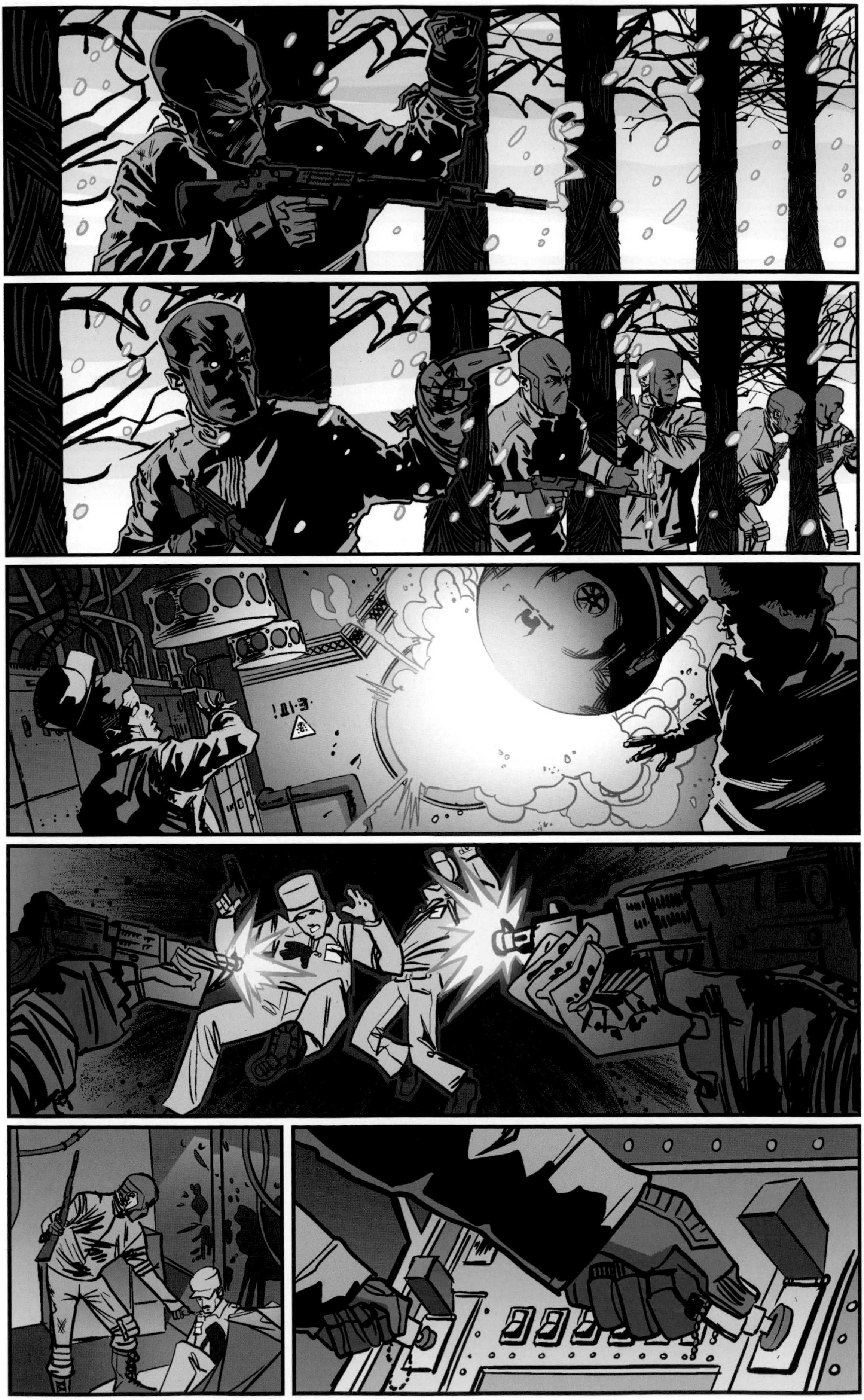

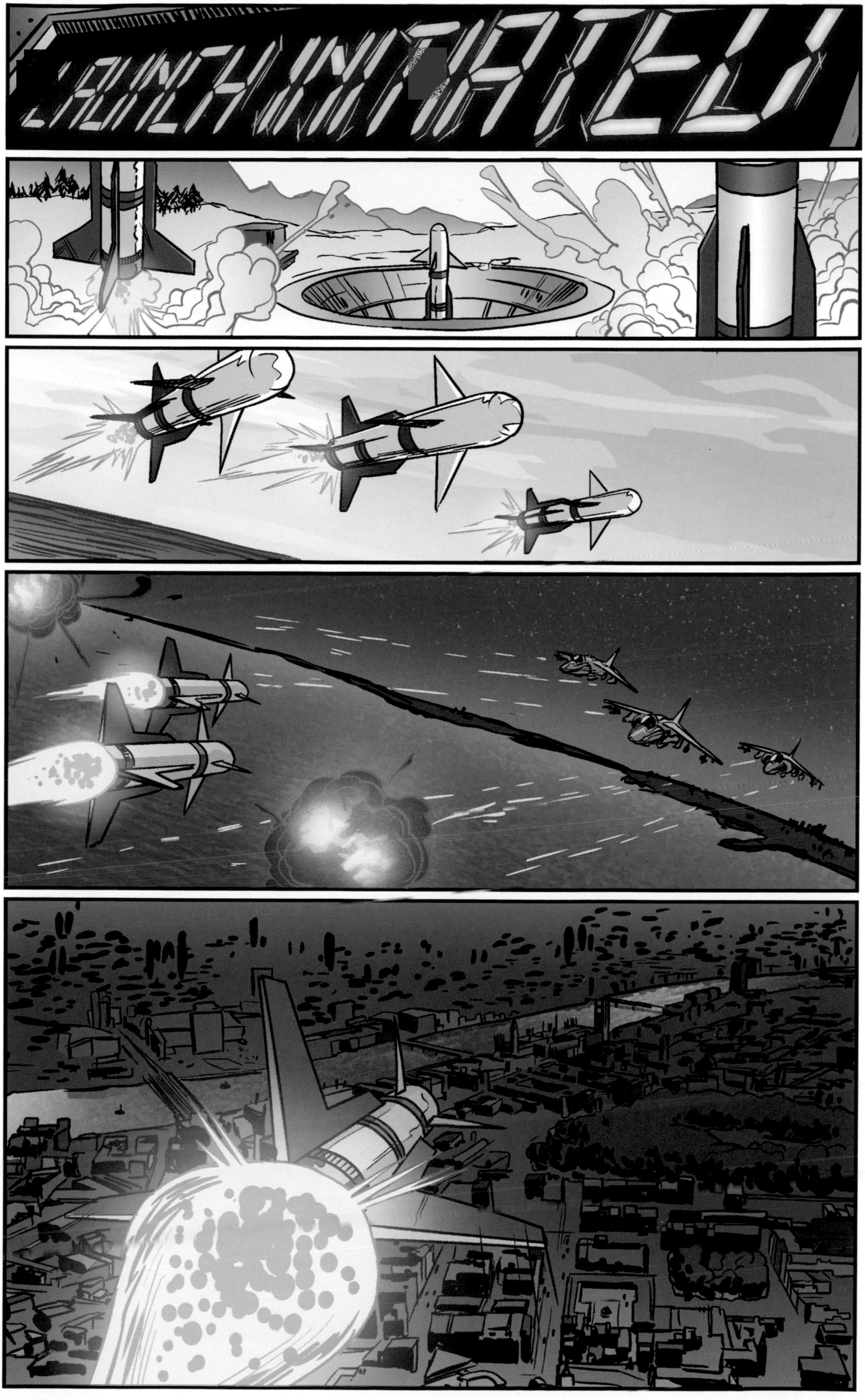
[redacted]AUNCH INITIATED

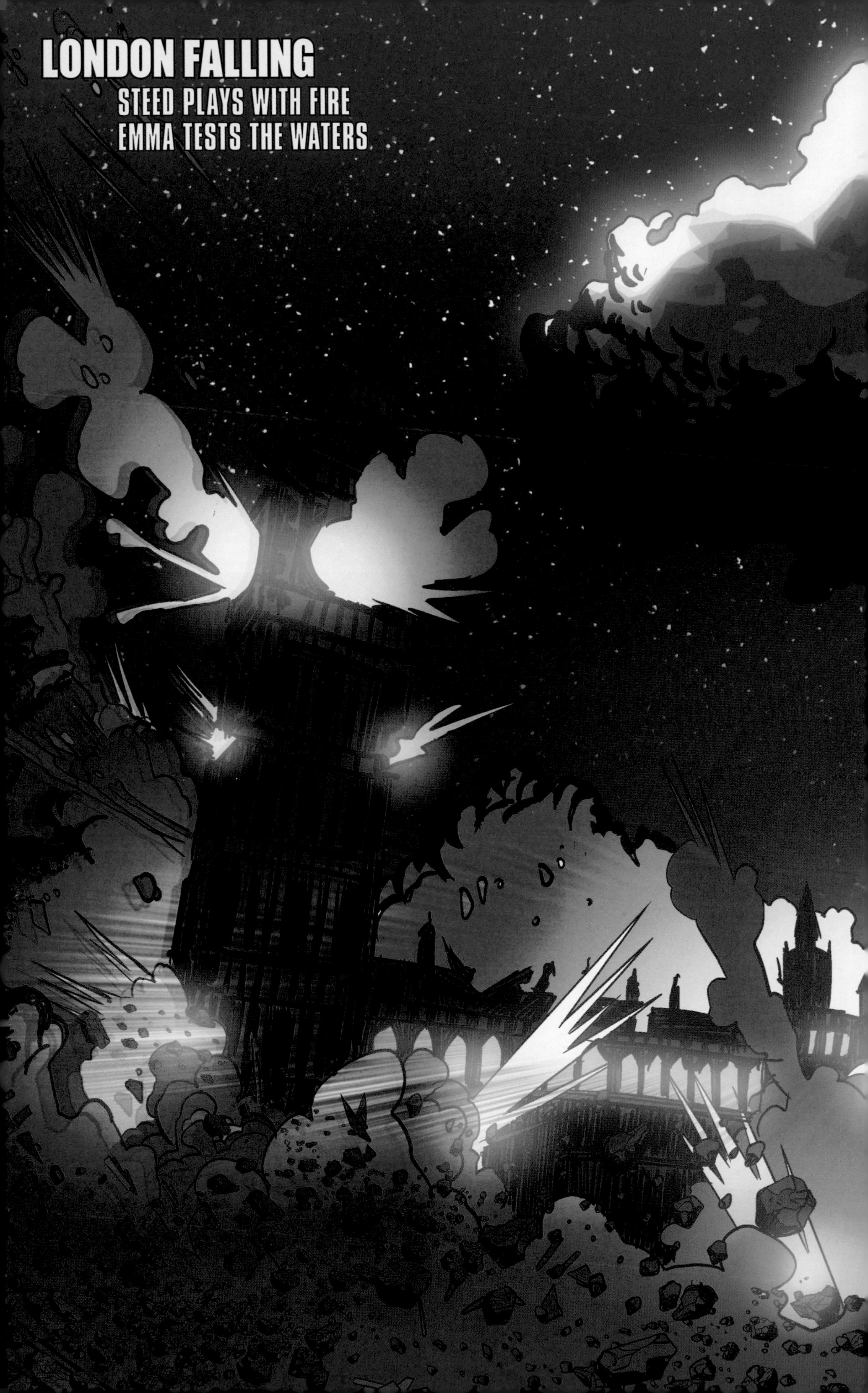
LONDON FALLING
STEED PLAYS WITH FIRE
EMMA TESTS THE WATERS

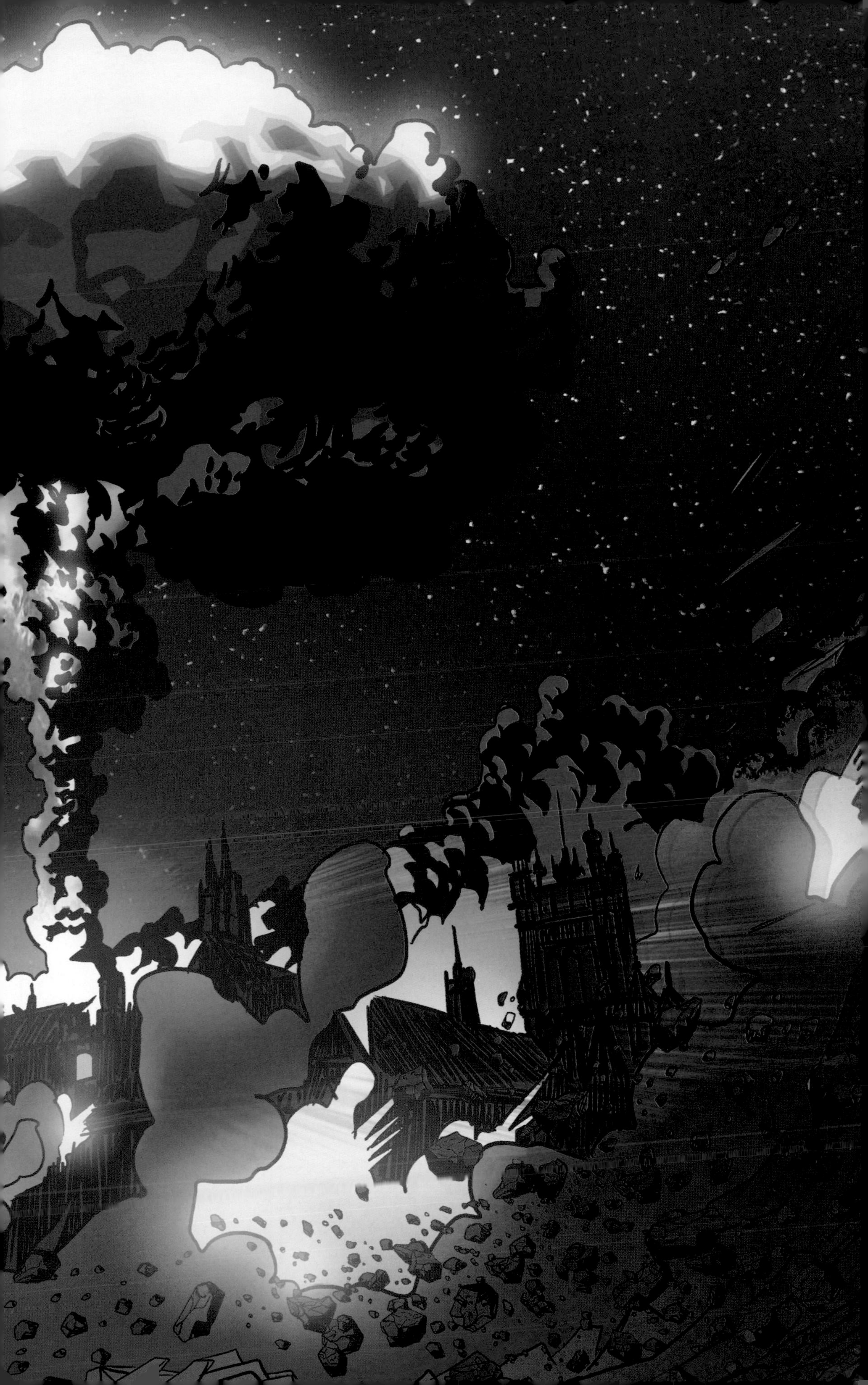

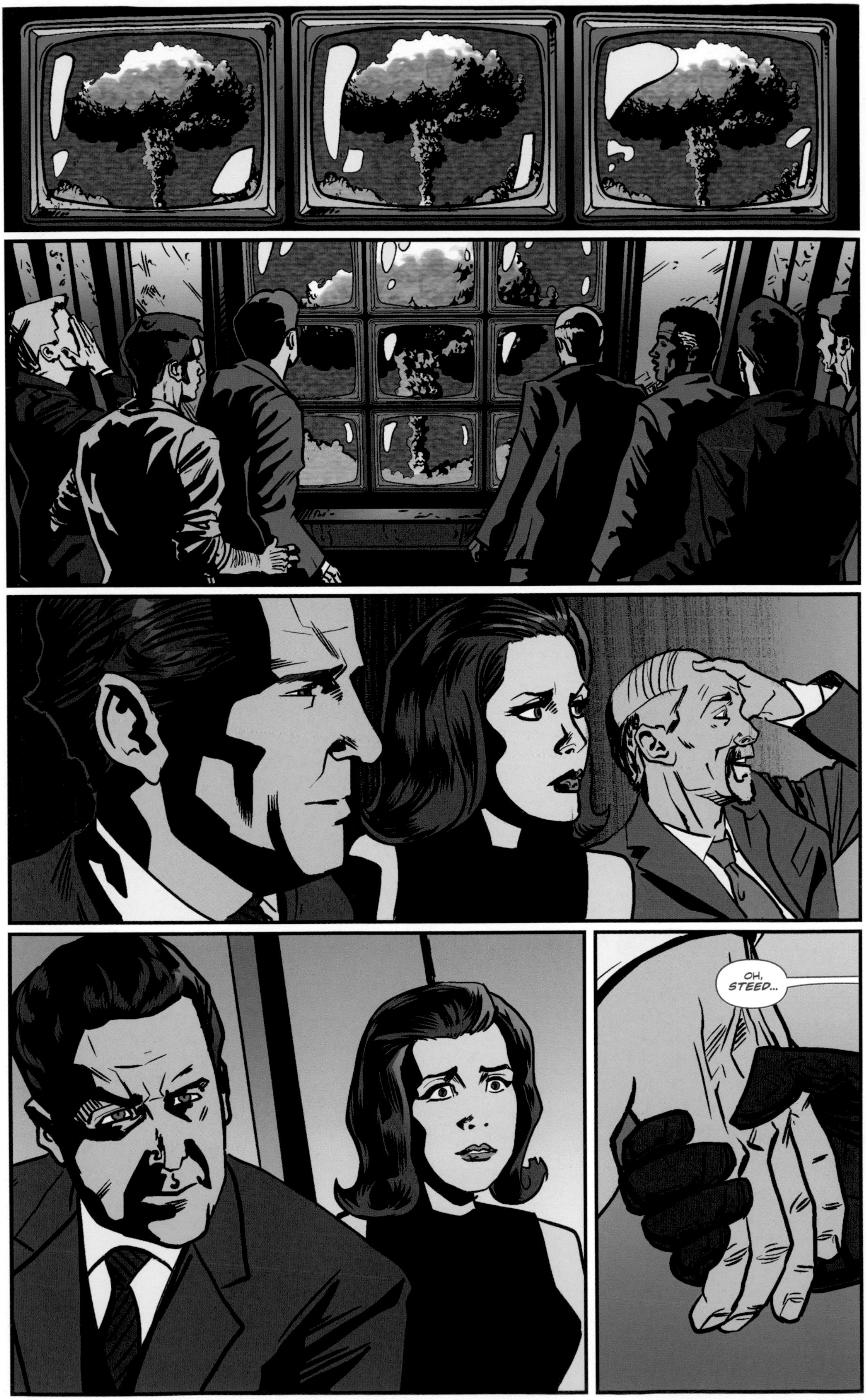
OH, STEED...

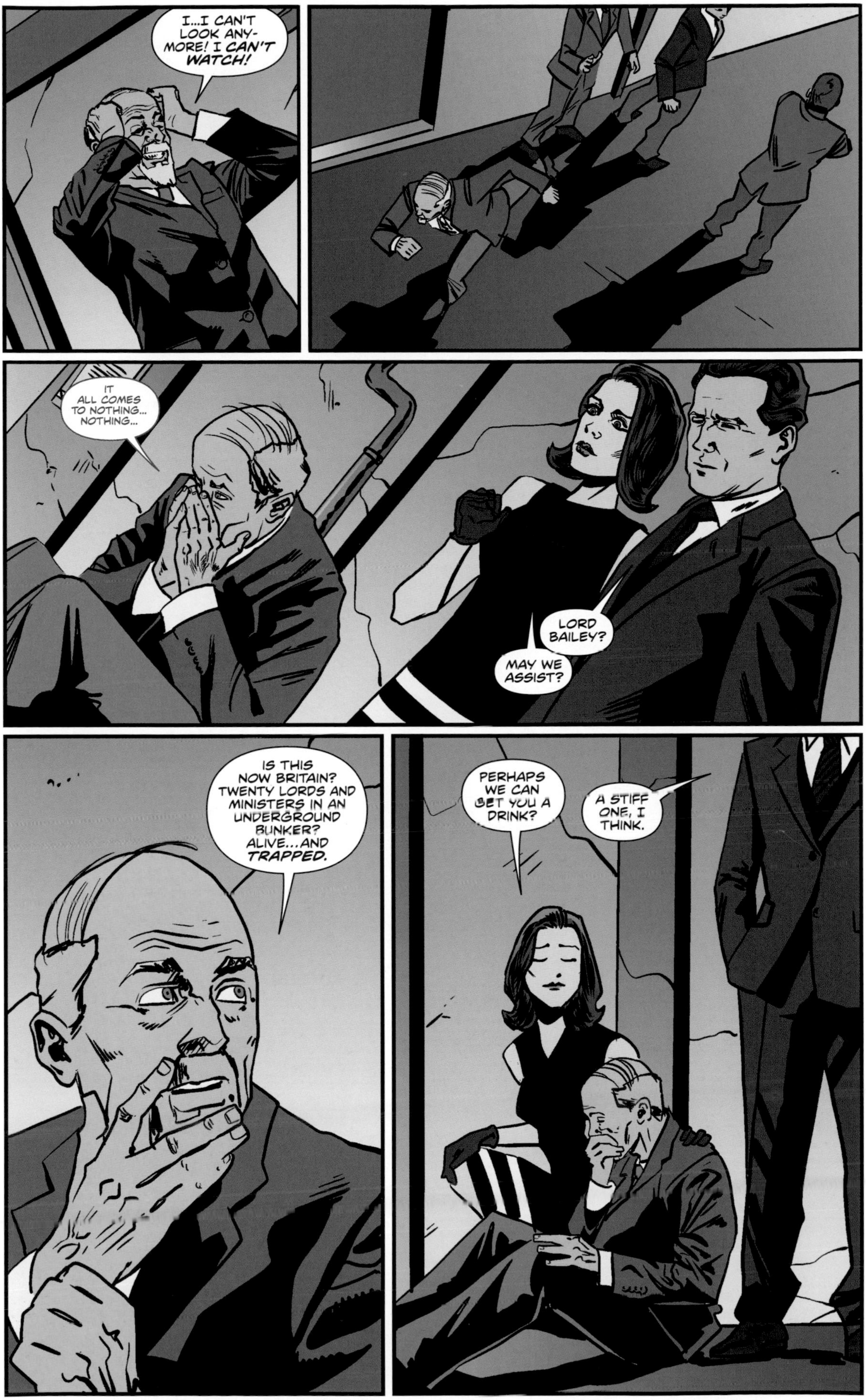
I...I CAN'T LOOK ANY-MORE! I *CAN'T WATCH!*
IT ALL COMES TO NOTHING... NOTHING...
LORD BAILEY?
MAY WE ASSIST?
IS THIS NOW BRITAIN? TWENTY LORDS AND MINISTERS IN AN UNDERGROUND BUNKER? ALIVE...AND *TRAPPED.*
PERHAPS WE CAN GET YOU A DRINK?
A STIFF ONE, I THINK.

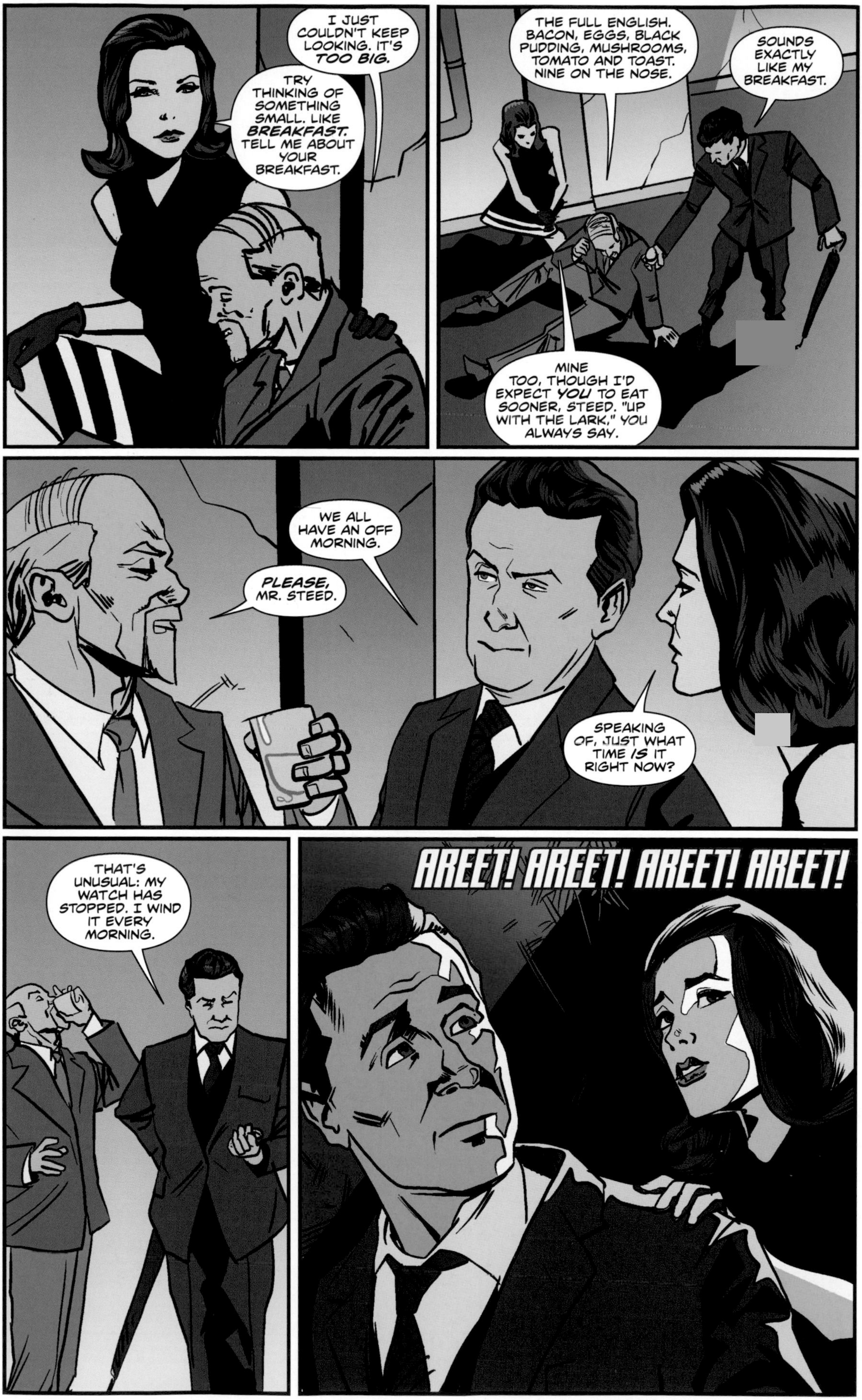
I JUST COULDN'T KEEP LOOKING. IT'S TOO BIG.
TRY THINKING OF SOMETHING SMALL. LIKE BREAKFAST. TELL ME ABOUT YOUR BREAKFAST.
THE FULL ENGLISH. BACON, EGGS, BLACK PUDDING, MUSHROOMS, TOMATO AND TOAST. NINE ON THE NOSE.
SOUNDS EXACTLY LIKE MY BREAKFAST.
MINE TOO, THOUGH I'D EXPECT YOU TO EAT SOONER, STEED. "UP WITH THE LARK," YOU ALWAYS SAY.
WE ALL HAVE AN OFF MORNING.
PLEASE, MR. STEED.
SPEAKING OF, JUST WHAT TIME IS IT RIGHT NOW?
THAT'S UNUSUAL: MY WATCH HAS STOPPED. I WIND IT EVERY MORNING.
AREET! AREET! AREET! AREET!

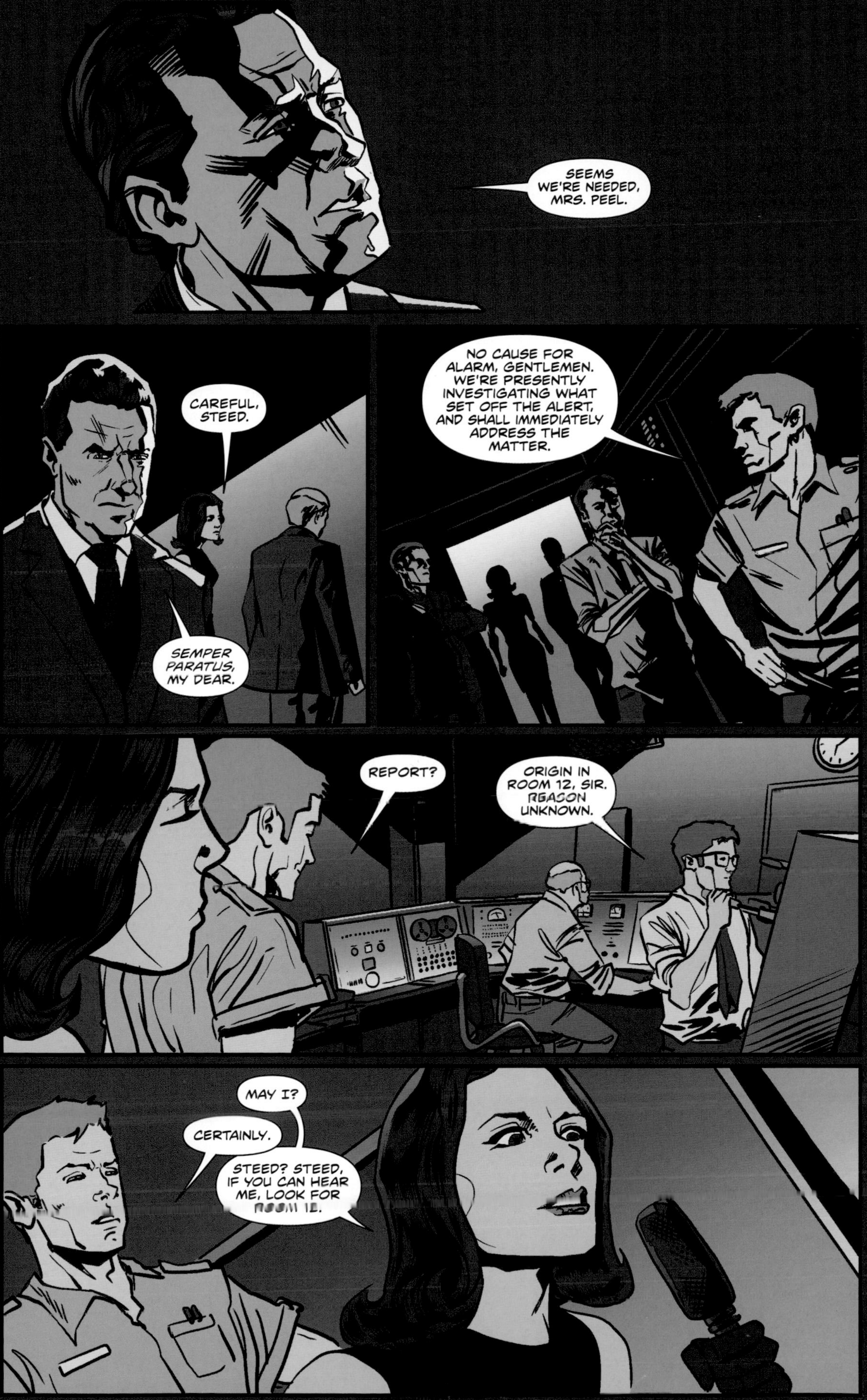
SEEMS WE'RE NEEDED, MRS. PEEL.
CAREFUL, STEED.
SEMPER PARATUS, MY DEAR.
NO CAUSE FOR ALARM, GENTLEMEN. WE'RE PRESENTLY INVESTIGATING WHAT SET OFF THE ALERT, AND SHALL IMMEDIATELY ADDRESS THE MATTER.
REPORT?
ORIGIN IN ROOM 12, SIR. REASON UNKNOWN.
MAY I?
CERTAINLY.
STEED? STEED, IF YOU CAN HEAR ME, LOOK FOR

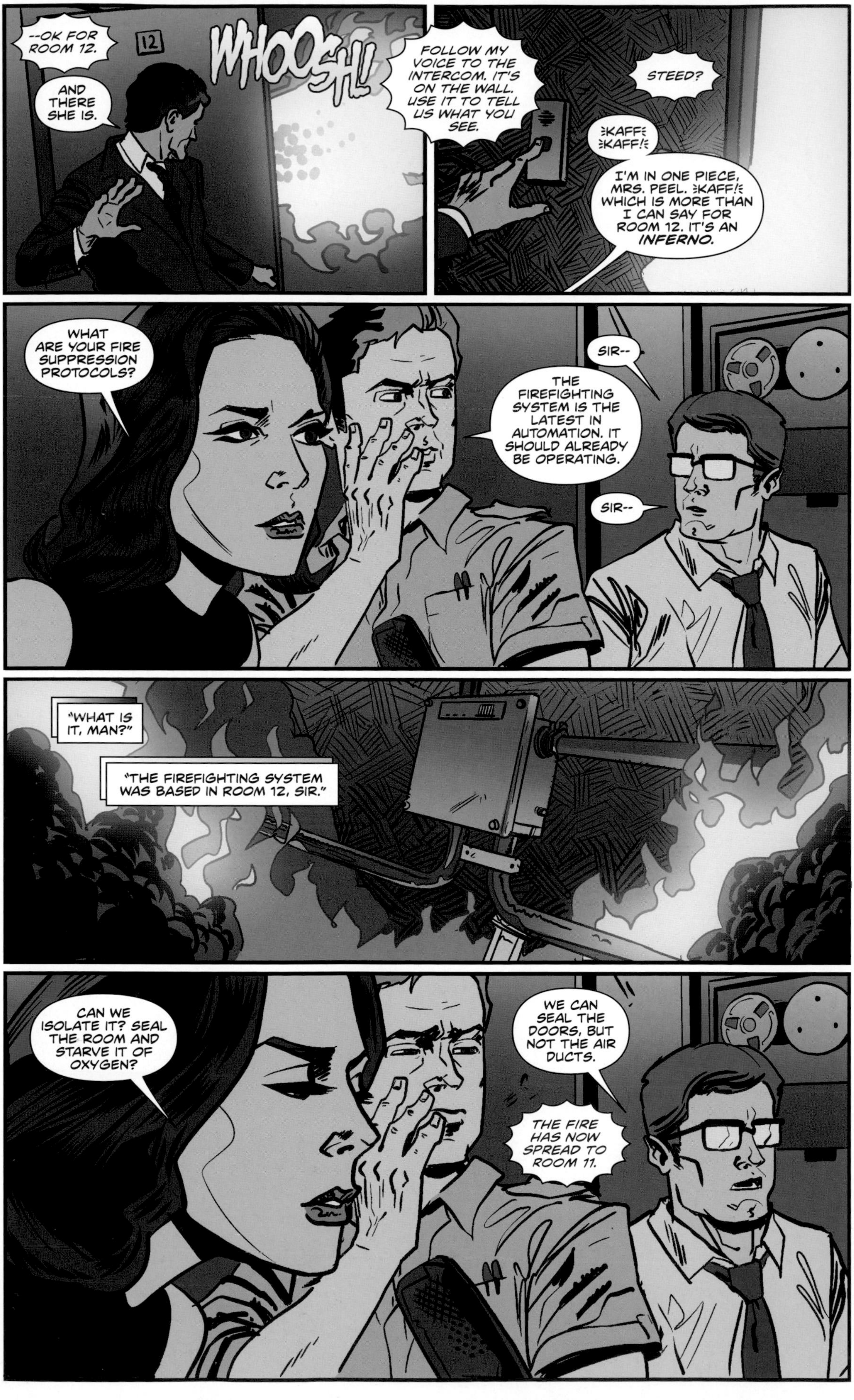
--OK FOR ROOM 12.
12
AND THERE SHE IS.
WHOOSH!
FOLLOW MY VOICE TO THE INTERCOM. IT'S ON THE WALL. USE IT TO TELL US WHAT YOU SEE.
STEED?
KAFF KAFF!
I'M IN ONE PIECE, MRS. PEEL. KAFF! WHICH IS MORE THAN I CAN SAY FOR ROOM 12. IT'S AN INFERNO.
WHAT ARE YOUR FIRE SUPPRESSION PROTOCOLS?
SIR--
THE FIREFIGHTING SYSTEM IS THE LATEST IN AUTOMATION. IT SHOULD ALREADY BE OPERATING.
SIR--
"WHAT IS IT, MAN?"
"THE FIREFIGHTING SYSTEM WAS BASED IN ROOM 12, SIR."
CAN WE ISOLATE IT? SEAL THE ROOM AND STARVE IT OF OXYGEN?
WE CAN SEAL THE DOORS, BUT NOT THE AIR DUCTS.
THE FIRE HAS NOW SPREAD TO ROOM 11.

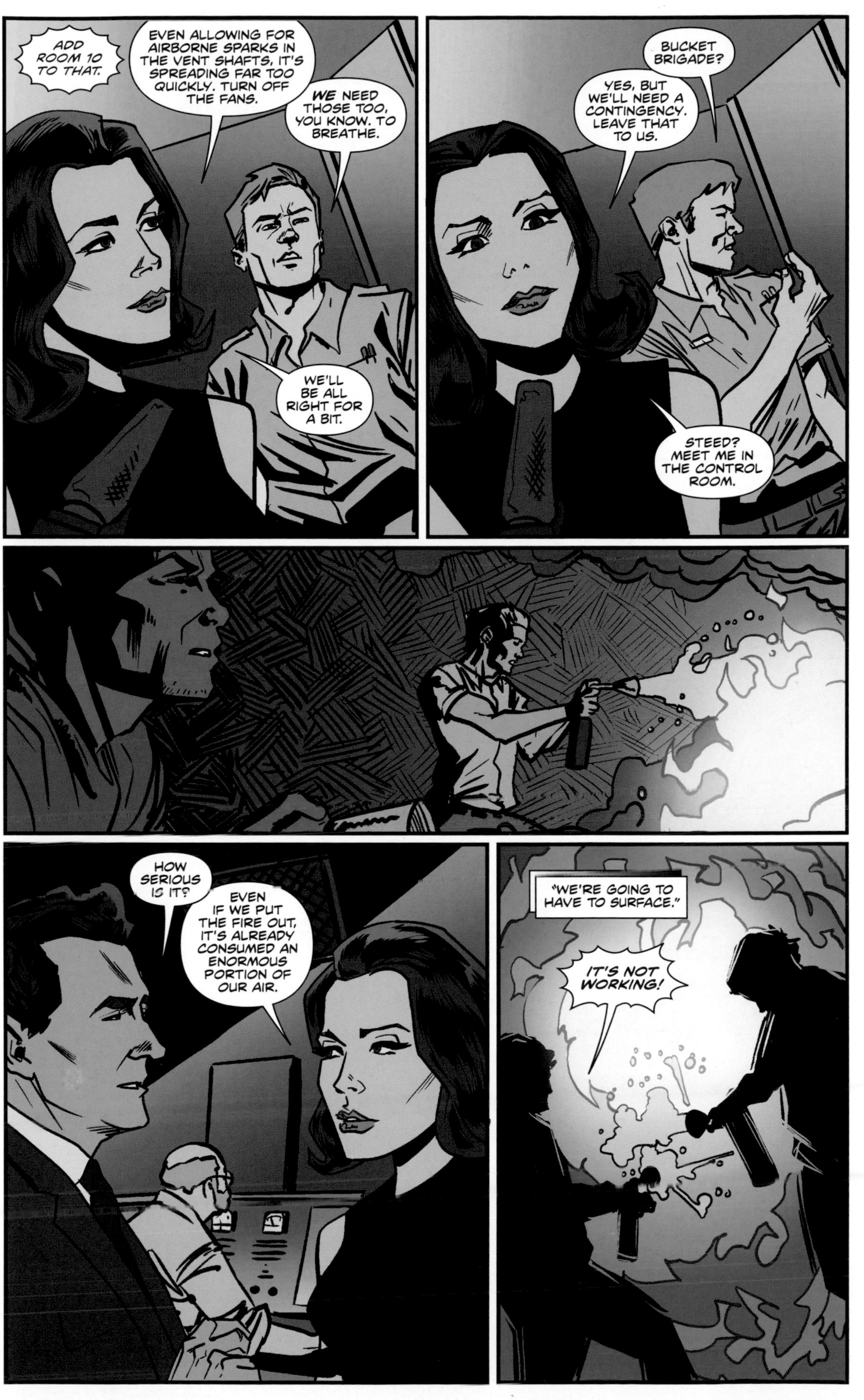
ADD ROOM 10 TO THAT.
EVEN ALLOWING FOR AIRBORNE SPARKS IN THE VENT SHAFTS, IT'S SPREADING FAR TOO QUICKLY. TURN OFF THE FANS.
WE NEED THOSE TOO, YOU KNOW. TO BREATHE.
WE'LL BE ALL RIGHT FOR A BIT.
BUCKET BRIGADE?
YES, BUT WE'LL NEED A CONTINGENCY. LEAVE THAT TO US.
STEED? MEET ME IN THE CONTROL ROOM.
HOW SERIOUS IS IT?
EVEN IF WE PUT THE FIRE OUT, IT'S ALREADY CONSUMED AN ENORMOUS PORTION OF OUR AIR.
"WE'RE GOING TO HAVE TO SURFACE."
IT'S NOT WORKING!

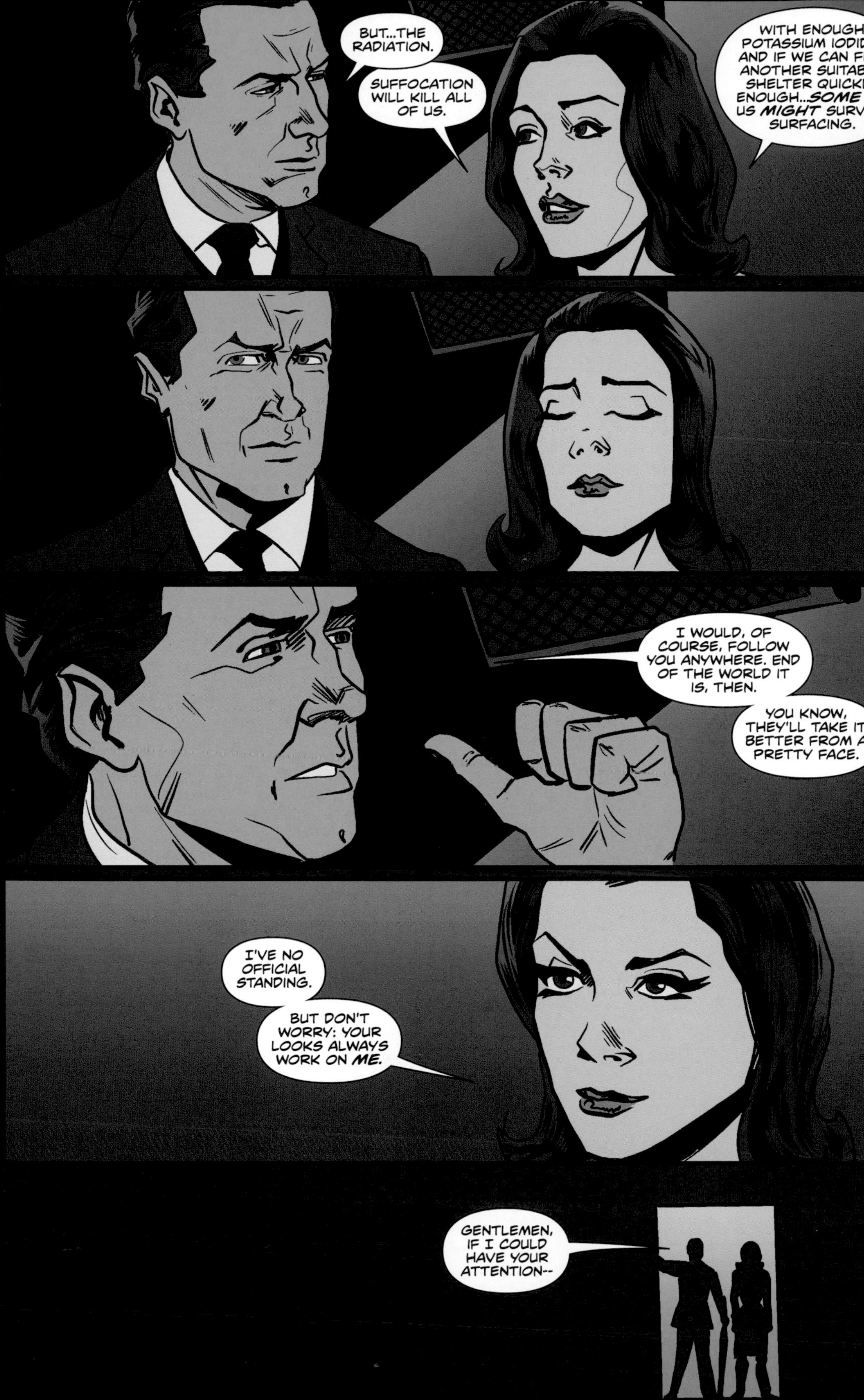
BUT...THE RADIATION.
SUFFOCATION WILL KILL ALL OF US.
WITH ENOUGH POTASSIUM IODIDE, AND IF WE CAN FIND ANOTHER SUITABLE SHELTER QUICKLY ENOUGH...SOME OF US MIGHT SURVIVE SURFACING.
I WOULD, OF COURSE, FOLLOW YOU ANYWHERE. END OF THE WORLD IT IS, THEN.
YOU KNOW, THEY'LL TAKE IT BETTER FROM A PRETTY FACE.
I'VE NO OFFICIAL STANDING.
BUT DON'T WORRY: YOUR LOOKS ALWAYS WORK ON ME.
GENTLEMEN, IF I COULD HAVE YOUR ATTENTION--

YOU'VE ALL BEEN GIVEN A BOTTLE OF POTASSIUM IODIDE AND HAVE TAKEN YOUR FIRST DOSE. ALL THAT'S LEFT, THEN...

...IS THE *ASCENT.*

AS ALWAYS, SCIENCE LEADS THE HUMAN ENDEAVOUR. GEOFFREY HERE AND MY COLLEAGUE MRS. PEEL SHALL GO FIRST, TO TAKE ENVIRONMENTAL READINGS.

THEN THE REST OF US SHALL FOLLOW.

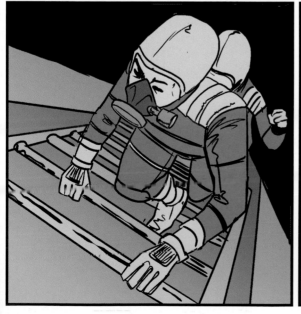

I DO SO ADMIRE PROGRESS.

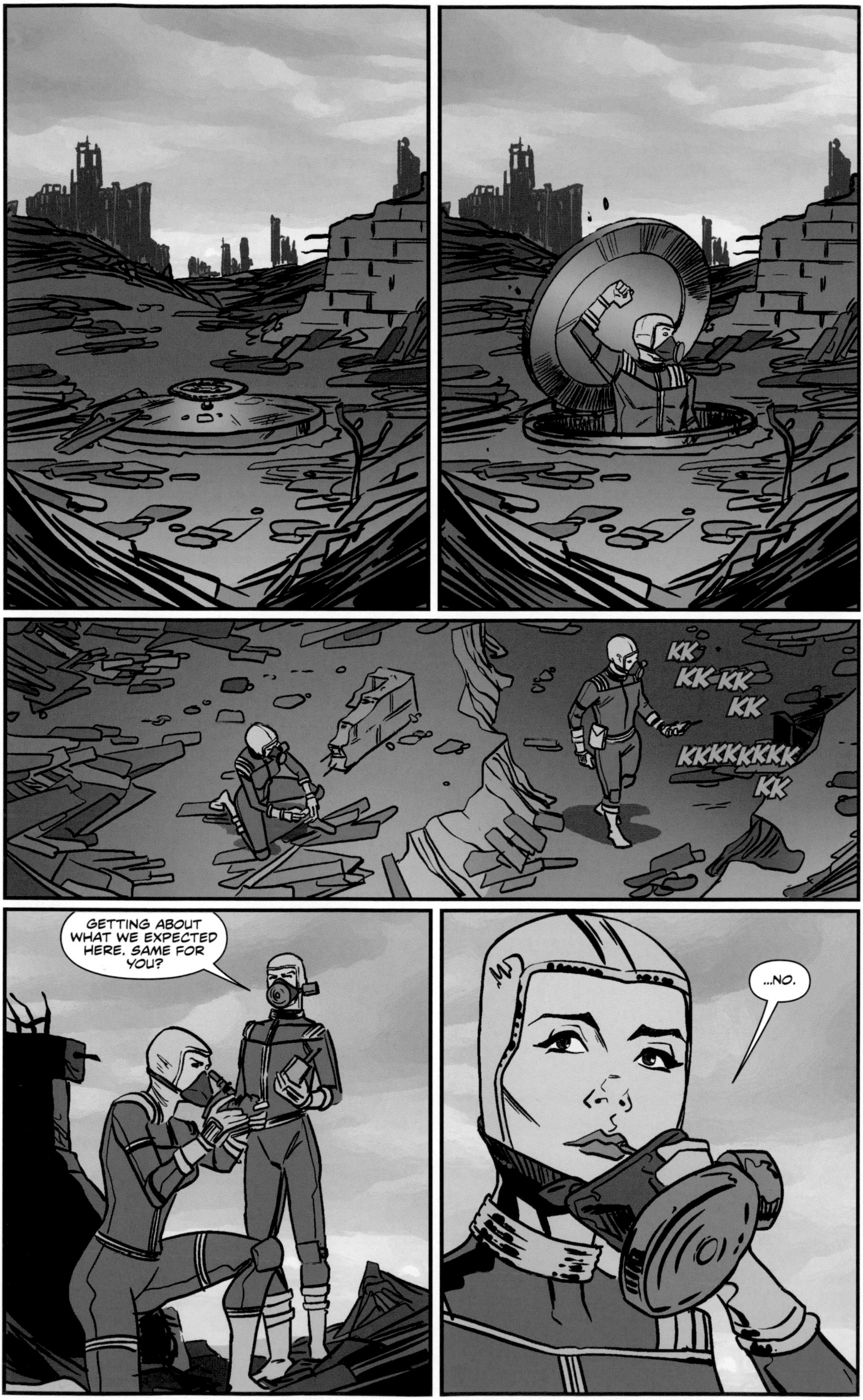
KK
KK-KK
KK
KKKKKKKK
KK
GETTING ABOUT WHAT WE EXPECTED HERE. SAME FOR YOU?
...NO.

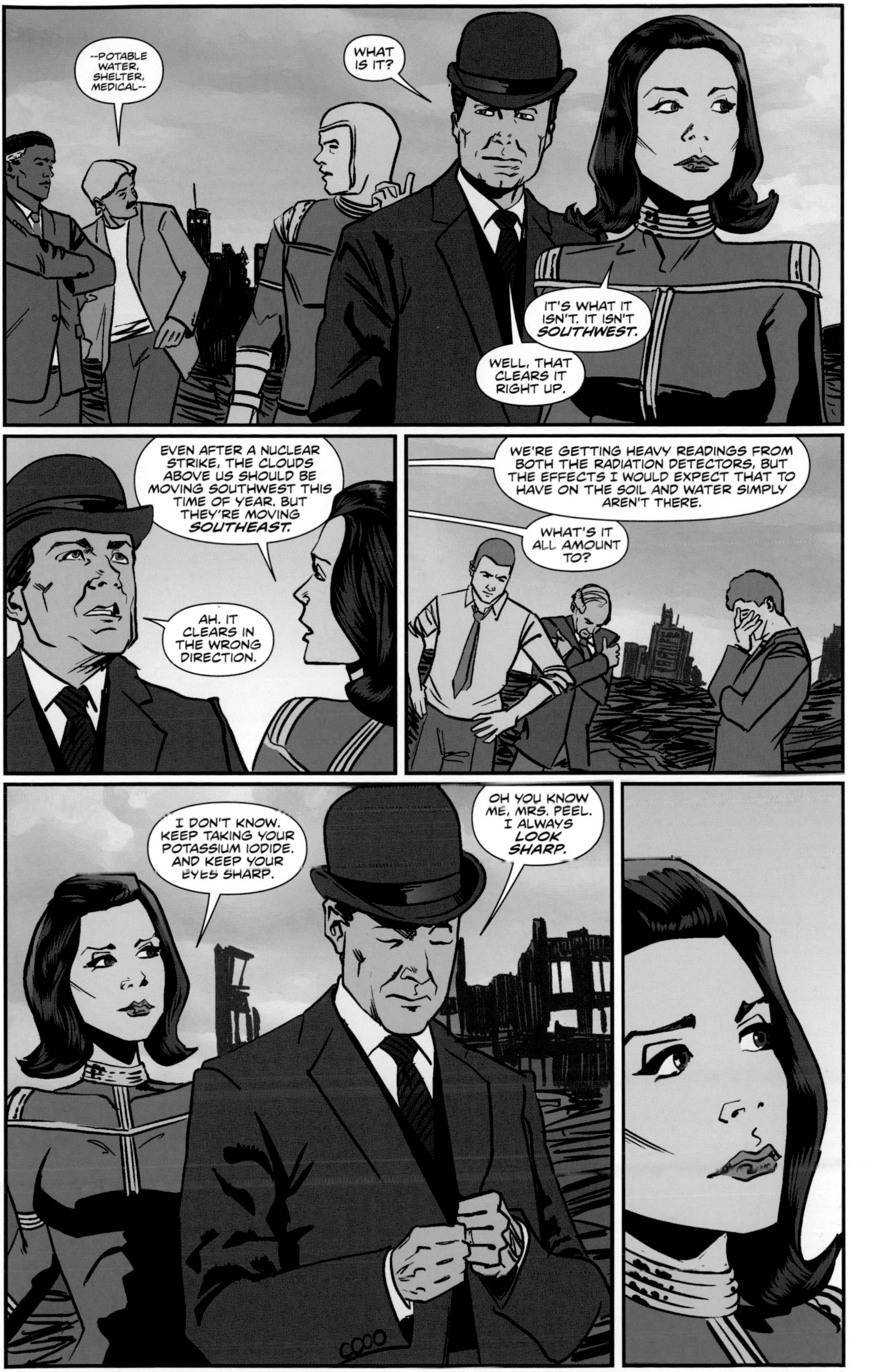
--POTABLE WATER, SHELTER, MEDICAL--
WHAT IS IT?
IT'S WHAT IT ISN'T. IT ISN'T SOUTHWEST.
WELL, THAT CLEARS IT RIGHT UP.
EVEN AFTER A NUCLEAR STRIKE, THE CLOUDS ABOVE US SHOULD BE MOVING SOUTHWEST THIS TIME OF YEAR. BUT THEY'RE MOVING SOUTHEAST.
AH. IT CLEARS IN THE WRONG DIRECTION.
WE'RE GETTING HEAVY READINGS FROM BOTH THE RADIATION DETECTORS, BUT THE EFFECTS I WOULD EXPECT THAT TO HAVE ON THE SOIL AND WATER SIMPLY AREN'T THERE.
WHAT'S IT ALL AMOUNT TO?
I DON'T KNOW. KEEP TAKING YOUR POTASSIUM IODIDE. AND KEEP YOUR EYES SHARP.
OH YOU KNOW ME, MRS. PEEL. I ALWAYS LOOK SHARP.

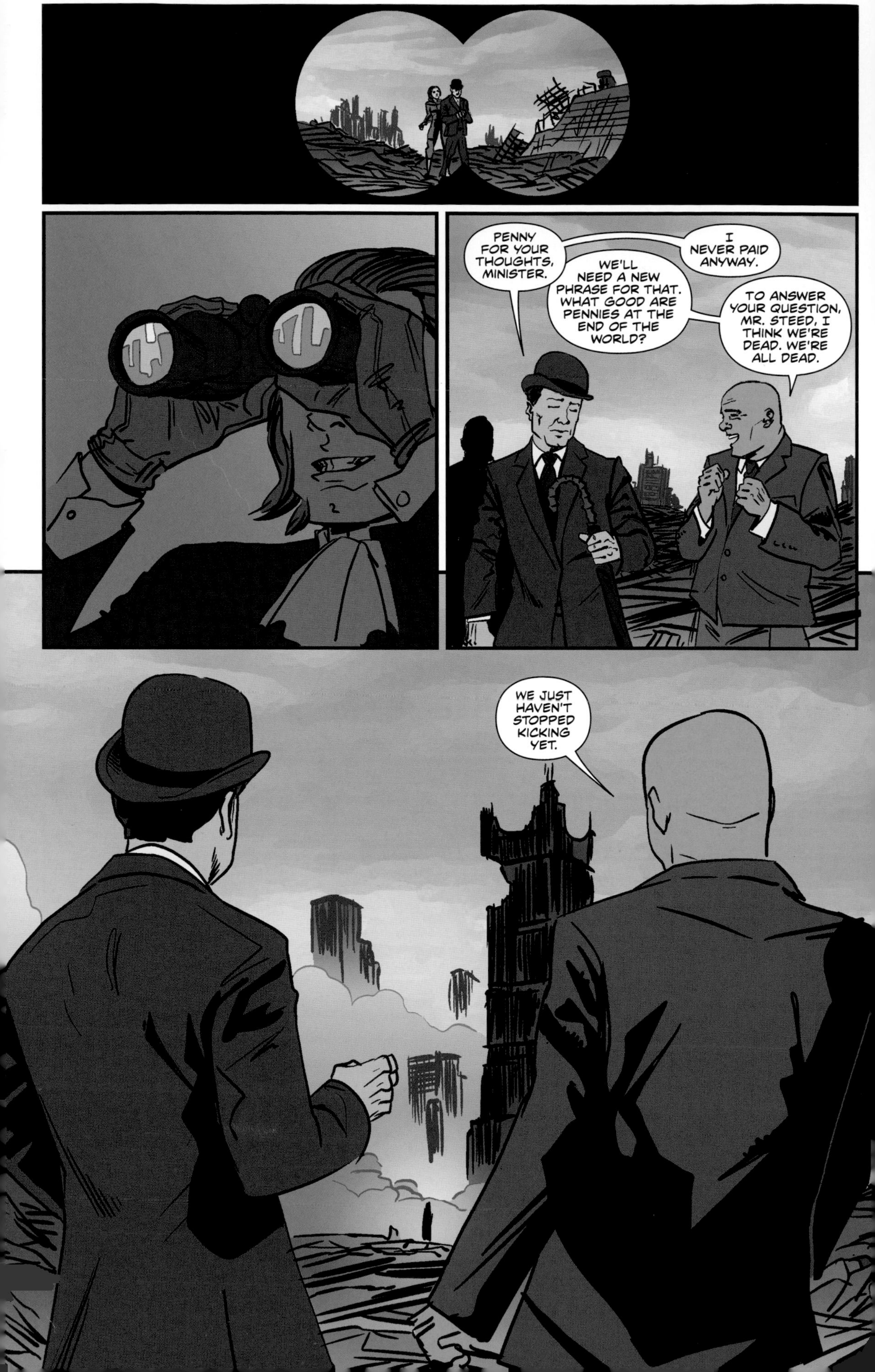
PENNY FOR YOUR THOUGHTS, MINISTER.
WE'LL NEED A NEW PHRASE FOR THAT. WHAT GOOD ARE PENNIES AT THE END OF THE WORLD?
I NEVER PAID ANYWAY.
TO ANSWER YOUR QUESTION, MR. STEED, I THINK WE'RE DEAD. WE'RE ALL DEAD.
WE JUST HAVEN'T STOPPED KICKING YET.

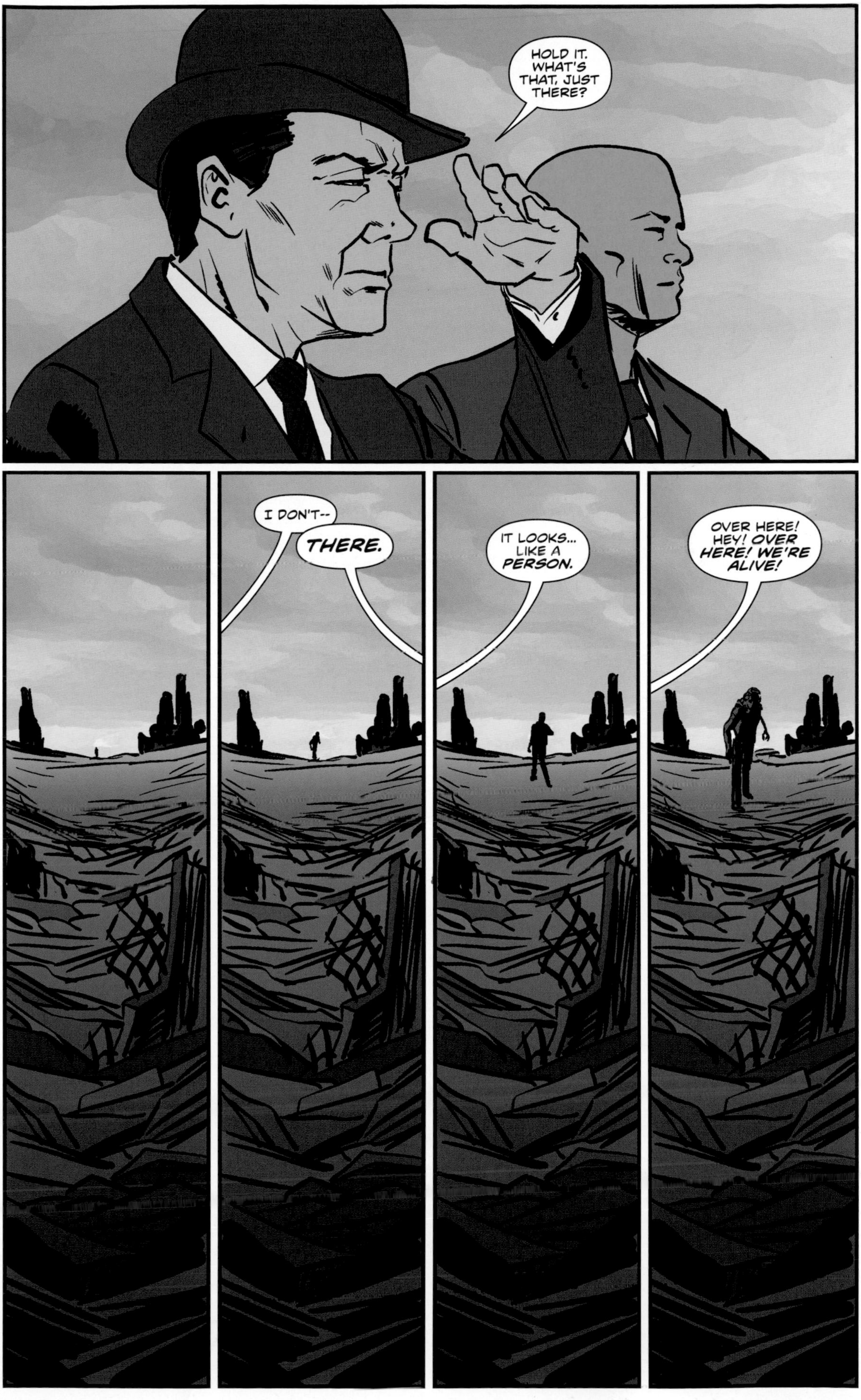
HOLD IT. WHAT'S THAT, JUST THERE?
I DON'T--
THERE.
IT LOOKS... LIKE A PERSON.
OVER HERE! HEY! OVER HERE! WE'RE ALIVE!

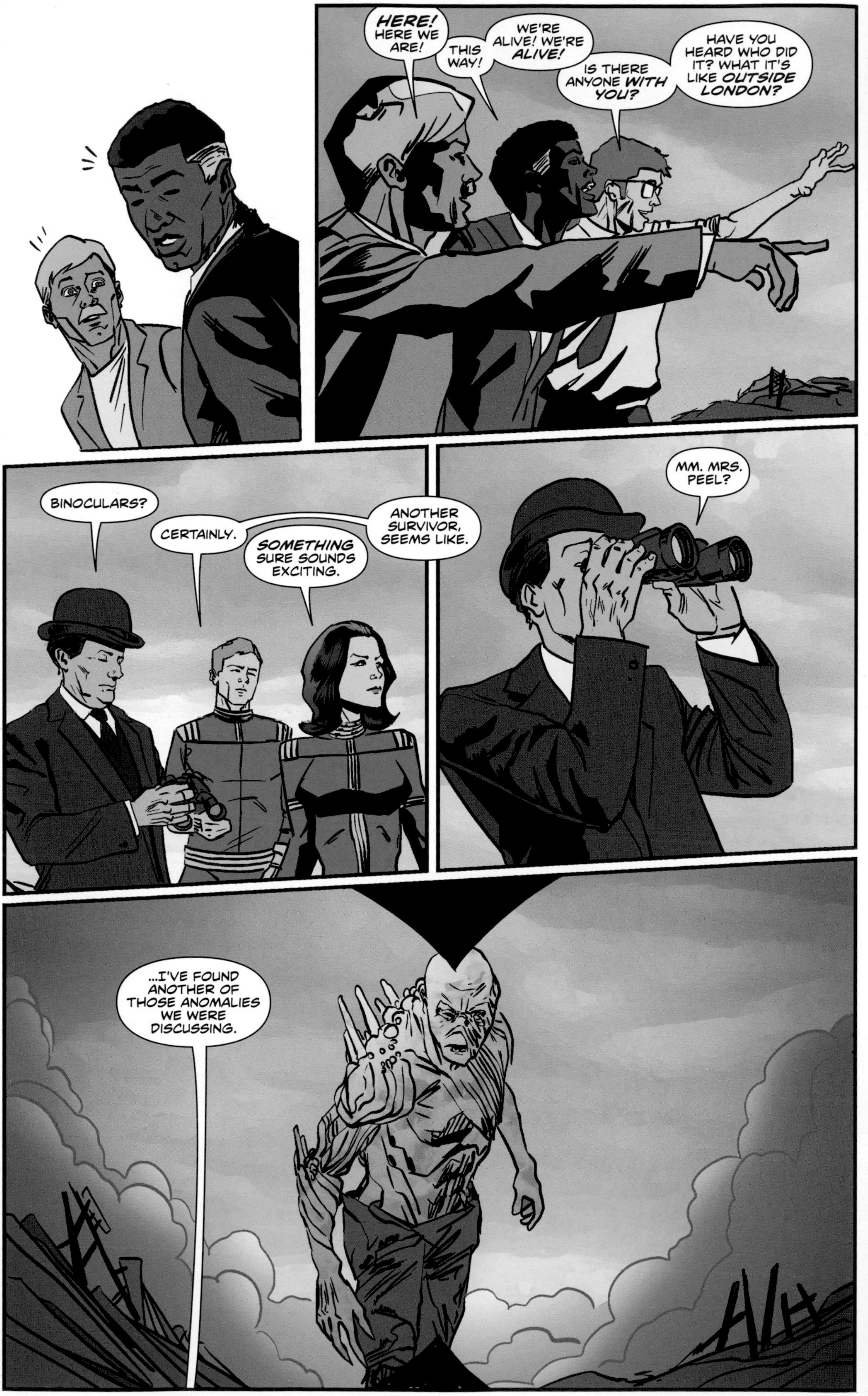
HERE! HERE WE ARE!
THIS WAY!
WE'RE ALIVE! WE'RE ALIVE!
IS THERE ANYONE WITH YOU?
HAVE YOU HEARD WHO DID IT? WHAT IT'S LIKE OUTSIDE LONDON?
BINOCULARS?
CERTAINLY.
ANOTHER SURVIVOR, SEEMS LIKE.
SOMETHING SURE SOUNDS EXCITING.
MM. MRS. PEEL?
...I'VE FOUND ANOTHER OF THOSE ANOMALIES WE WERE DISCUSSING.

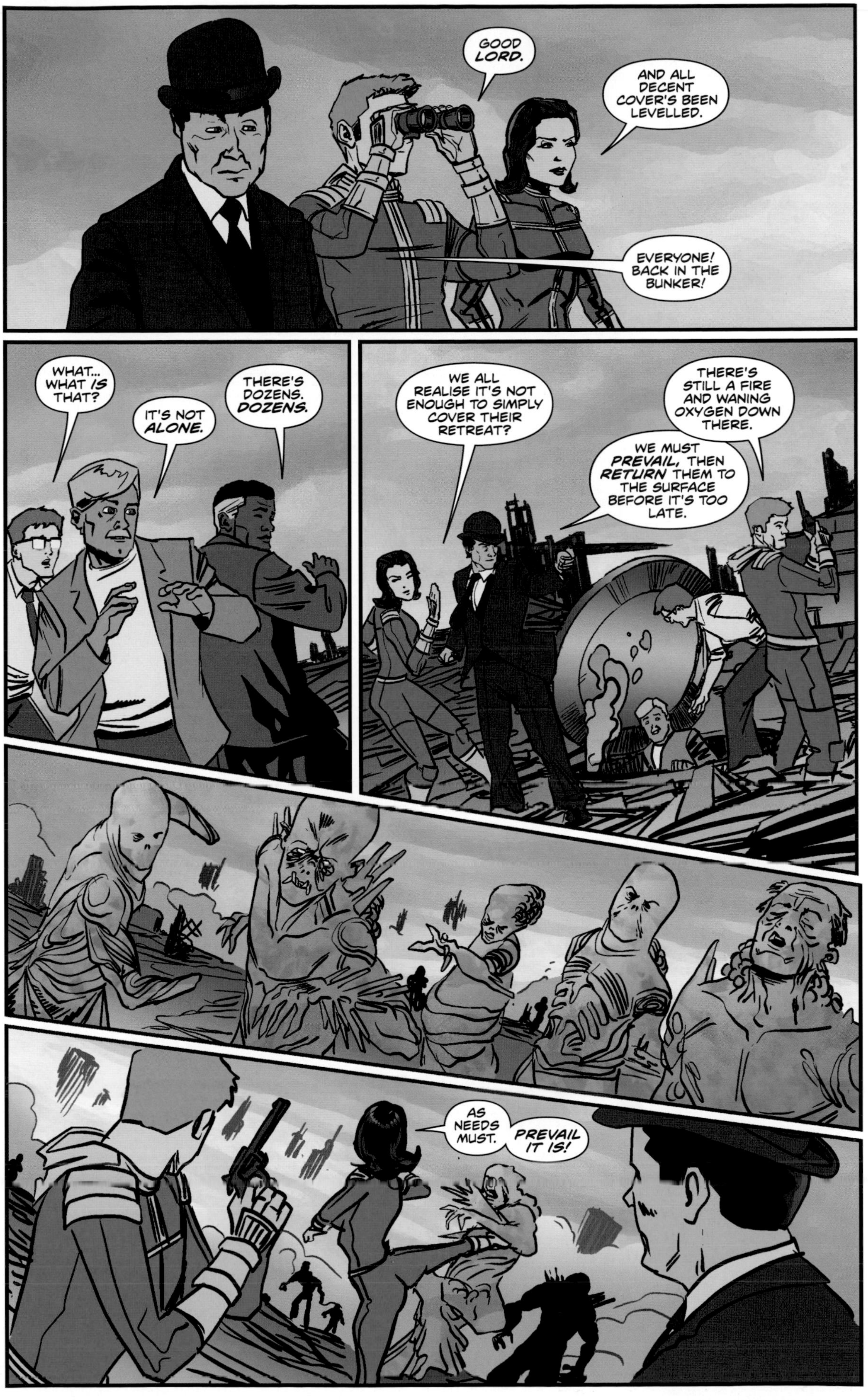
GOOD LORD.
AND ALL DECENT COVER'S BEEN LEVELLED.
EVERYONE! BACK IN THE BUNKER!
WHAT... WHAT IS THAT?
IT'S NOT ALONE.
THERE'S DOZENS. DOZENS.
WE ALL REALISE IT'S NOT ENOUGH TO SIMPLY COVER THEIR RETREAT?
THERE'S STILL A FIRE AND WANING OXYGEN DOWN THERE.
WE MUST PREVAIL, THEN RETURN THEM TO THE SURFACE BEFORE IT'S TOO LATE.
AS NEEDS MUST.
PREVAIL IT IS!

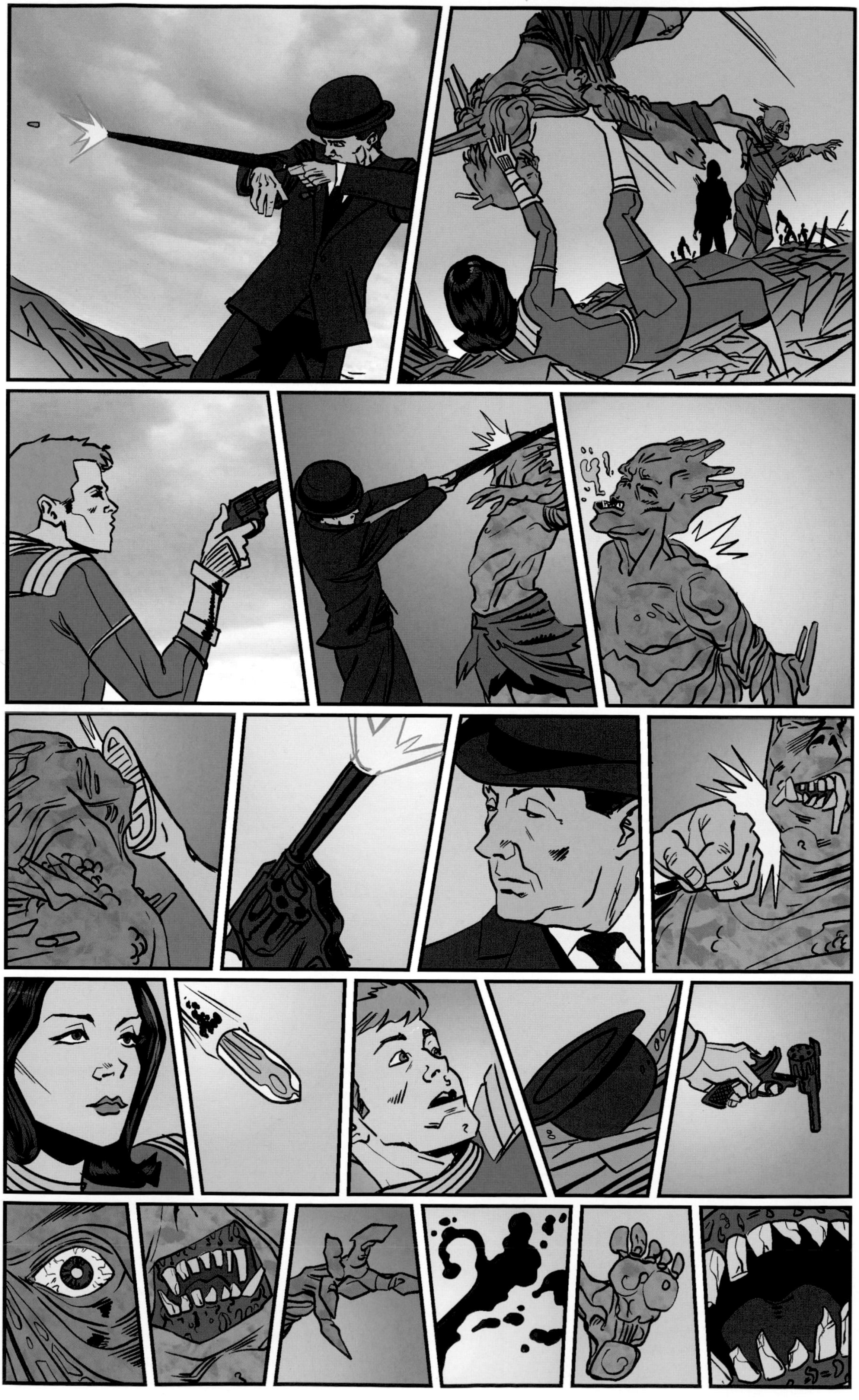

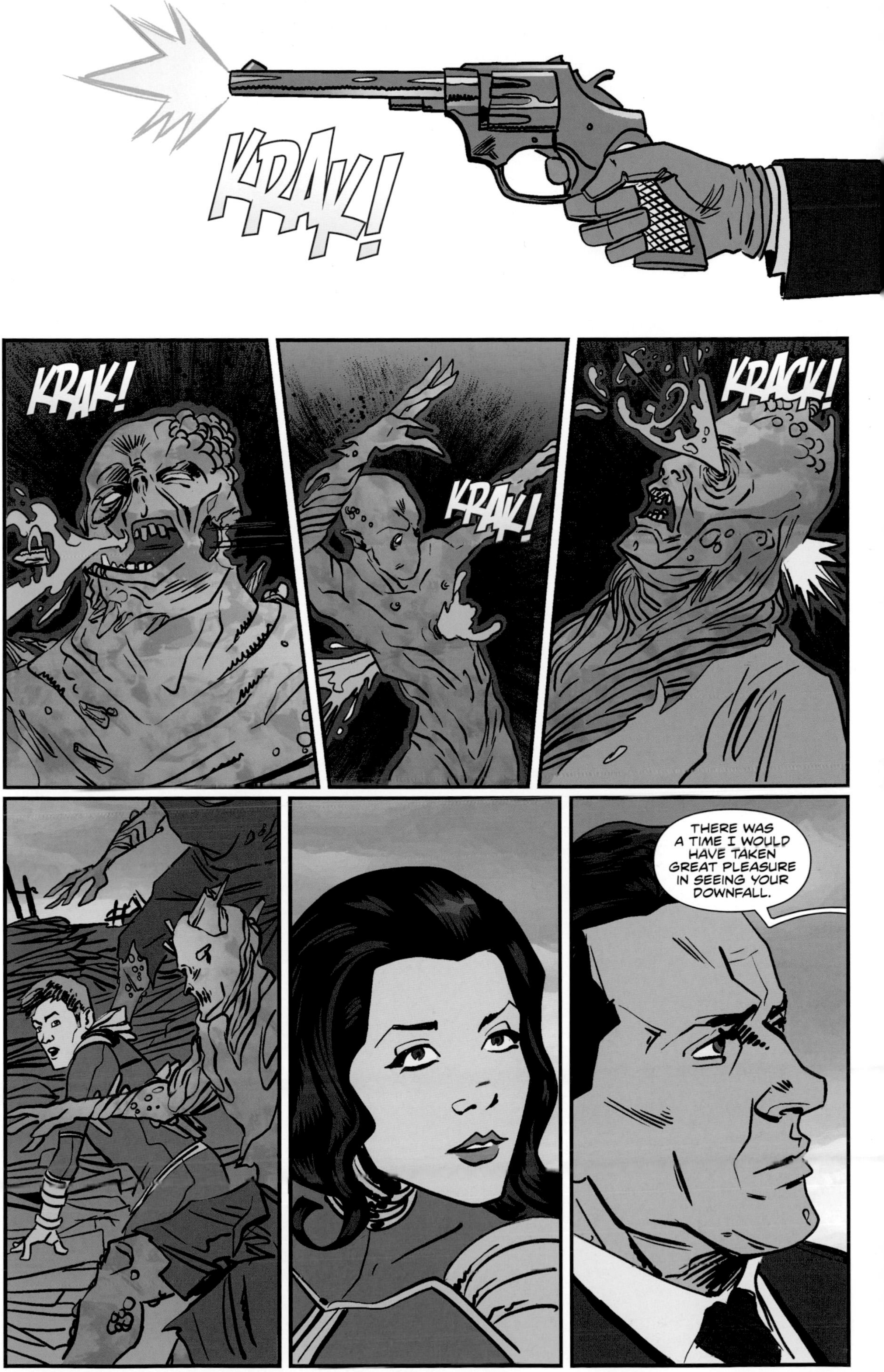
KRAK!
KRAK!
KRAK!
KRACK!
THERE WAS A TIME I WOULD HAVE TAKEN GREAT PLEASURE IN SEEING YOUR DOWNFALL.

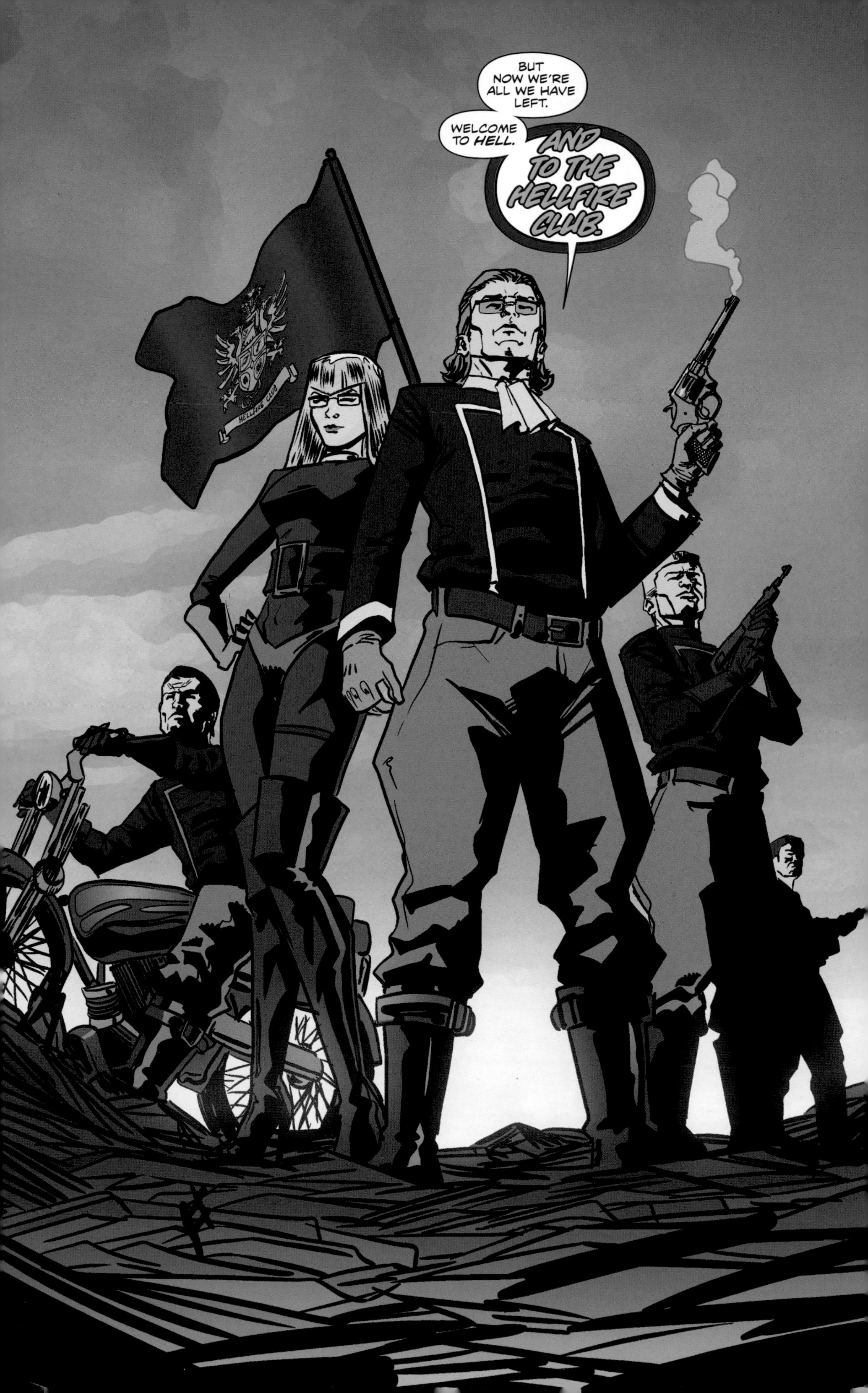
BUT NOW WE'RE ALL WE HAVE LEFT.
WELCOME TO HELL.
AND TO THE HELLFIRE CLUB.
HELLFIRE CLUB

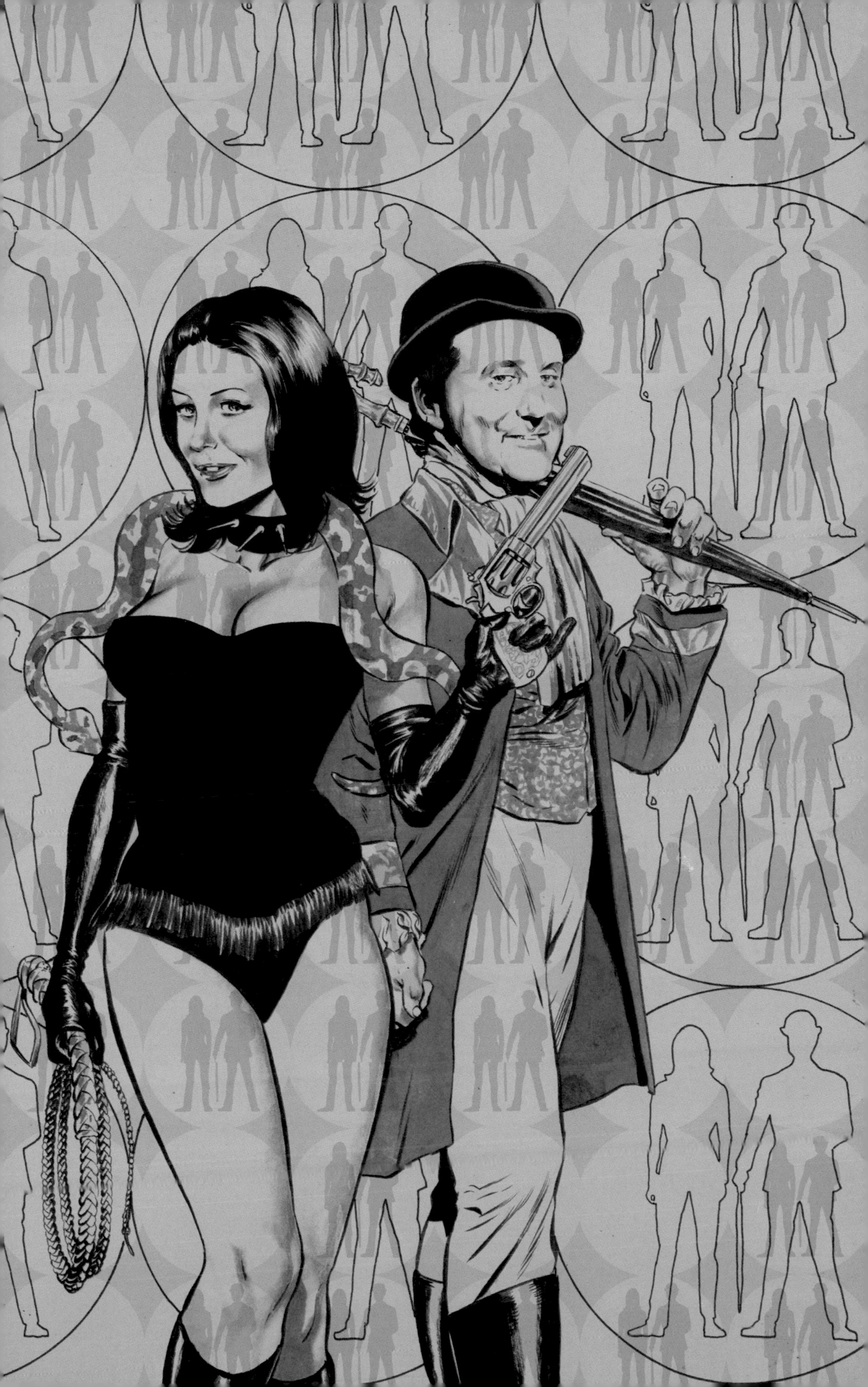

CHAPTER TWO

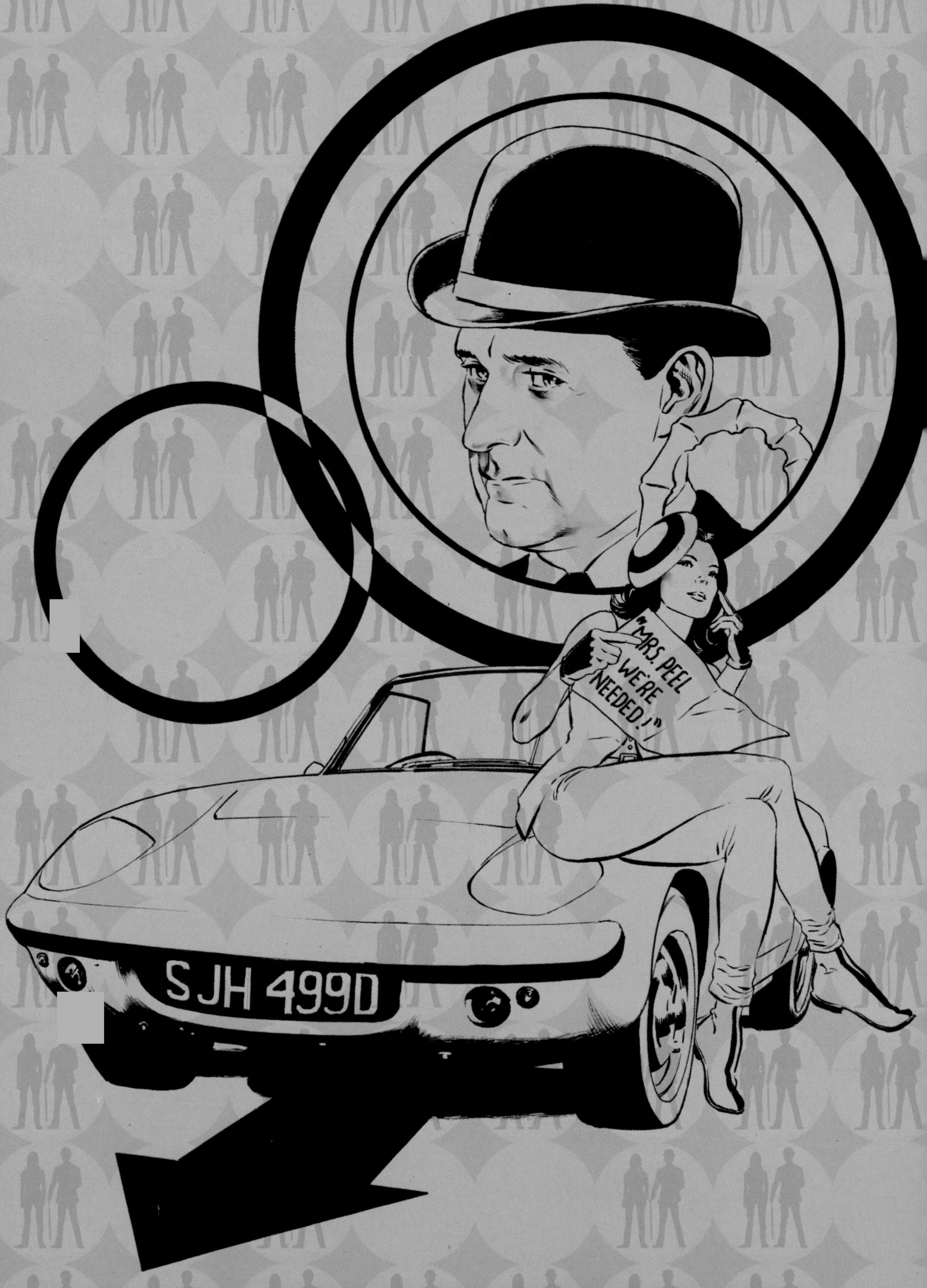
"MRS. PEEL WE'RE NEEDED!"
SJH 499D

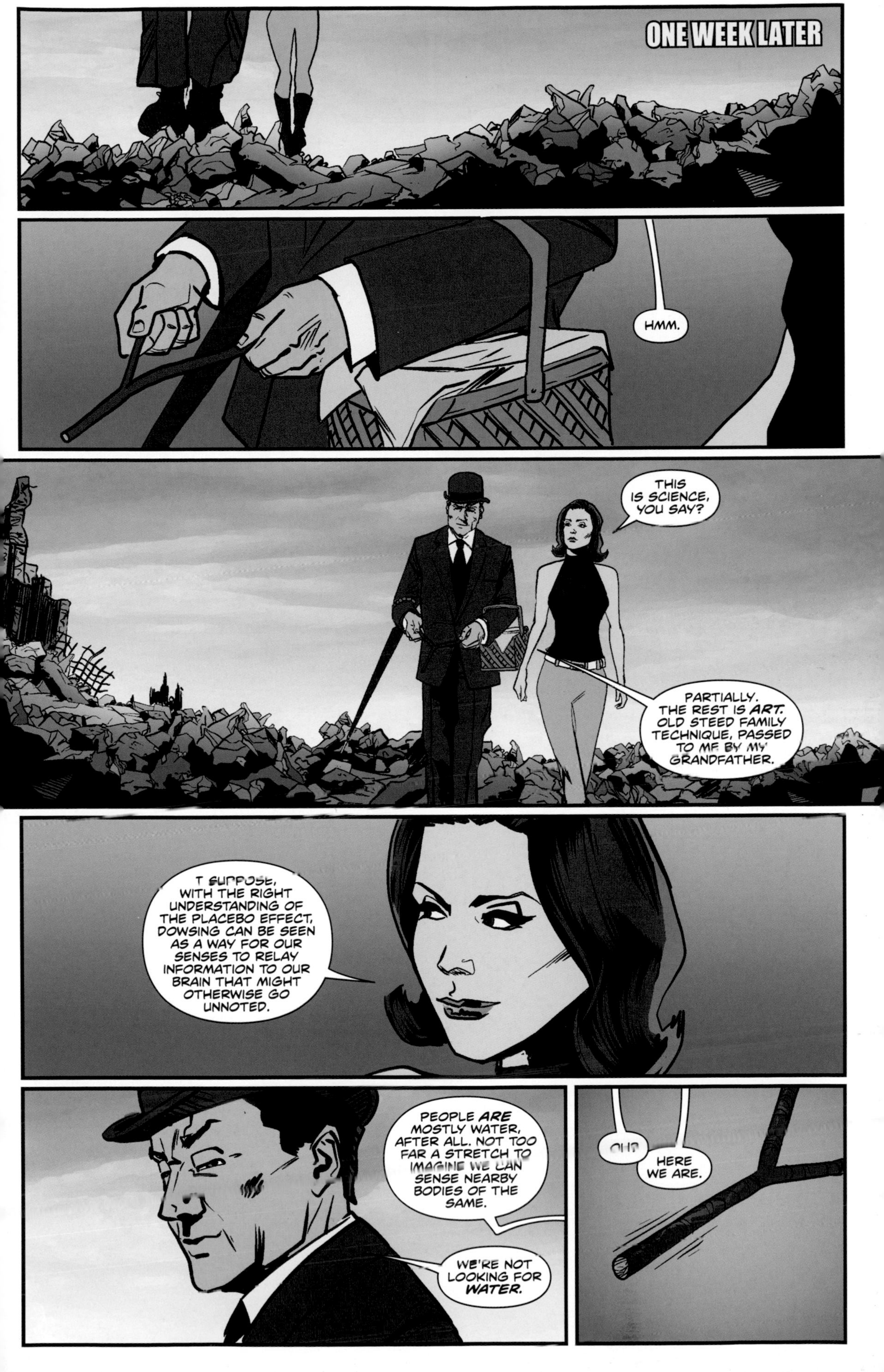
ONE WEEK LATER
HMM.
THIS IS SCIENCE, YOU SAY?
PARTIALLY. THE REST IS ART. OLD STEED FAMILY TECHNIQUE, PASSED TO ME BY MY GRANDFATHER.
I SUPPOSE, WITH THE RIGHT UNDERSTANDING OF THE PLACEBO EFFECT, DOWSING CAN BE SEEN AS A WAY FOR OUR SENSES TO RELAY INFORMATION TO OUR BRAIN THAT MIGHT OTHERWISE GO UNNOTED.
PEOPLE ARE MOSTLY WATER, AFTER ALL. NOT TOO FAR A STRETCH TO IMAGINE WE CAN SENSE NEARBY BODIES OF THE SAME.
WE'RE NOT LOOKING FOR WATER.
OH?
HERE WE ARE.

WOULD YOU?
NOW, A LITTLE DIRT UNDER THE NAILS...
AH.
IT BECOMES APPARENT.
INDEED. AN HONEST REWARD FOR AN HONEST DAY'S LABOUR.

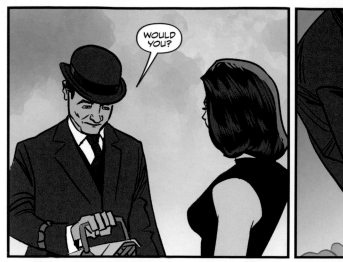

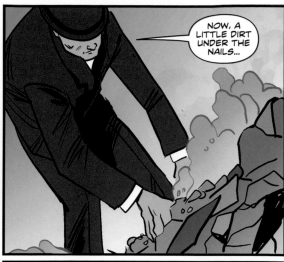

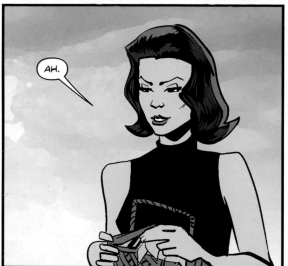

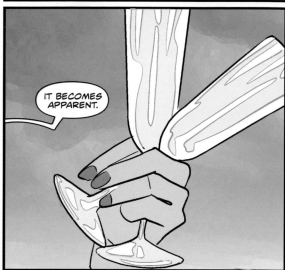

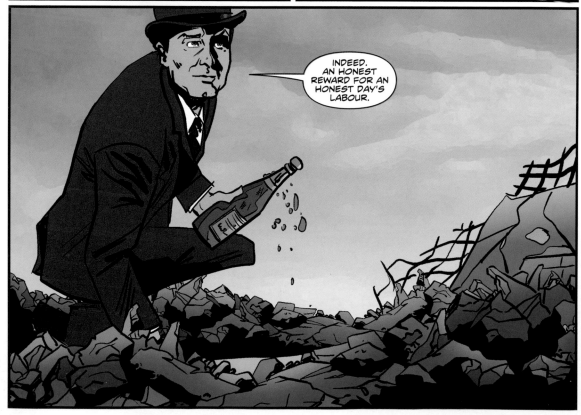

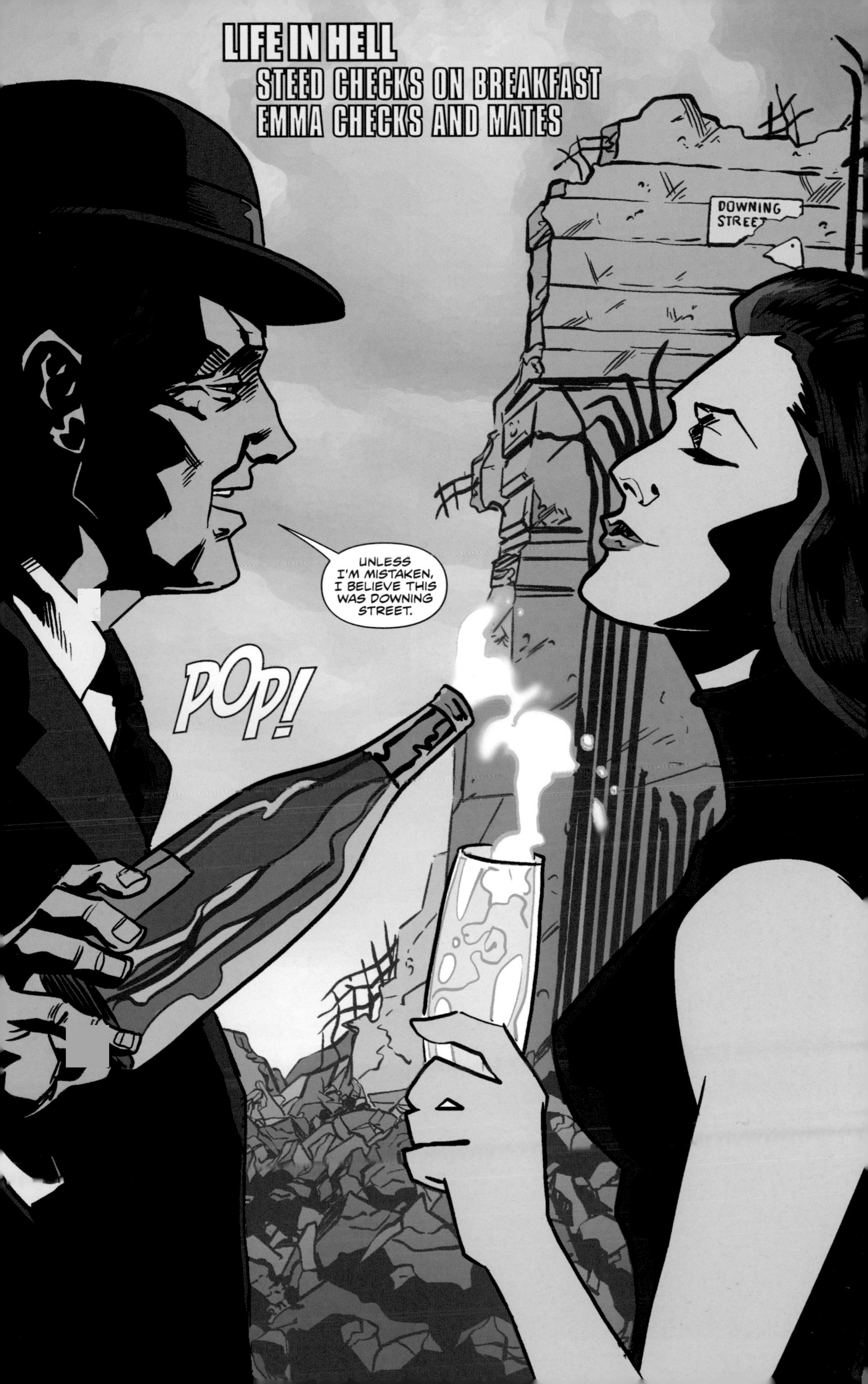
LIFE IN HELL
STEED CHECKS ON BREAKFAST
EMMA CHECKS AND MATES
DOWNING STREET
UNLESS I'M MISTAKEN, I BELIEVE THIS WAS DOWNING STREET.
POP!

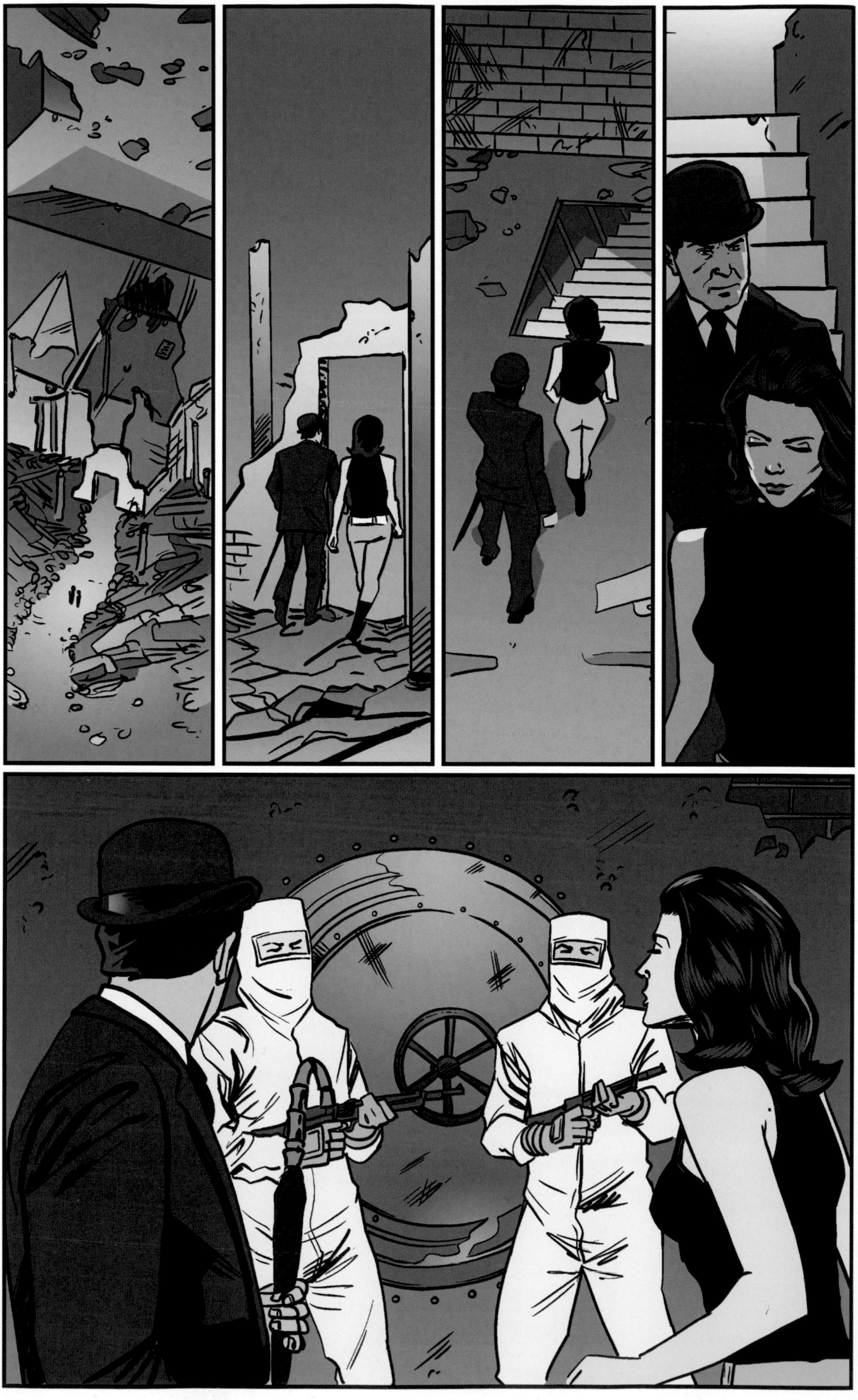

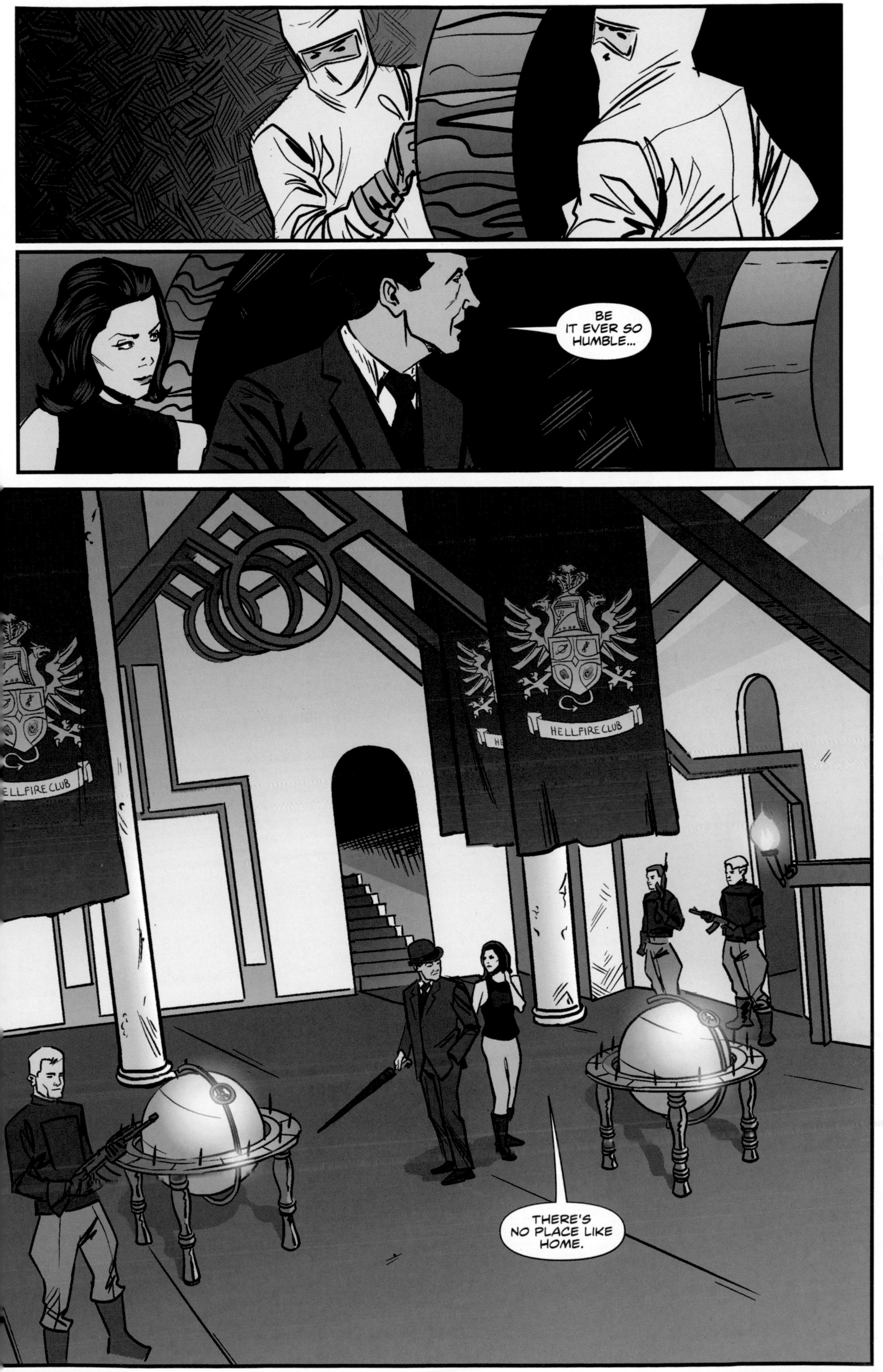
BE IT EVER SO HUMBLE...
HELLFIRE CLUB
HELLFIRE CLUB
THERE'S NO PLACE LIKE HOME.

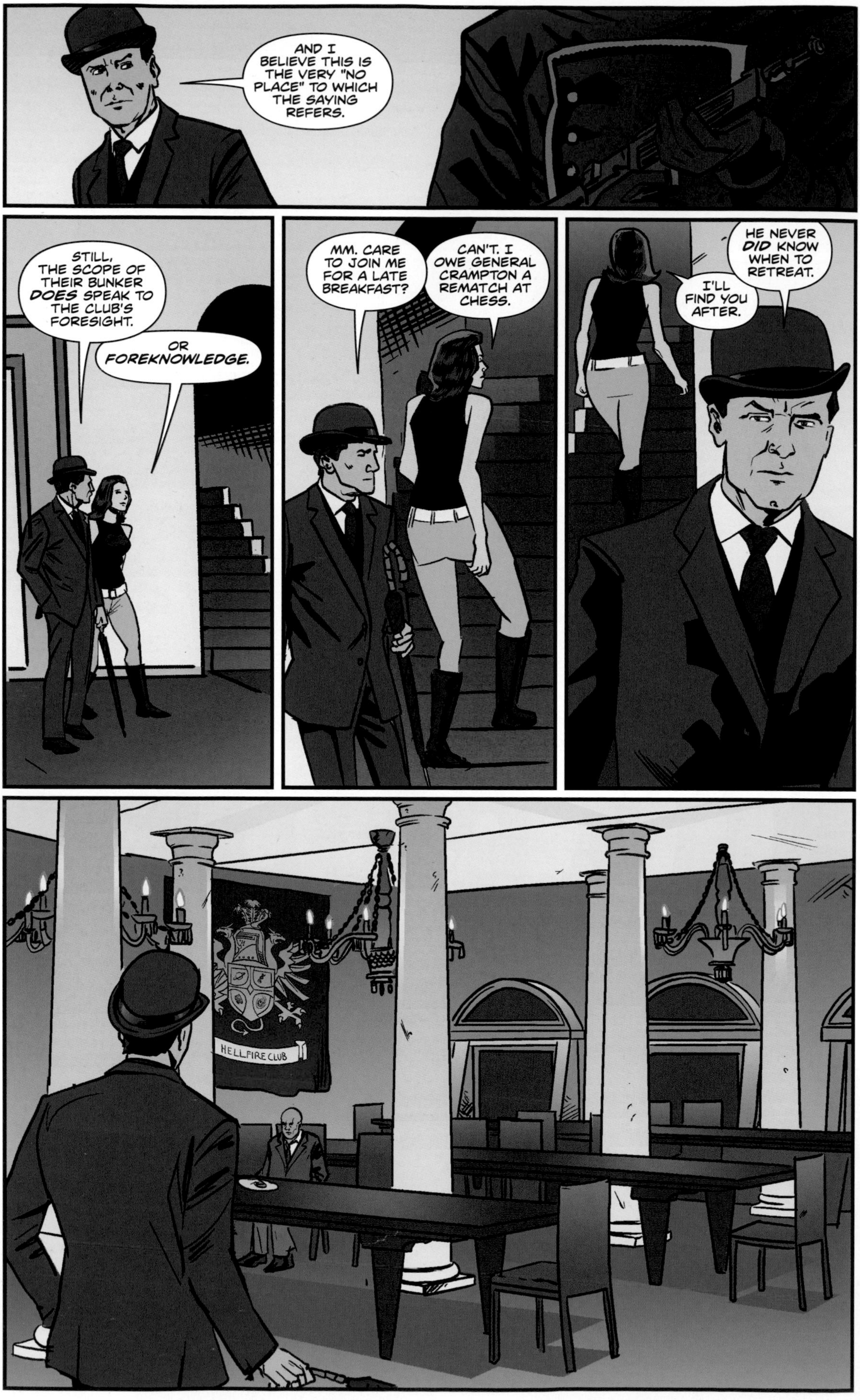
AND I BELIEVE THIS IS THE VERY "NO PLACE" TO WHICH THE SAYING REFERS.
STILL, THE SCOPE OF THEIR BUNKER DOES SPEAK TO THE CLUB'S FORESIGHT.
OR FOREKNOWLEDGE.
MM. CARE TO JOIN ME FOR A LATE BREAKFAST?
CAN'T. I OWE GENERAL CRAMPTON A REMATCH AT CHESS.
I'LL FIND YOU AFTER.
HE NEVER DID KNOW WHEN TO RETREAT.
HELLFIRE CLUB

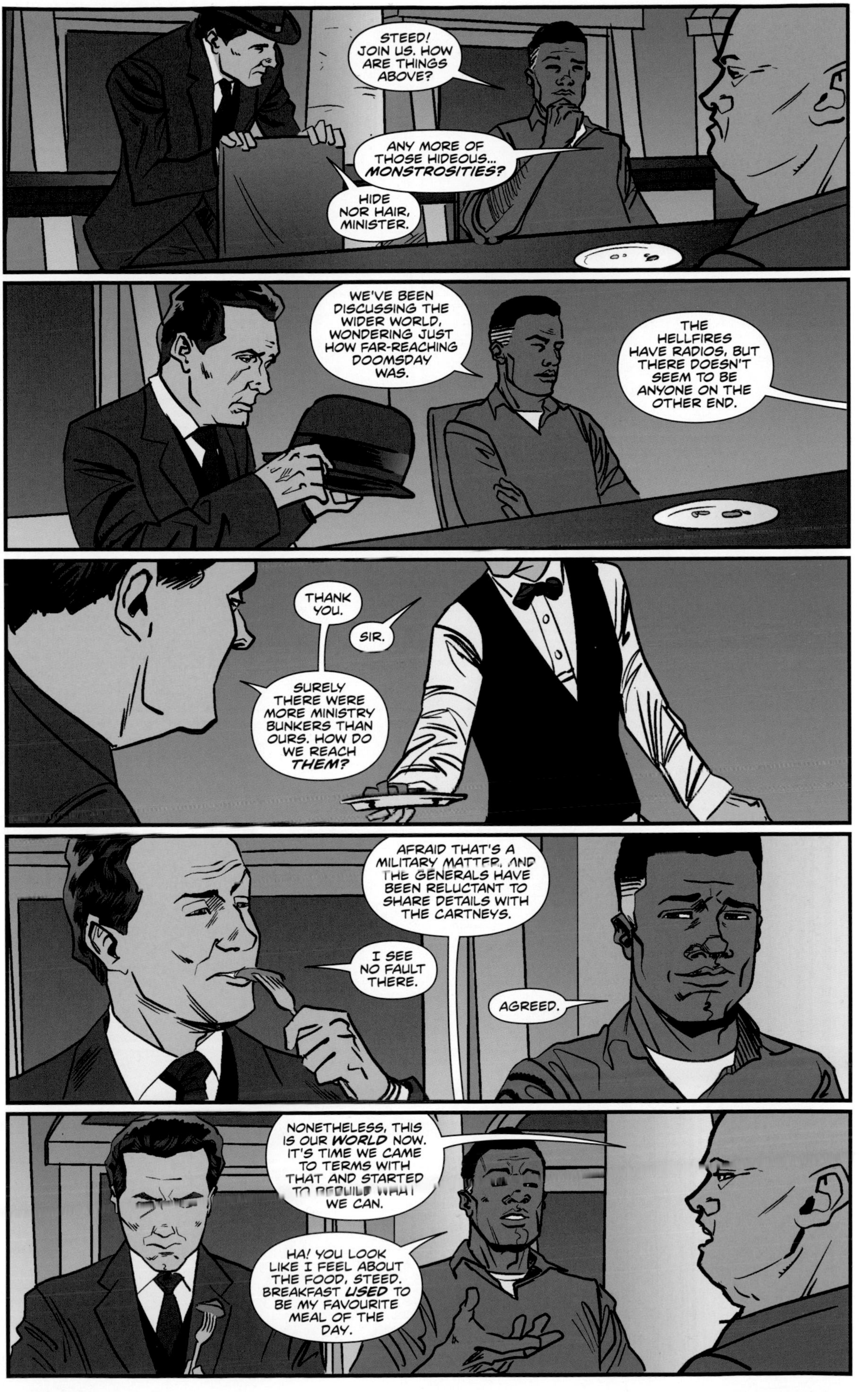
STEED! JOIN US. HOW ARE THINGS ABOVE?
ANY MORE OF THOSE HIDEOUS... *MONSTROSITIES?*
HIDE NOR HAIR, MINISTER.
WE'VE BEEN DISCUSSING THE WIDER WORLD, WONDERING JUST HOW FAR-REACHING DOOMSDAY WAS.
THE HELLFIRES HAVE RADIOS, BUT THERE DOESN'T SEEM TO BE ANYONE ON THE OTHER END.
THANK YOU.
SIR.
SURELY THERE WERE MORE MINISTRY BUNKERS THAN OURS. HOW DO WE REACH *THEM?*
AFRAID THAT'S A MILITARY MATTER, AND THE GENERALS HAVE BEEN RELUCTANT TO SHARE DETAILS WITH THE CARTNEYS.
I SEE NO FAULT THERE.
AGREED.
NONETHELESS, THIS IS OUR *WORLD* NOW. IT'S TIME WE CAME TO TERMS WITH THAT AND STARTED TO REBUILD WHAT WE CAN.
HA! YOU LOOK LIKE I FEEL ABOUT THE FOOD, STEED. BREAKFAST *USED* TO BE MY FAVOURITE MEAL OF THE DAY.

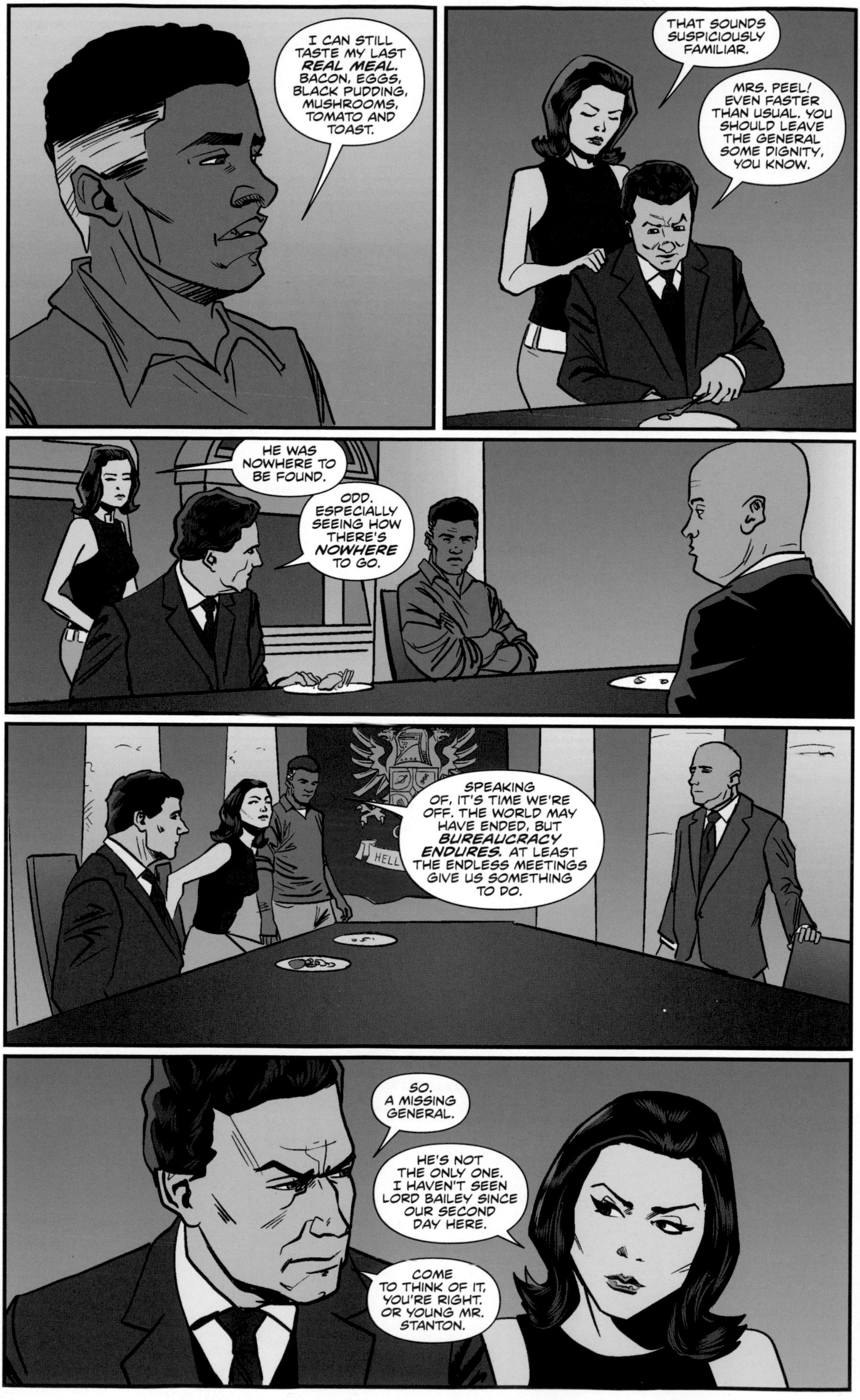

I CAN STILL TASTE MY LAST **REAL MEAL.** BACON, EGGS, BLACK PUDDING, MUSHROOMS, TOMATO AND TOAST.
THAT SOUNDS SUSPICIOUSLY FAMILIAR.
MRS. PEEL! EVEN FASTER THAN USUAL. YOU SHOULD LEAVE THE GENERAL SOME DIGNITY, YOU KNOW.
HE WAS NOWHERE TO BE FOUND.
ODD. ESPECIALLY SEEING HOW THERE'S ***NOWHERE*** TO GO.
SPEAKING OF, IT'S TIME WE'RE OFF. THE WORLD MAY HAVE ENDED, BUT ***BUREAUCRACY ENDURES.*** AT LEAST THE ENDLESS MEETINGS GIVE US SOMETHING TO DO.
SO. A MISSING GENERAL.
HE'S NOT THE ONLY ONE. I HAVEN'T SEEN LORD BAILEY SINCE OUR SECOND DAY HERE.
COME TO THINK OF IT, YOU'RE RIGHT. OR YOUNG MR. STANTON.

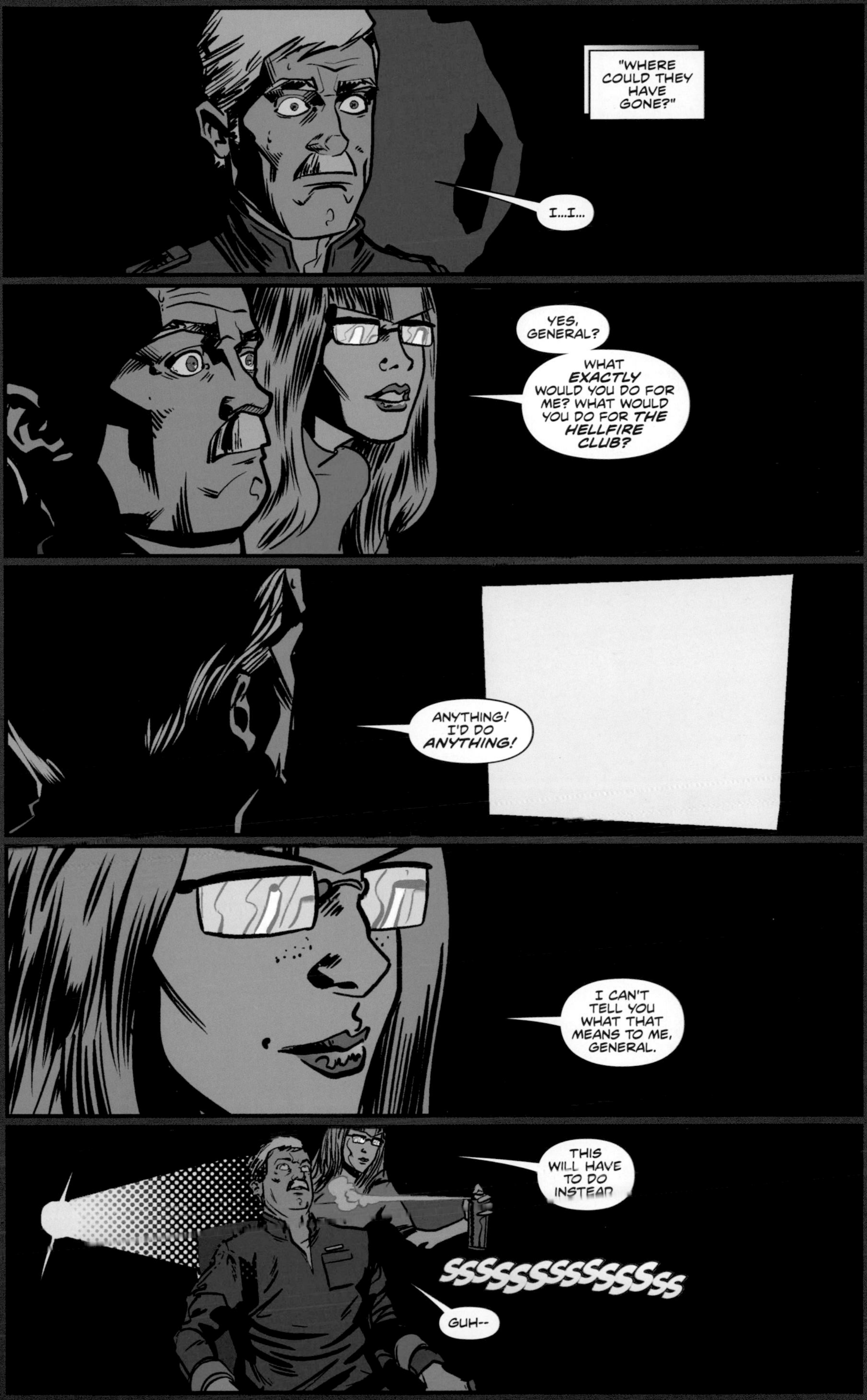
"WHERE COULD THEY HAVE GONE?"
I...I...
YES, GENERAL?
WHAT *EXACTLY* WOULD YOU DO FOR ME? WHAT WOULD YOU DO FOR *THE HELLFIRE CLUB?*
ANYTHING! I'D DO *ANYTHING!*
I CAN'T TELL YOU WHAT THAT MEANS TO ME, GENERAL.
THIS WILL HAVE TO DO INSTEAD
SSSSSSSSSSSSss
GUH--

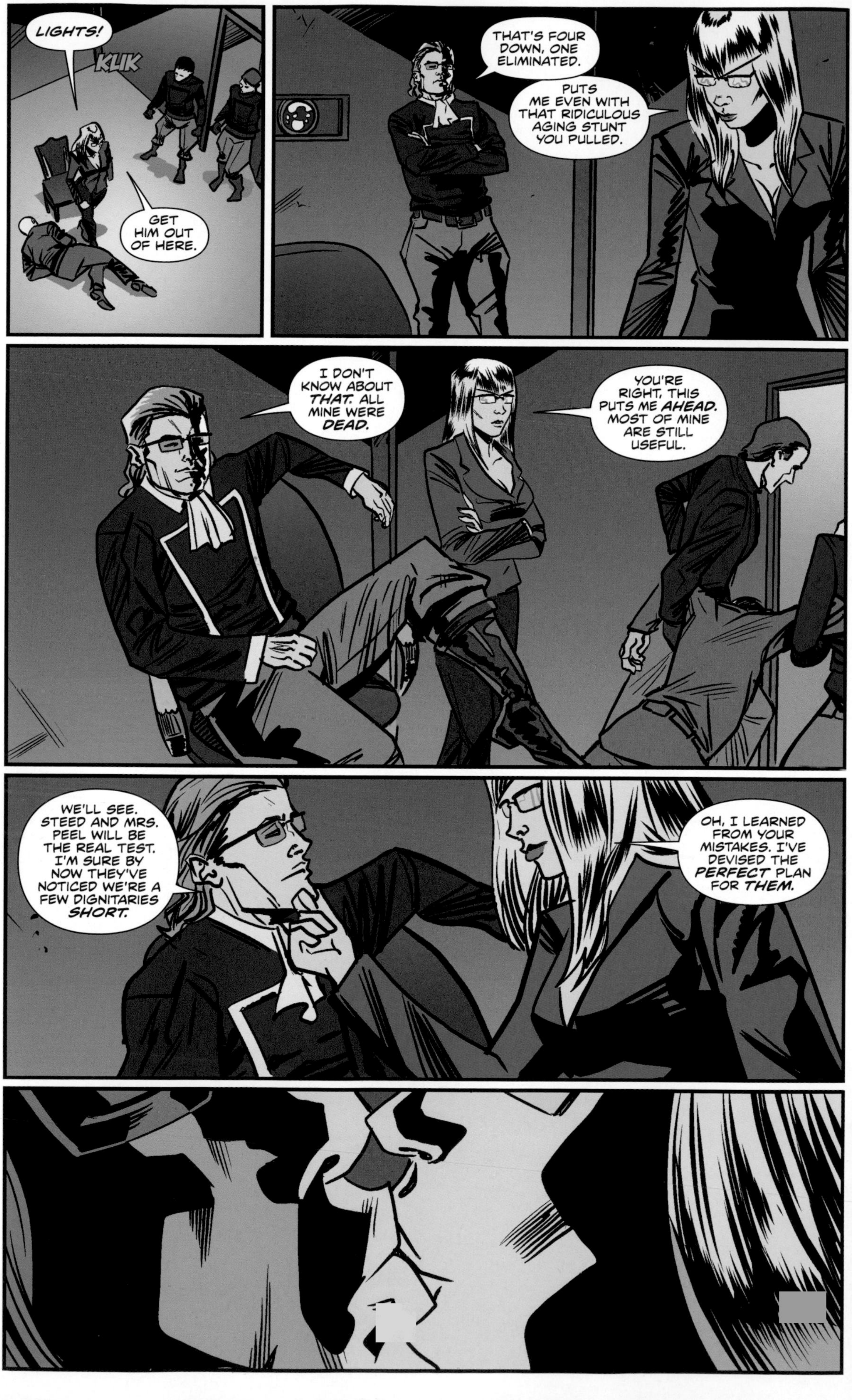
LIGHTS!
KLIK
GET HIM OUT OF HERE.
THAT'S FOUR DOWN, ONE ELIMINATED.
PUTS ME EVEN WITH THAT RIDICULOUS AGING STUNT YOU PULLED.
I DON'T KNOW ABOUT THAT. ALL MINE WERE DEAD.
YOU'RE RIGHT, THIS PUTS ME AHEAD. MOST OF MINE ARE STILL USEFUL.
WE'LL SEE. STEED AND MRS. PEEL WILL BE THE REAL TEST. I'M SURE BY NOW THEY'VE NOTICED WE'RE A FEW DIGNITARIES SHORT.
OH, I LEARNED FROM YOUR MISTAKES. I'VE DEVISED THE PERFECT PLAN FOR THEM.

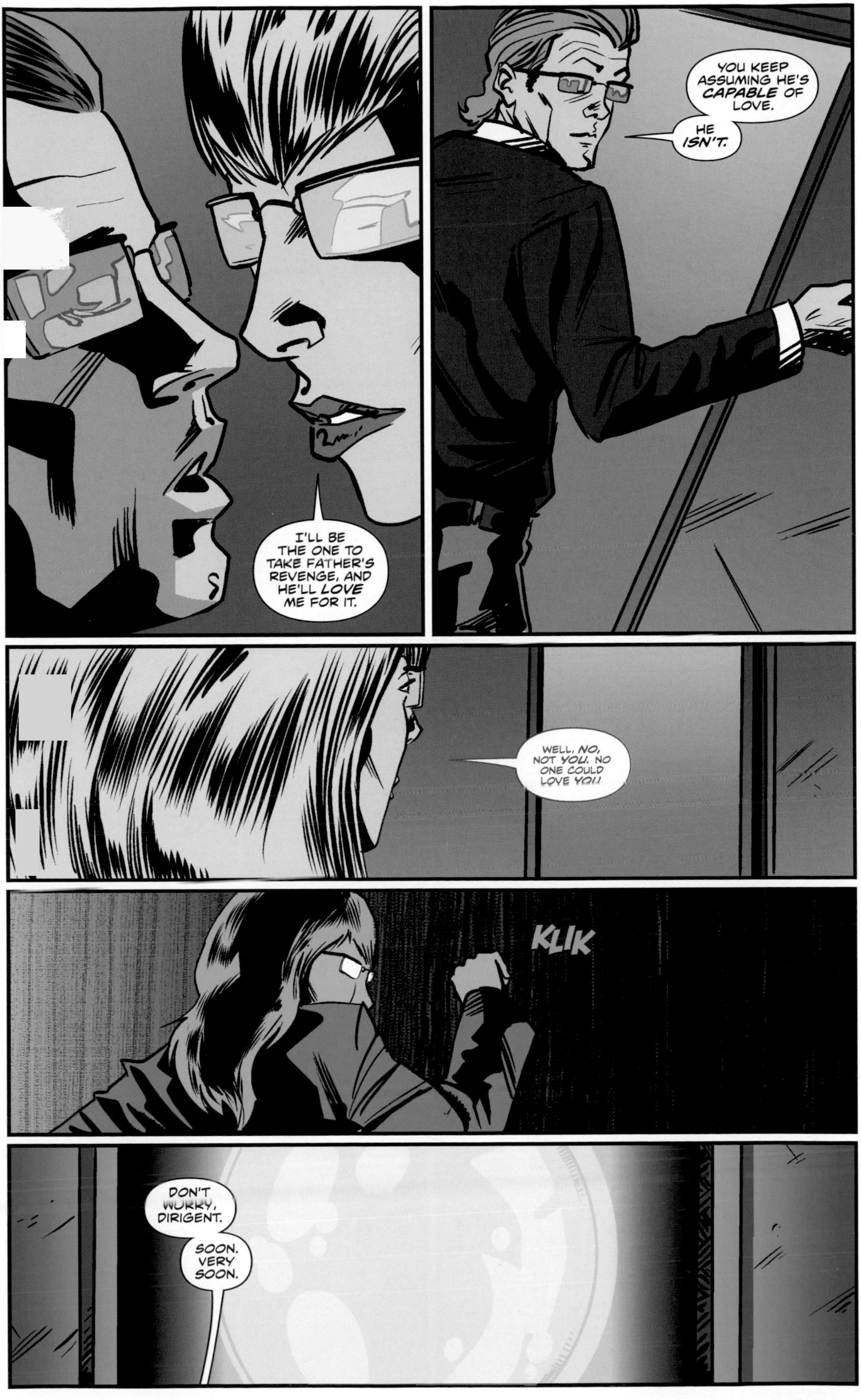
I'LL BE THE ONE TO TAKE FATHER'S REVENGE, AND HE'LL LOVE ME FOR IT.
YOU KEEP ASSUMING HE'S CAPABLE OF LOVE.
HE ISN'T.
WELL, NO, NOT YOU. NO ONE COULD LOVE YOU.
KLIK
DON'T WORRY, DIRIGENT.
SOON. VERY SOON.

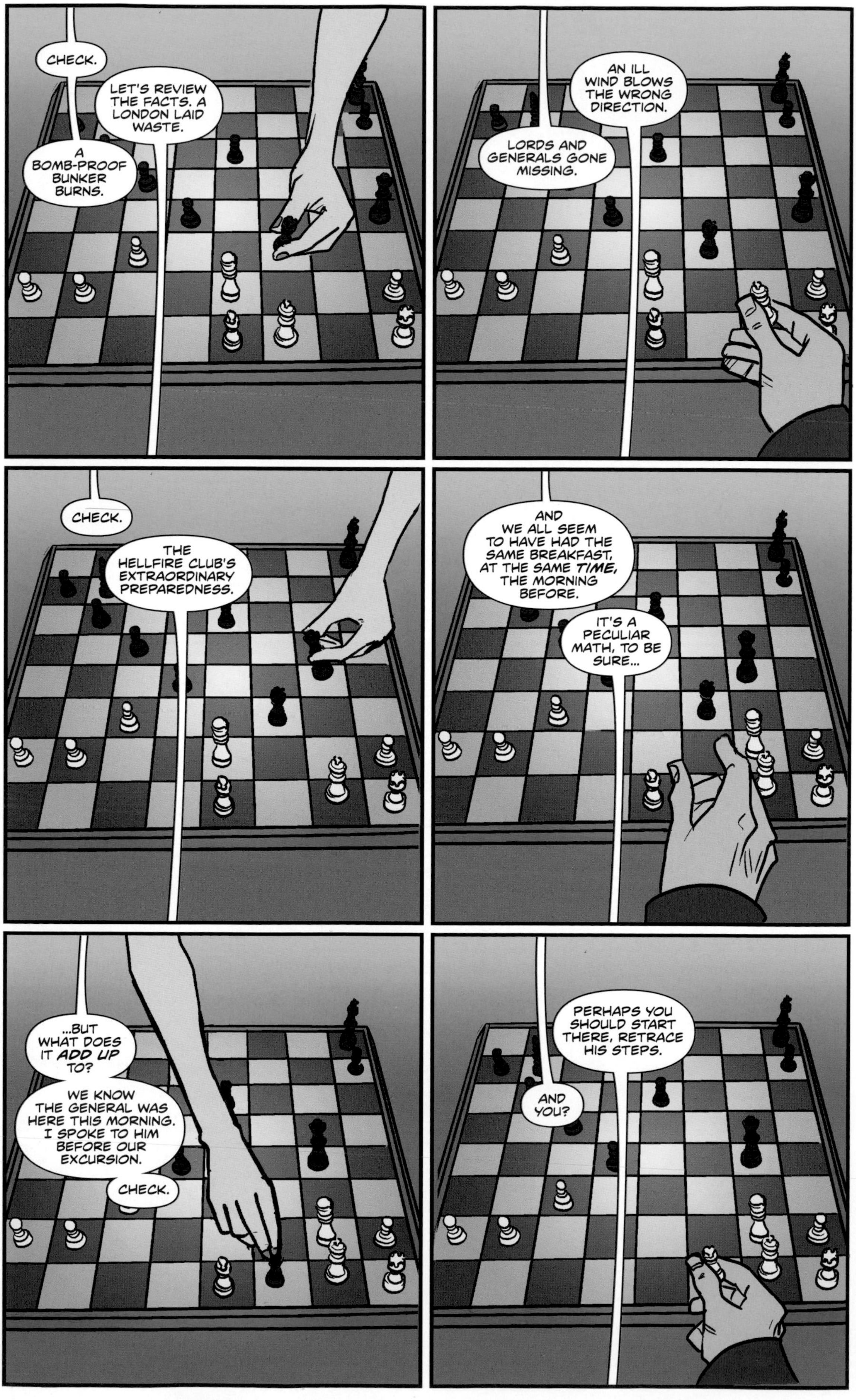
CHECK.
LET'S REVIEW THE FACTS. A LONDON LAID WASTE.
A BOMB-PROOF BUNKER BURNS.
AN ILL WIND BLOWS THE WRONG DIRECTION.
LORDS AND GENERALS GONE MISSING.
CHECK.
THE HELLFIRE CLUB'S EXTRAORDINARY PREPAREDNESS.
AND WE ALL SEEM TO HAVE HAD THE SAME BREAKFAST, AT THE SAME *TIME*, THE MORNING BEFORE.
IT'S A PECULIAR MATH, TO BE SURE...
...BUT WHAT DOES IT **ADD UP** TO?
WE KNOW THE GENERAL WAS HERE THIS MORNING. I SPOKE TO HIM BEFORE OUR EXCURSION.
CHECK.
PERHAPS YOU SHOULD START THERE, RETRACE HIS STEPS.
AND YOU?

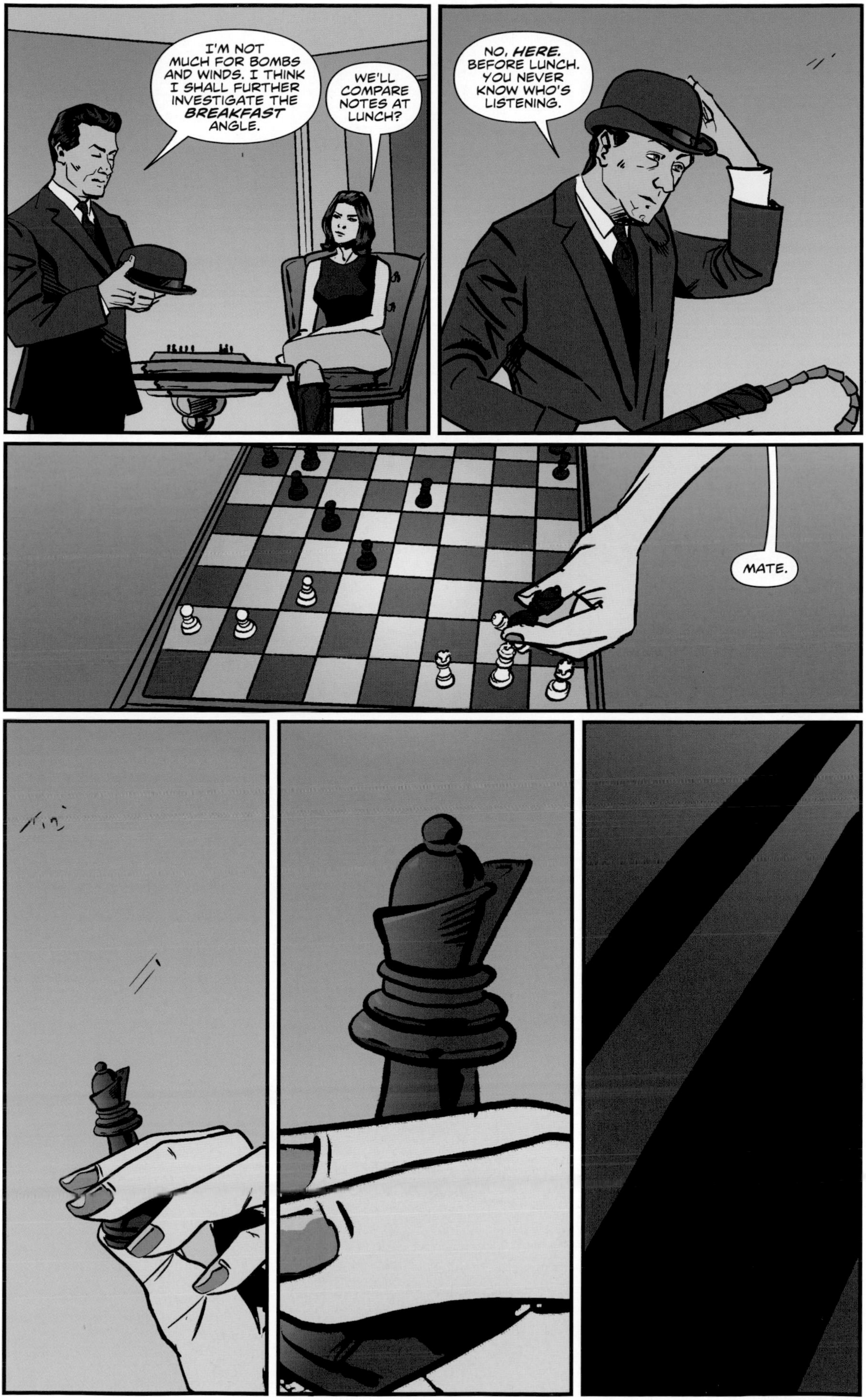
I'M NOT MUCH FOR BOMBS AND WINDS. I THINK I SHALL FURTHER INVESTIGATE THE *BREAKFAST* ANGLE.
WE'LL COMPARE NOTES AT LUNCH?
NO, *HERE.* BEFORE LUNCH. YOU NEVER KNOW WHO'S LISTENING.
MATE.

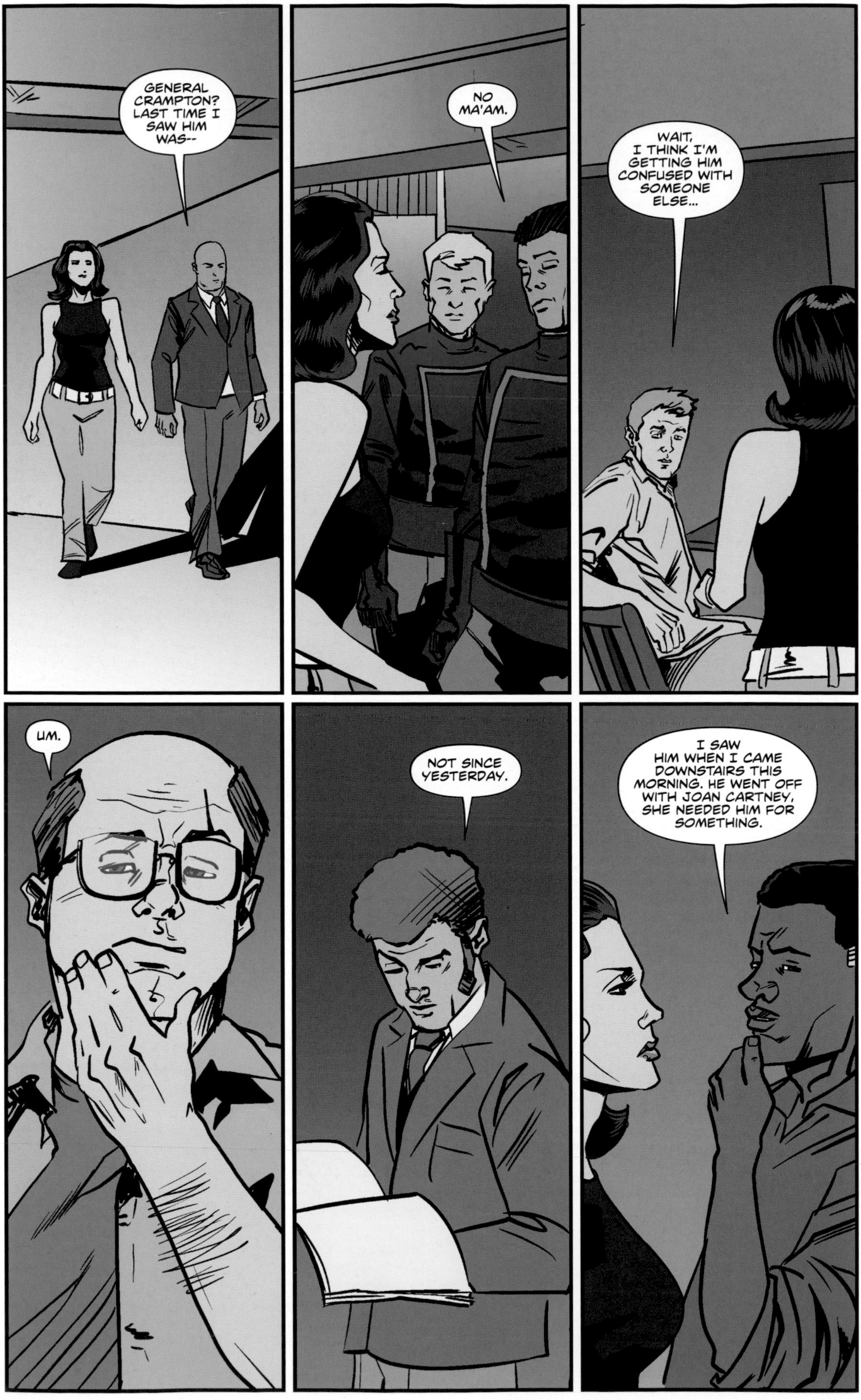
GENERAL CRAMPTON? LAST TIME I SAW HIM WAS--
NO MA'AM.
WAIT, I THINK I'M GETTING HIM CONFUSED WITH SOMEONE ELSE...
UM.
NOT SINCE YESTERDAY.
I SAW HIM WHEN I CAME DOWNSTAIRS THIS MORNING. HE WENT OFF WITH JOAN CARTNEY, SHE NEEDED HIM FOR SOMETHING.

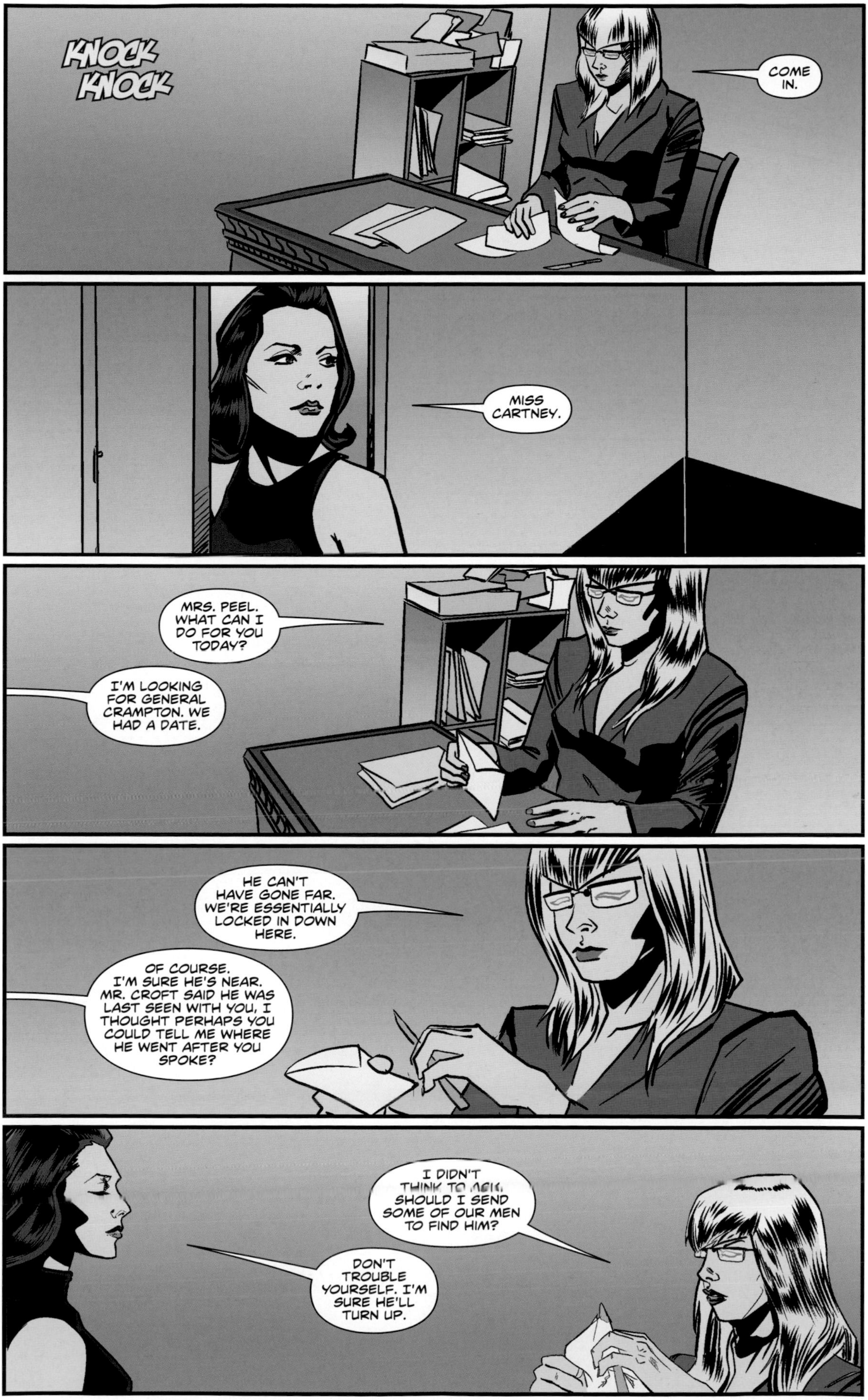
KNOCK KNOCK
COME IN.
MISS CARTNEY.
MRS. PEEL. WHAT CAN I DO FOR YOU TODAY?
I'M LOOKING FOR GENERAL CRAMPTON. WE HAD A DATE.
HE CAN'T HAVE GONE FAR. WE'RE ESSENTIALLY LOCKED IN DOWN HERE.
OF COURSE. I'M SURE HE'S NEAR. MR. CROFT SAID HE WAS LAST SEEN WITH YOU, I THOUGHT PERHAPS YOU COULD TELL ME WHERE HE WENT AFTER YOU SPOKE?
I DIDN'T THINK TO ASK. SHOULD I SEND SOME OF OUR MEN TO FIND HIM?
DON'T TROUBLE YOURSELF. I'M SURE HE'LL TURN UP.

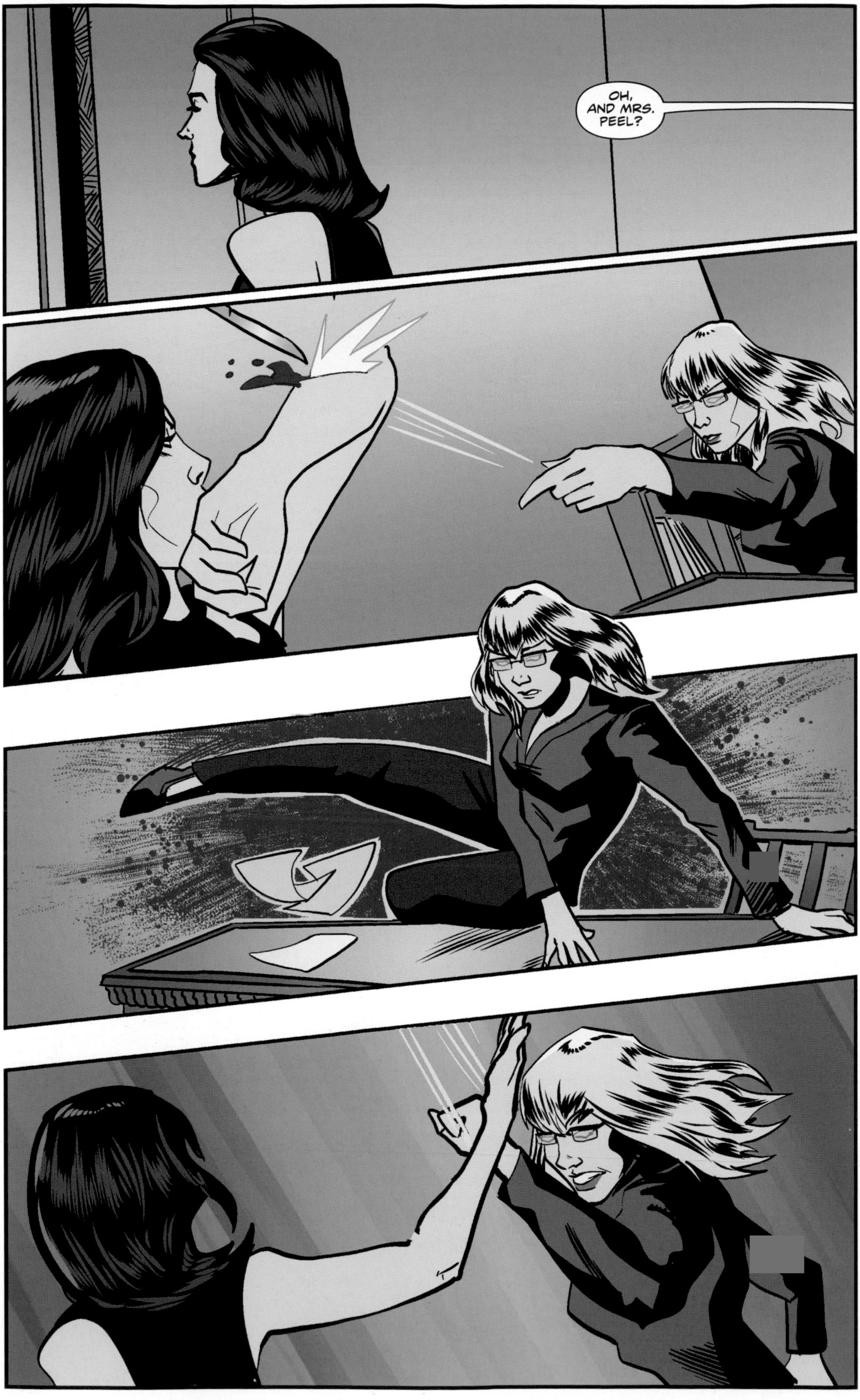
OH, AND MRS. PEEL?

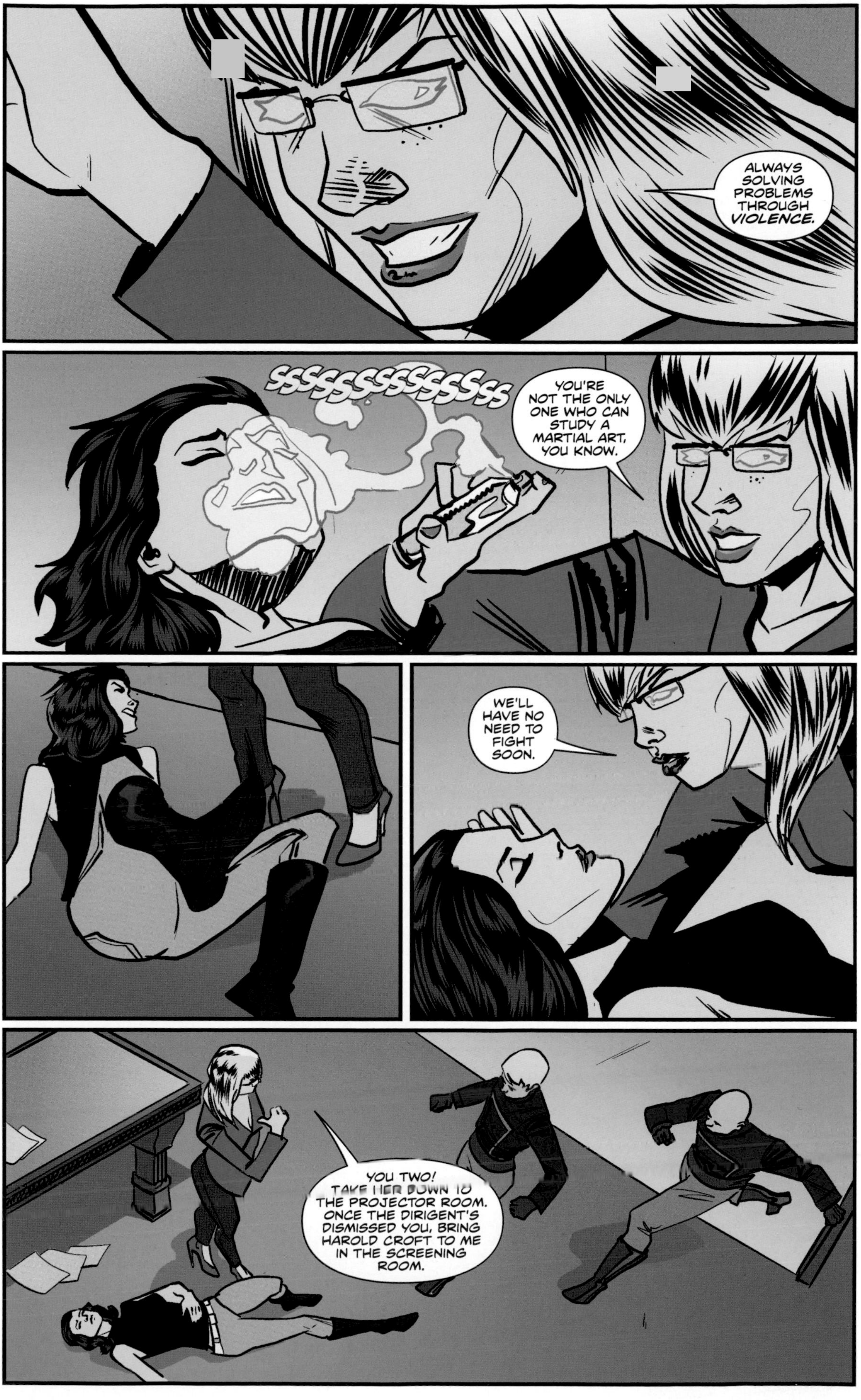
ALWAYS SOLVING PROBLEMS THROUGH *VIOLENCE.*
SSSSSSSSSSSSSS
YOU'RE NOT THE ONLY ONE WHO CAN STUDY A MARTIAL ART, YOU KNOW.
WE'LL HAVE NO NEED TO FIGHT SOON.
YOU TWO! TAKE HER DOWN TO THE PROJECTOR ROOM. ONCE THE DIRIGENT'S DISMISSED YOU, BRING HAROLD CROFT TO ME IN THE SCREENING ROOM.

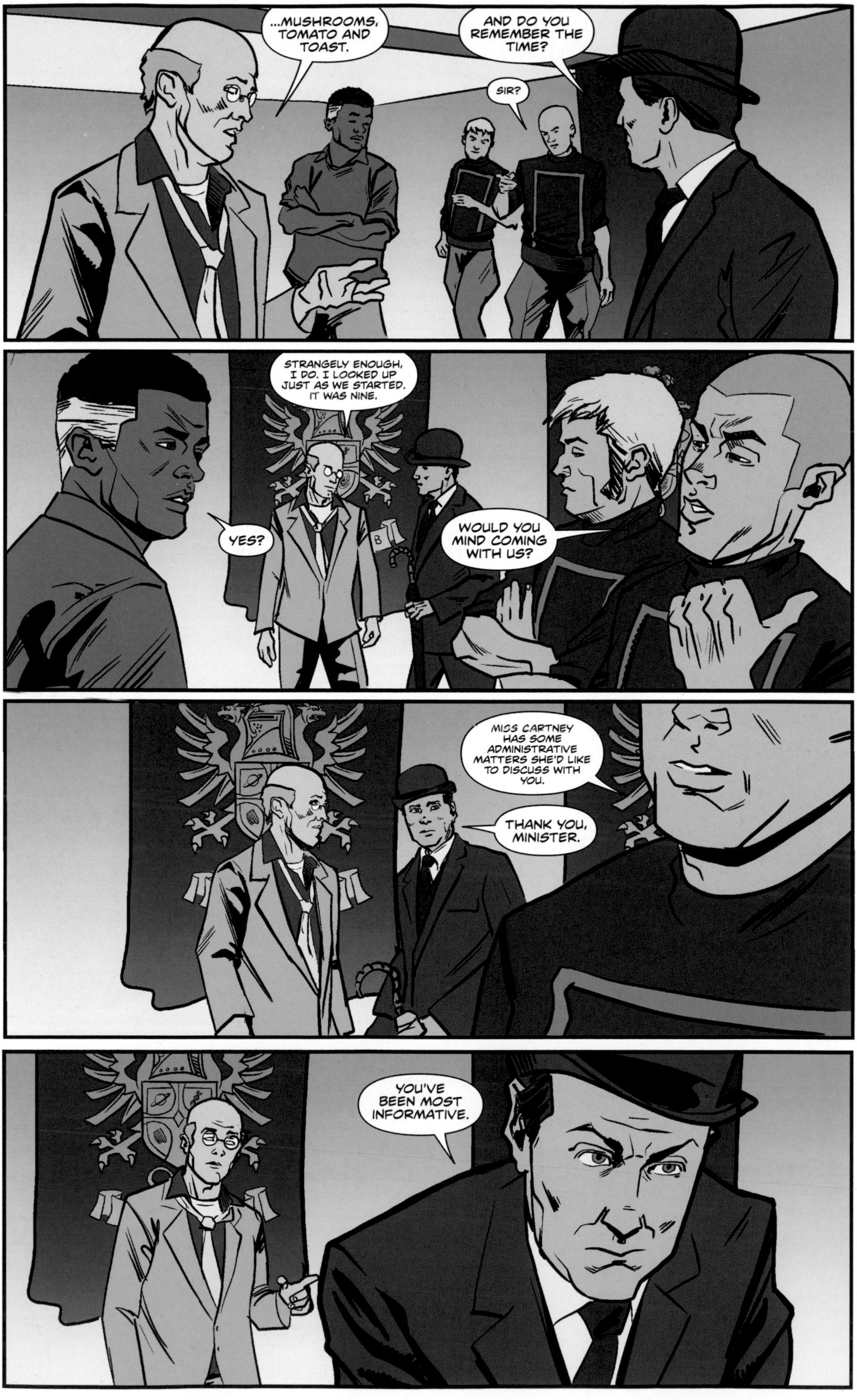
...MUSHROOMS, TOMATO AND TOAST.
AND DO YOU REMEMBER THE TIME?
SIR?
STRANGELY ENOUGH, I DO. I LOOKED UP JUST AS WE STARTED. IT WAS NINE.
YES?
WOULD YOU MIND COMING WITH US?
MISS CARTNEY HAS SOME ADMINISTRATIVE MATTERS SHE'D LIKE TO DISCUSS WITH YOU.
THANK YOU, MINISTER.
YOU'VE BEEN MOST INFORMATIVE.

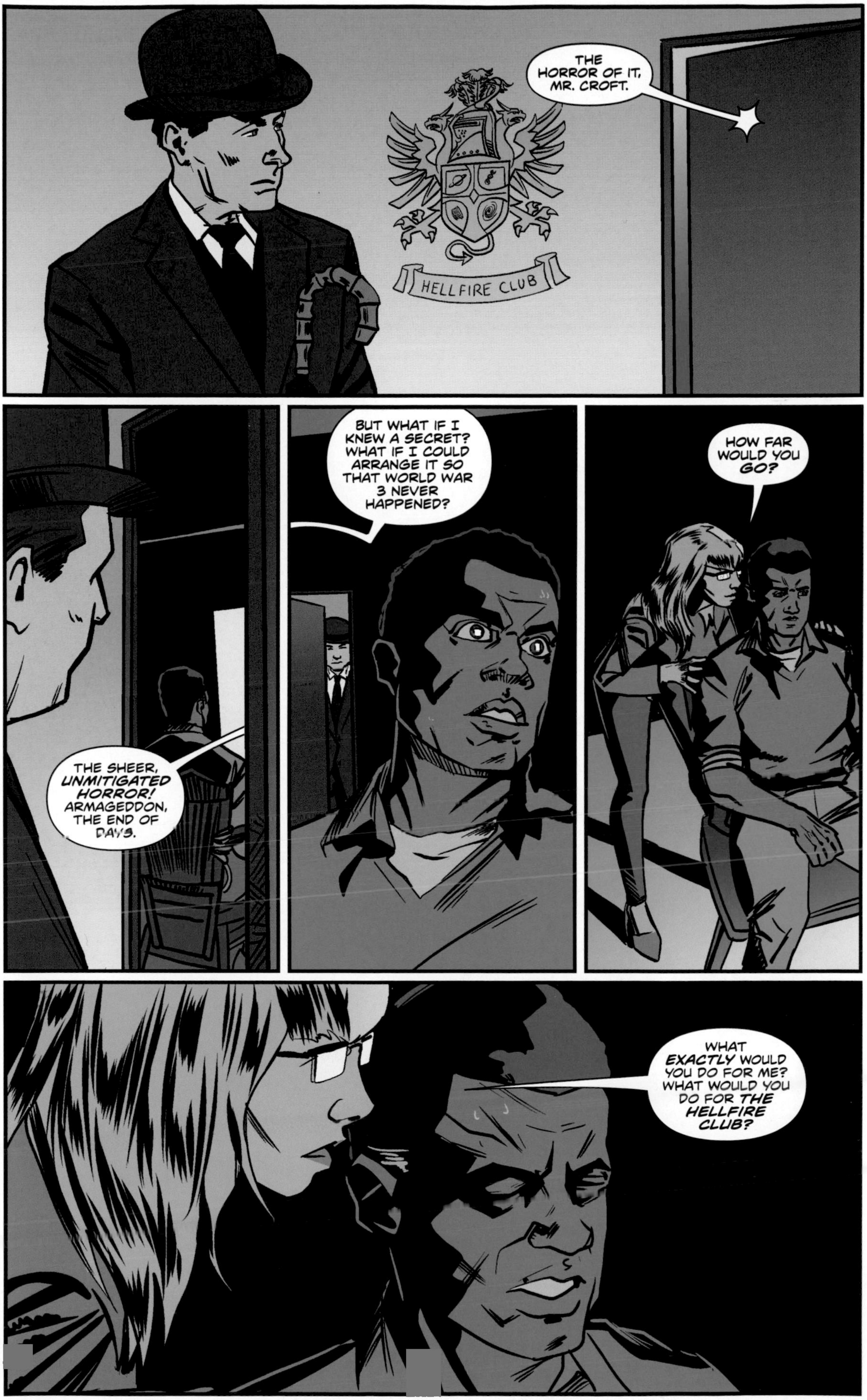
THE HORROR OF IT, MR. CROFT.
HELLFIRE CLUB
THE SHEER, *UNMITIGATED HORROR!* ARMAGEDDON, THE END OF DAYS.
BUT WHAT IF I KNEW A SECRET? WHAT IF I COULD ARRANGE IT SO THAT WORLD WAR 3 NEVER HAPPENED?
HOW FAR WOULD YOU *GO?*
WHAT *EXACTLY* WOULD YOU DO FOR ME? WHAT WOULD YOU DO FOR *THE HELLFIRE CLUB?*

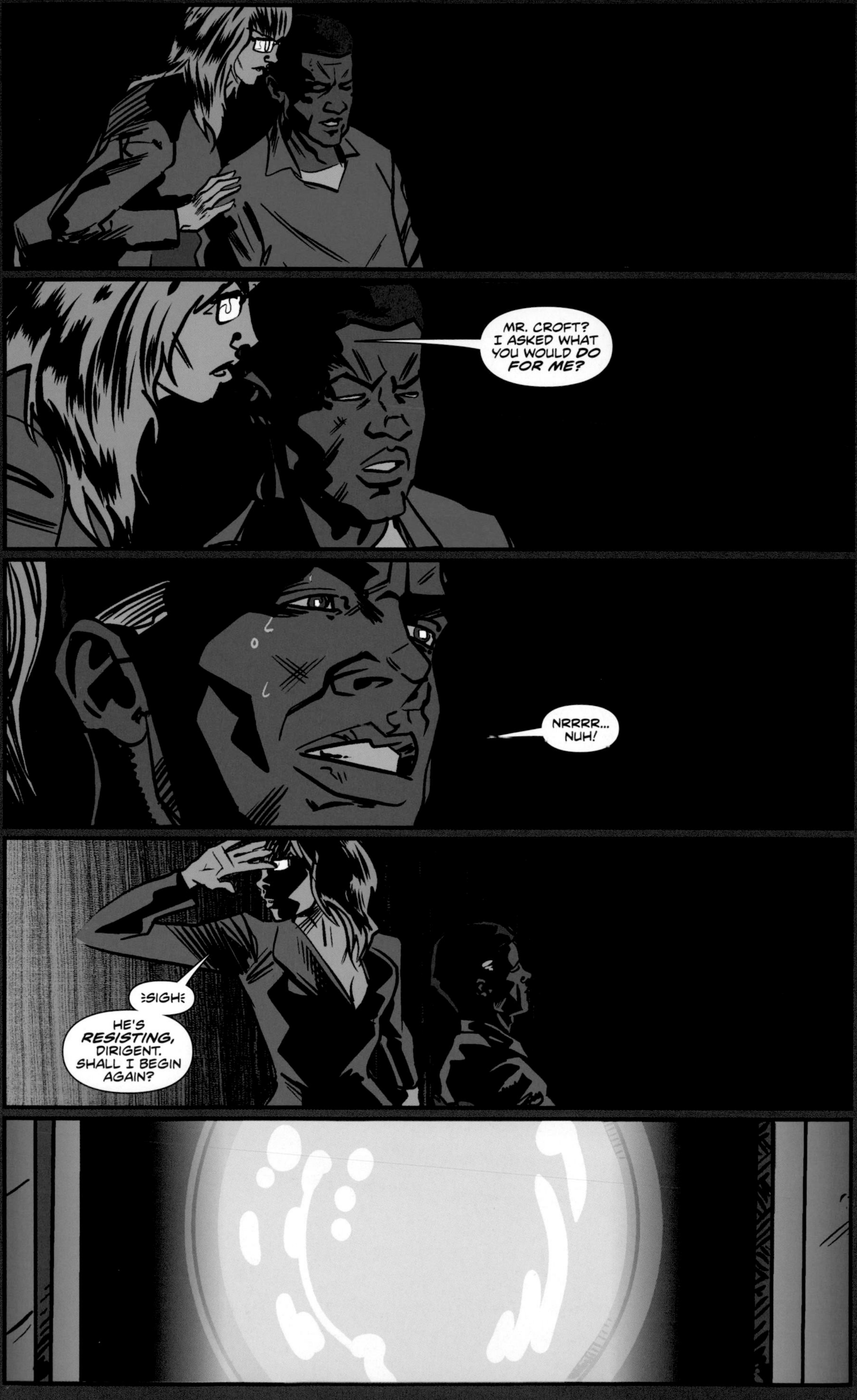
MR. CROFT? I ASKED WHAT YOU WOULD DO FOR ME?
NRRRR... NUH!
SIGH
HE'S RESISTING, DIRIGENT. SHALL I BEGIN AGAIN?

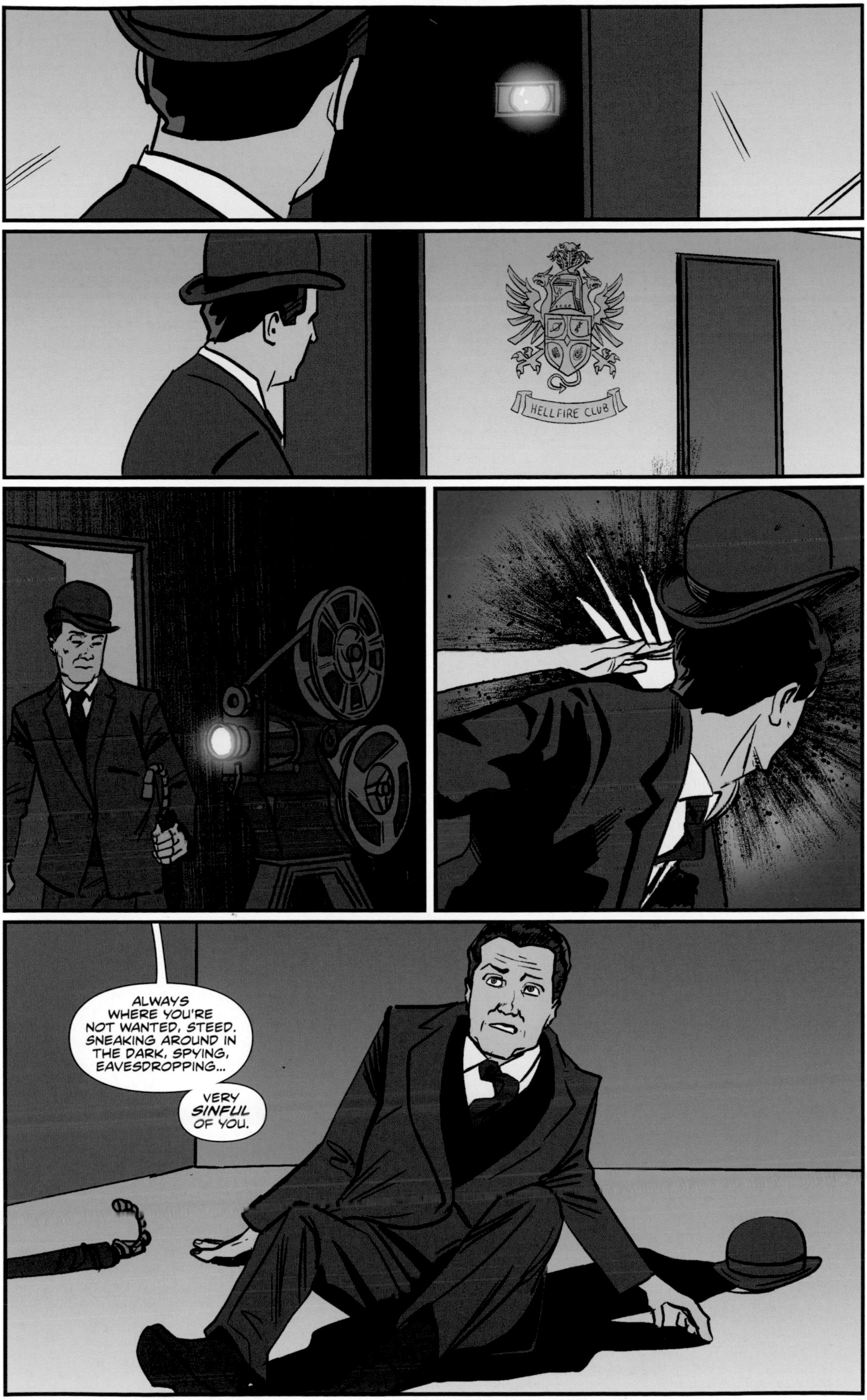
HELLFIRE CLUB
ALWAYS WHERE YOU'RE NOT WANTED, STEED. SNEAKING AROUND IN THE DARK, SPYING, EAVESDROPPING...
VERY *SINFUL* OF YOU.

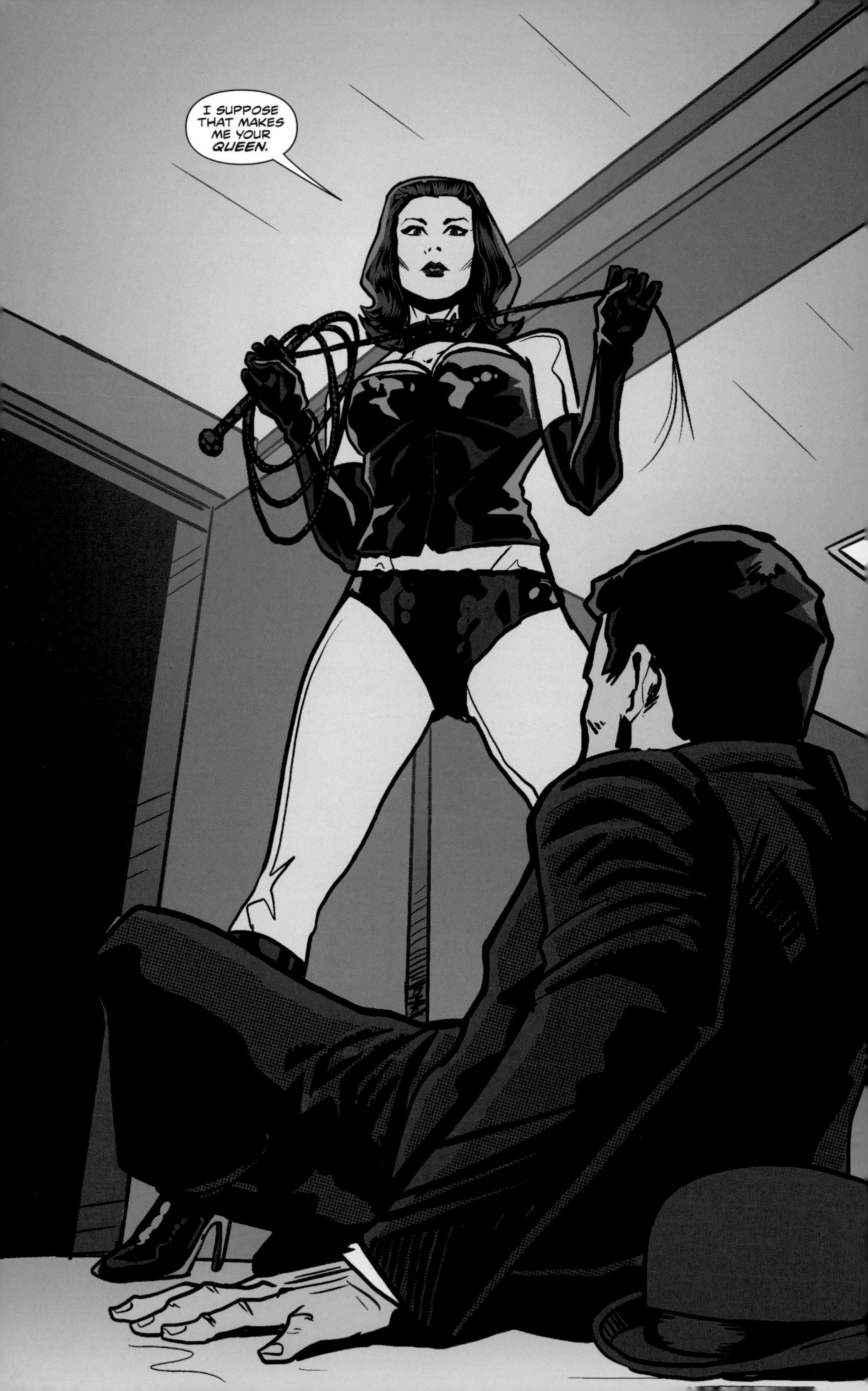
I SUPPOSE THAT MAKES ME YOUR QUEEN.

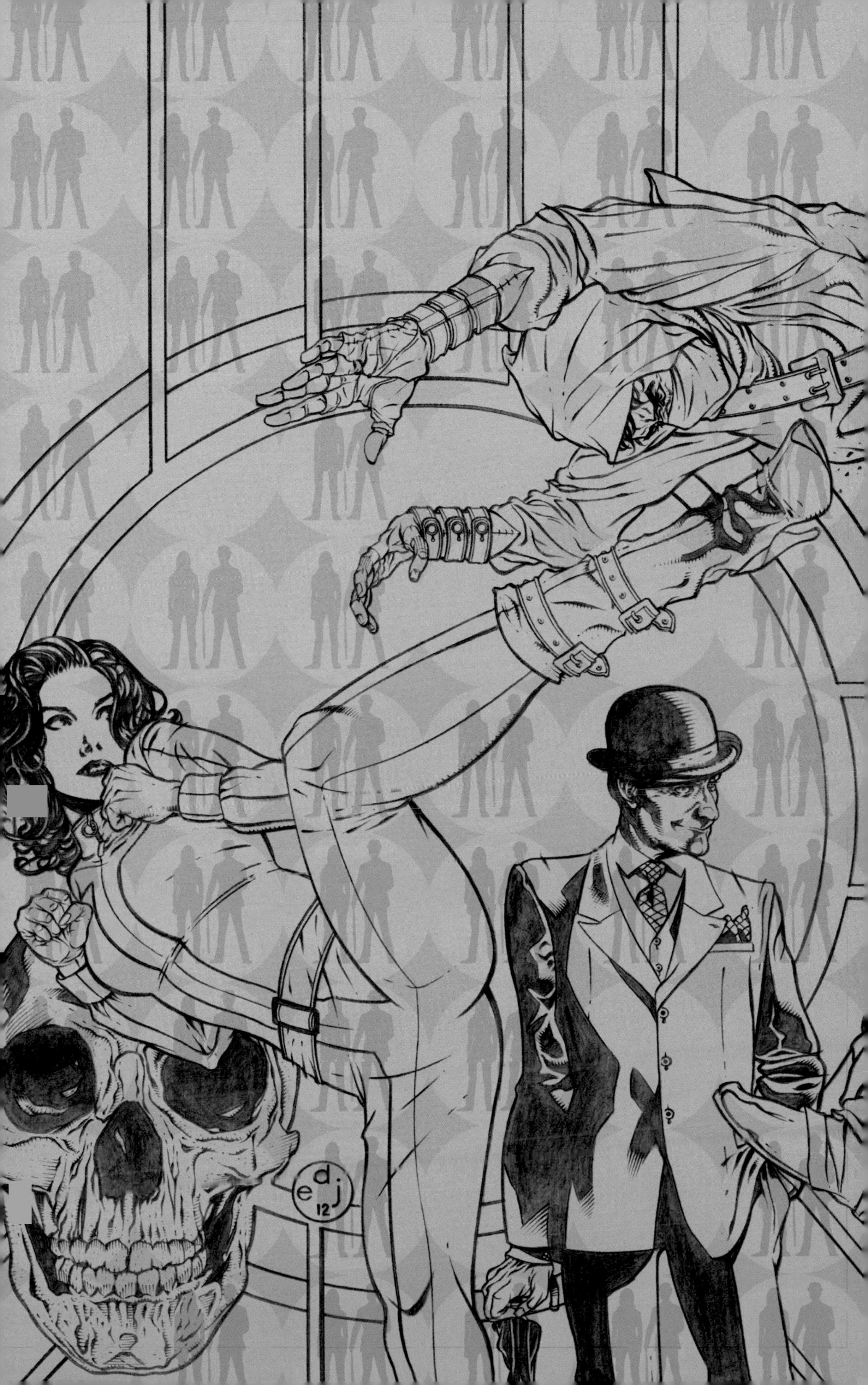

CHAPTER THREE

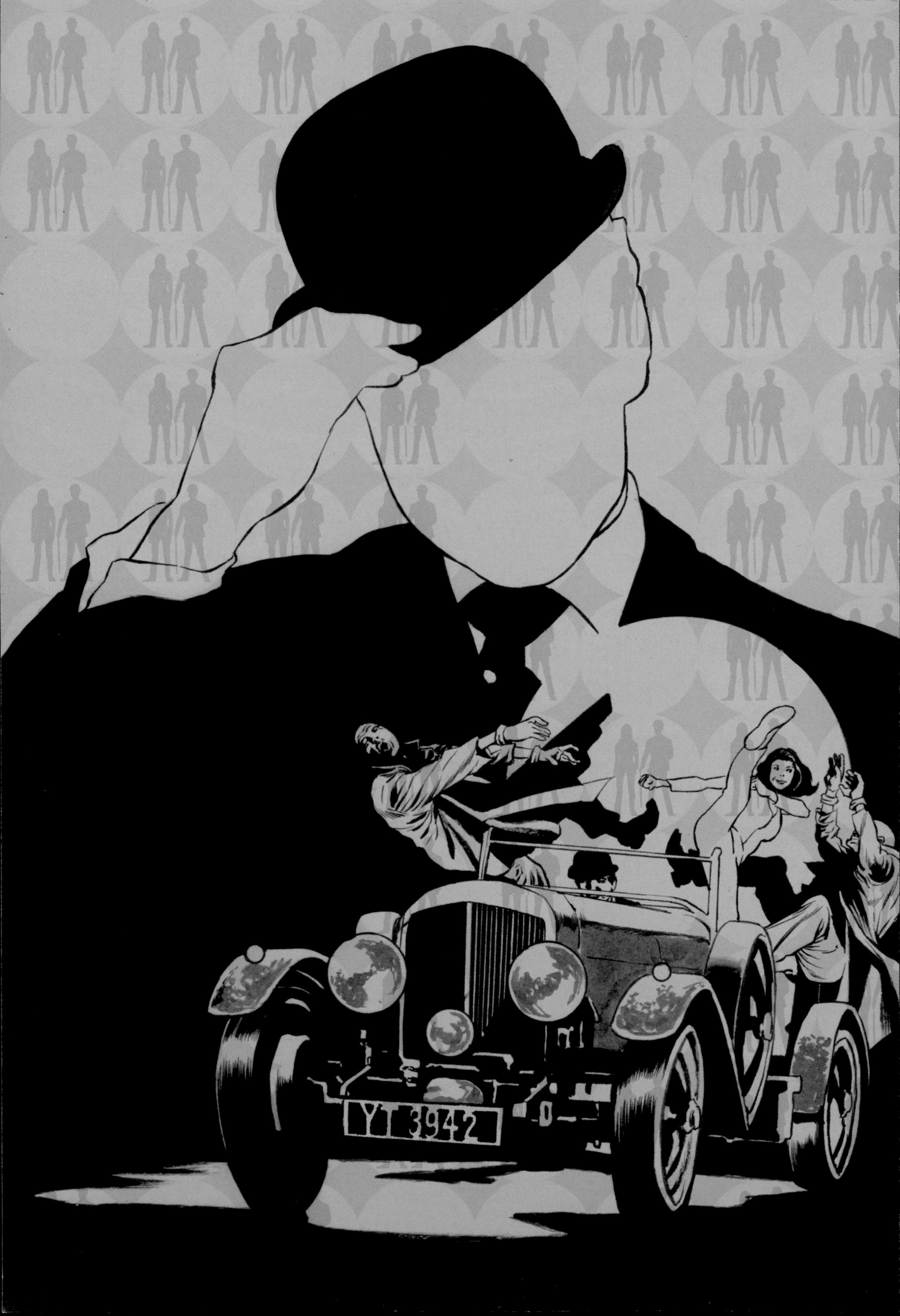
YT 3942

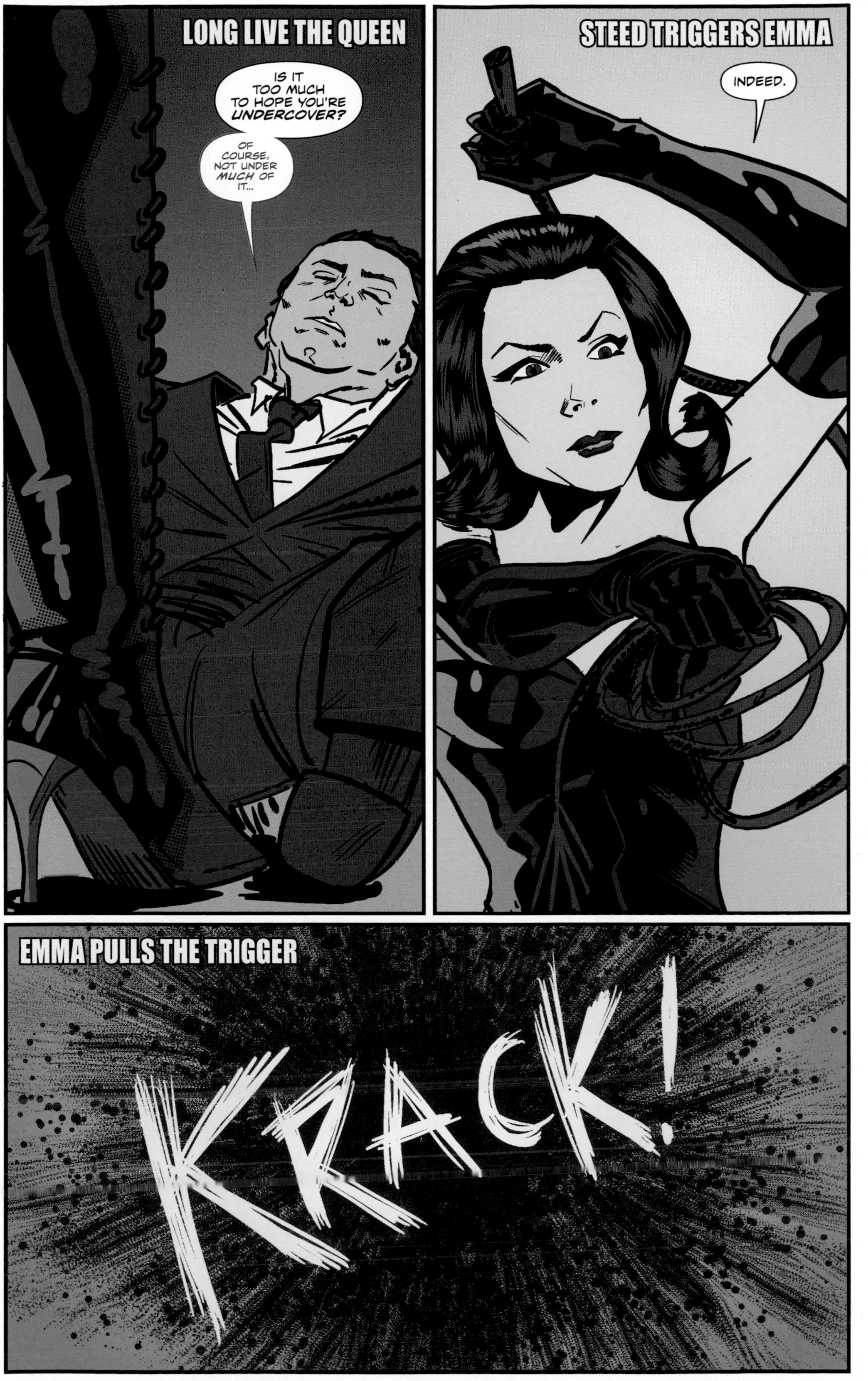
LONG LIVE THE QUEEN
IS IT TOO MUCH TO HOPE YOU'RE UNDERCOVER?
OF COURSE, NOT UNDER MUCH OF IT...
STEED TRIGGERS EMMA
INDEED.
EMMA PULLS THE TRIGGER
KRACK!

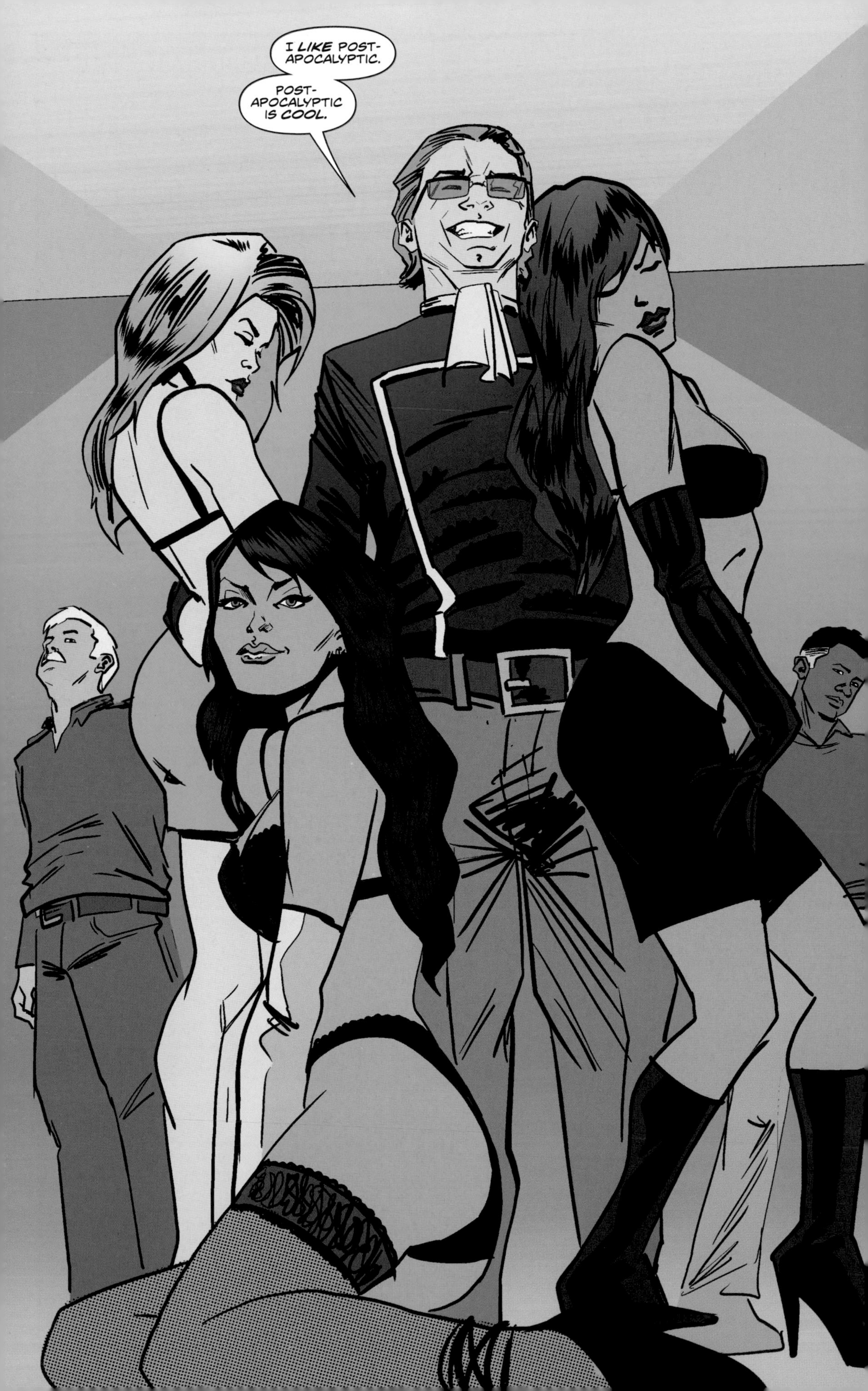
I LIKE POST-APOCALYPTIC.
POST-APOCALYPTIC IS COOL.

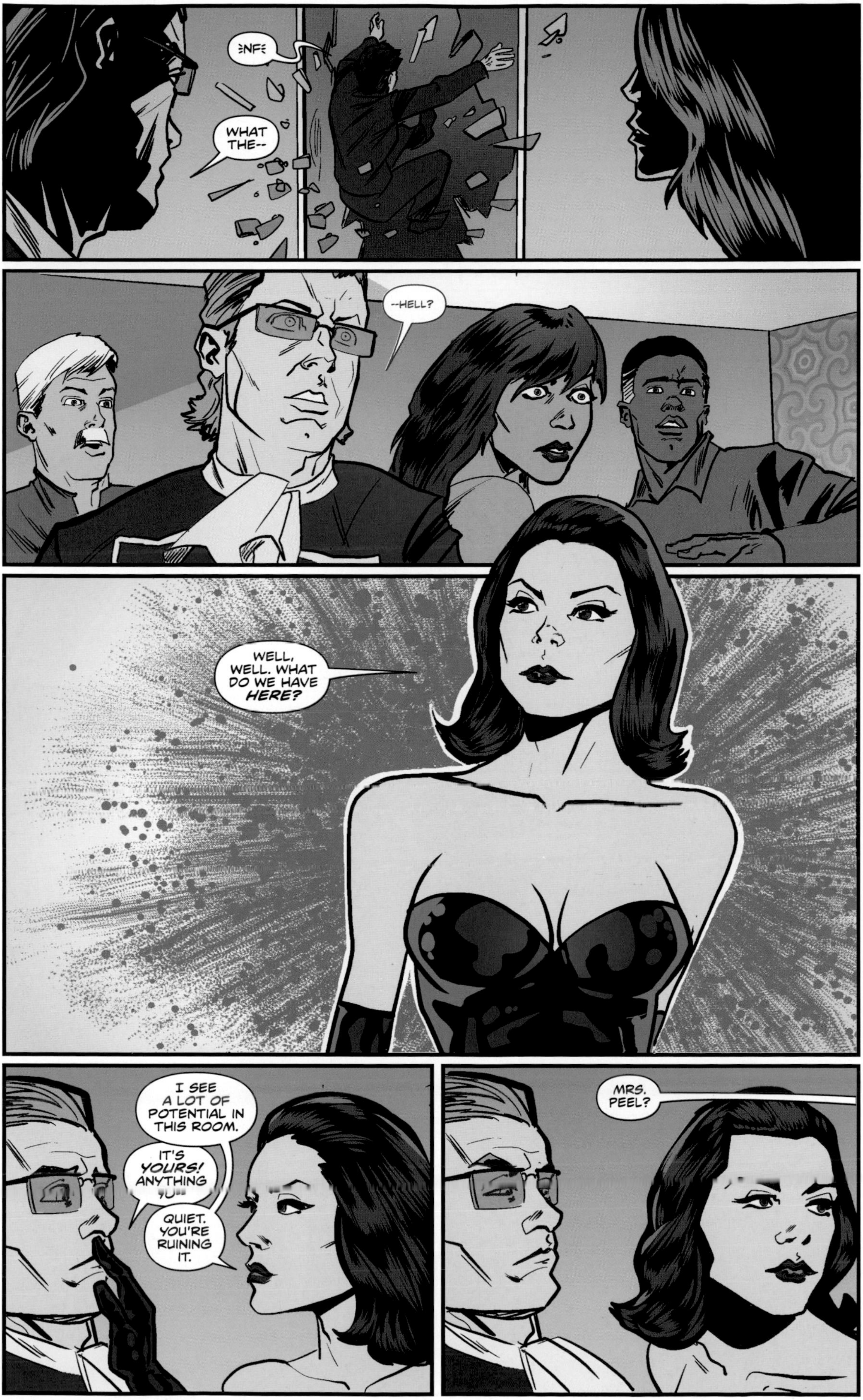

ƎNFƐ
WHAT THE--
--HELL?
WELL, WELL. WHAT DO WE HAVE HERE?
I SEE A LOT OF POTENTIAL IN THIS ROOM.
IT'S YOURS! ANYTHING YU--
QUIET. YOU'RE RUINING IT.
MRS. PEEL?

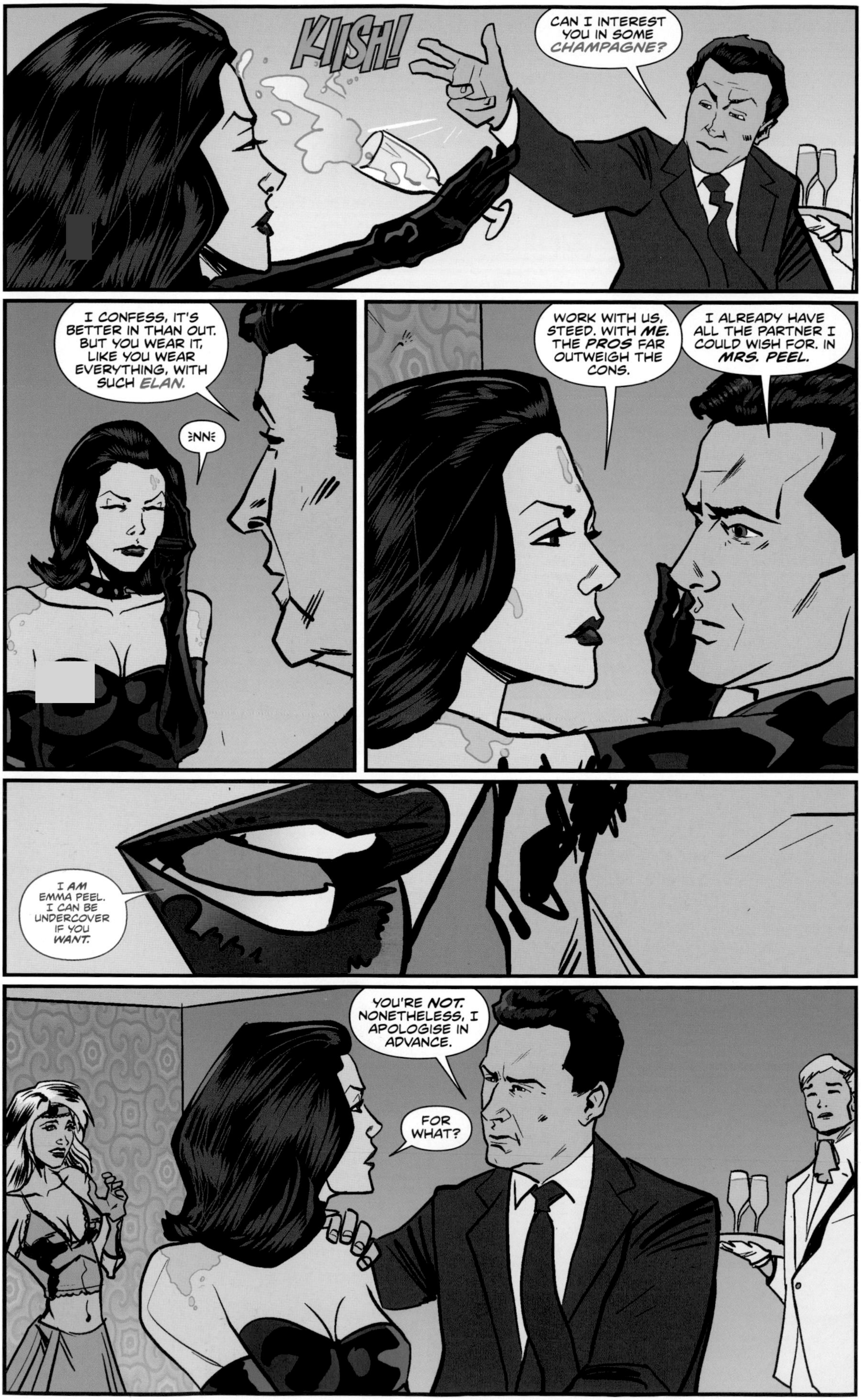
KLISH!
CAN I INTEREST YOU IN SOME CHAMPAGNE?
I CONFESS, IT'S BETTER IN THAN OUT. BUT YOU WEAR IT, LIKE YOU WEAR EVERYTHING, WITH SUCH ELAN.
NN
WORK WITH US, STEED. WITH ME. THE PROS FAR OUTWEIGH THE CONS.
I ALREADY HAVE ALL THE PARTNER I COULD WISH FOR. IN MRS. PEEL.
I AM EMMA PEEL. I CAN BE UNDERCOVER IF YOU WANT.
YOU'RE NOT. NONETHELESS, I APOLOGISE IN ADVANCE.
FOR WHAT?

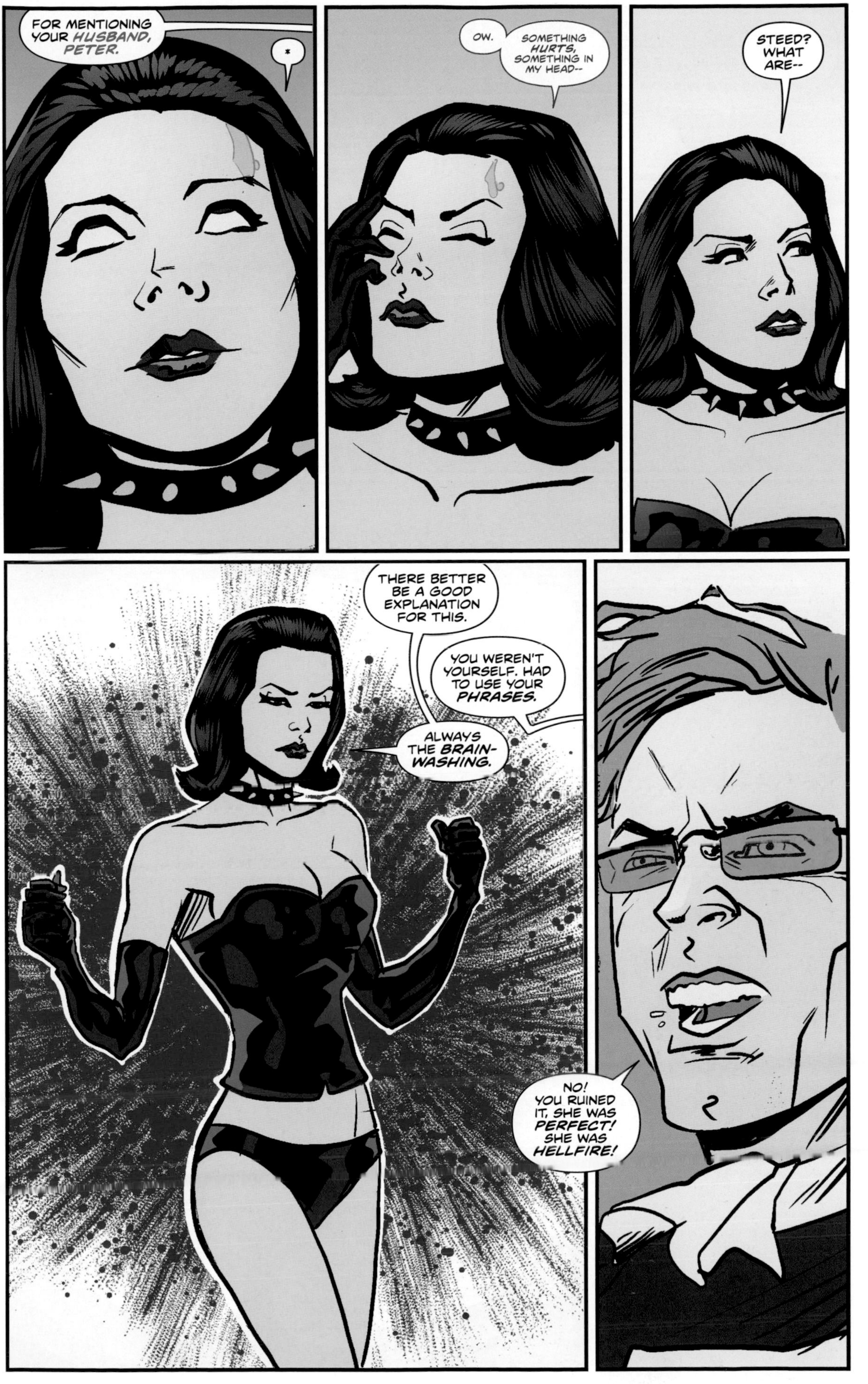
FOR MENTIONING YOUR HUSBAND, PETER.
*
OW.
SOMETHING HURTS, SOMETHING IN MY HEAD--
STEED? WHAT ARE--
THERE BETTER BE A GOOD EXPLANATION FOR THIS.
ALWAYS THE BRAIN-WASHING.
YOU WEREN'T YOURSELF. HAD TO USE YOUR PHRASES.
NO! YOU RUINED IT, SHE WAS PERFECT! SHE WAS HELLFIRE!

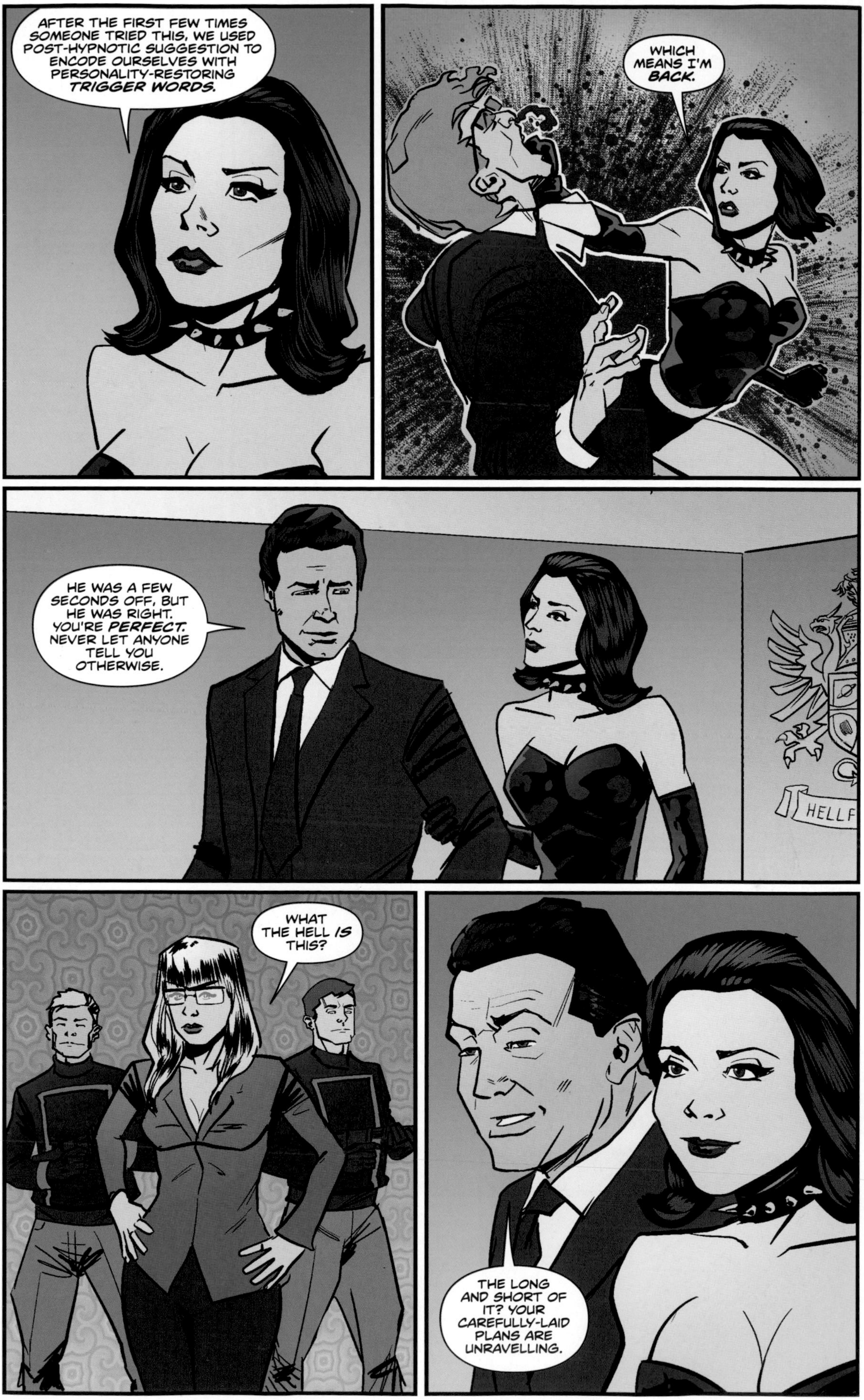
AFTER THE FIRST FEW TIMES SOMEONE TRIED THIS, WE USED POST-HYPNOTIC SUGGESTION TO ENCODE OURSELVES WITH PERSONALITY-RESTORING *TRIGGER WORDS.*
WHICH MEANS I'M *BACK.*
HE WAS A FEW SECONDS OFF, BUT HE WAS RIGHT. YOU'RE *PERFECT.* NEVER LET ANYONE TELL YOU OTHERWISE.
HELLF
WHAT THE HELL *IS* THIS?
THE LONG AND SHORT OF IT? YOUR CAREFULLY-LAID PLANS ARE UNRAVELLING.

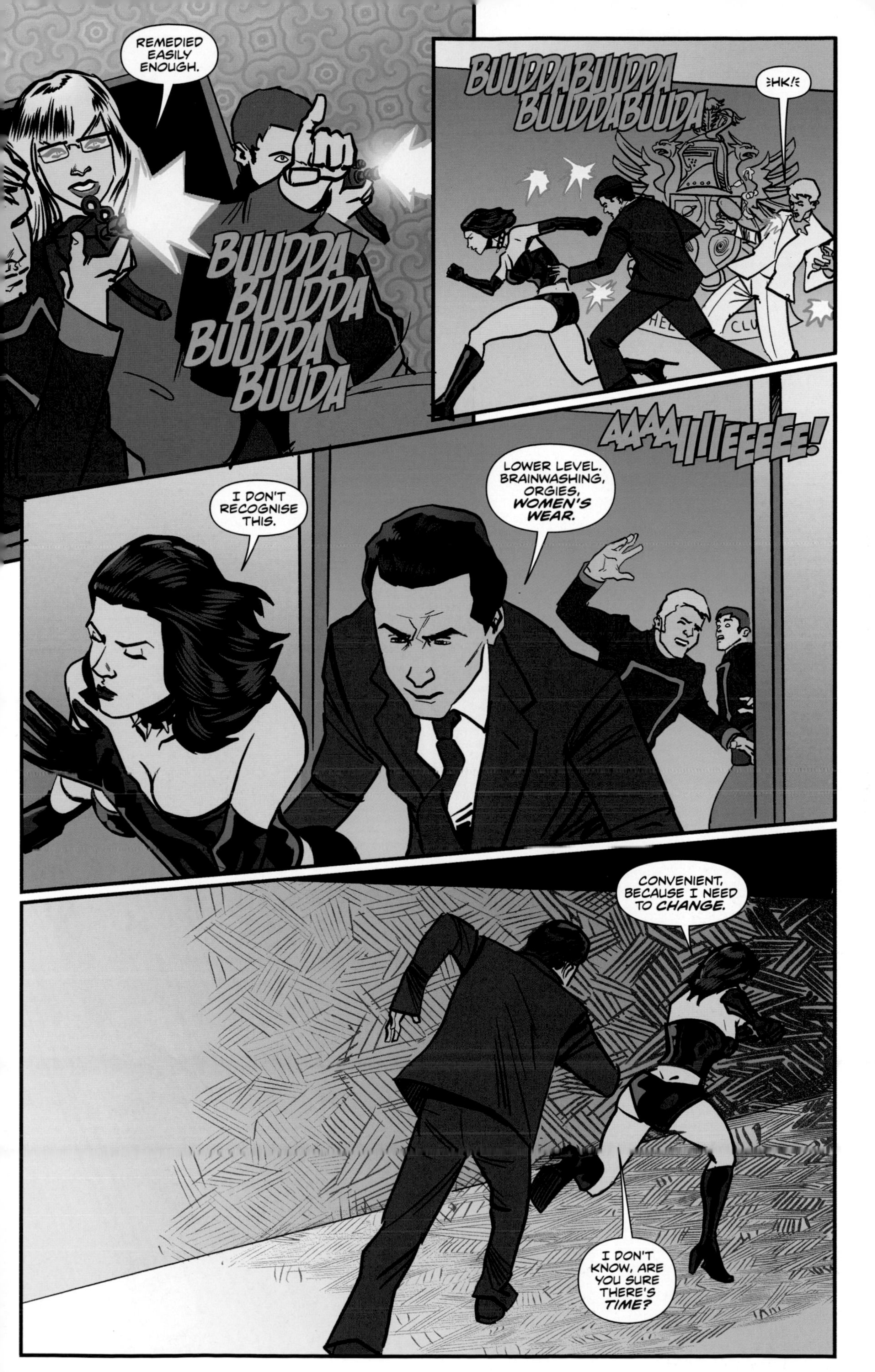
REMEDIED EASILY ENOUGH.
BUUDDA BUUDDA BUUDDA BUUDA
BUUDDABUUDDA BUUDDABUUDA
HK!
I DON'T RECOGNISE THIS.
LOWER LEVEL. BRAINWASHING, ORGIES, *WOMEN'S WEAR.*
AAAAIIIIEEEEE!
CONVENIENT, BECAUSE I NEED TO *CHANGE.*
I DON'T KNOW, ARE YOU SURE THERE'S *TIME?*

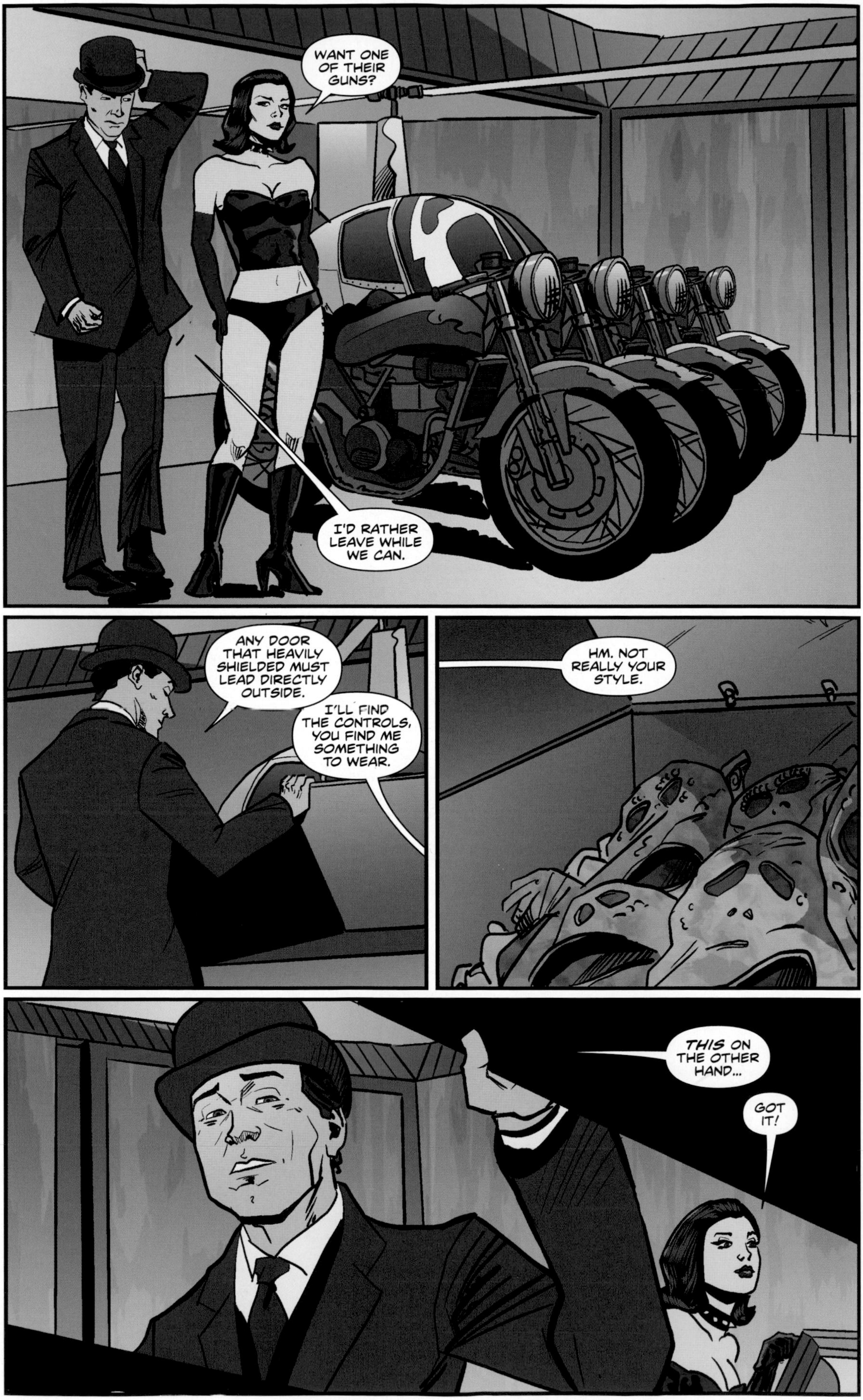
WANT ONE OF THEIR GUNS?
I'D RATHER LEAVE WHILE WE CAN.
ANY DOOR THAT HEAVILY SHIELDED MUST LEAD DIRECTLY OUTSIDE.
I'LL FIND THE CONTROLS, YOU FIND ME SOMETHING TO WEAR.
HM. NOT REALLY YOUR STYLE.
THIS ON THE OTHER HAND...
GOT IT!

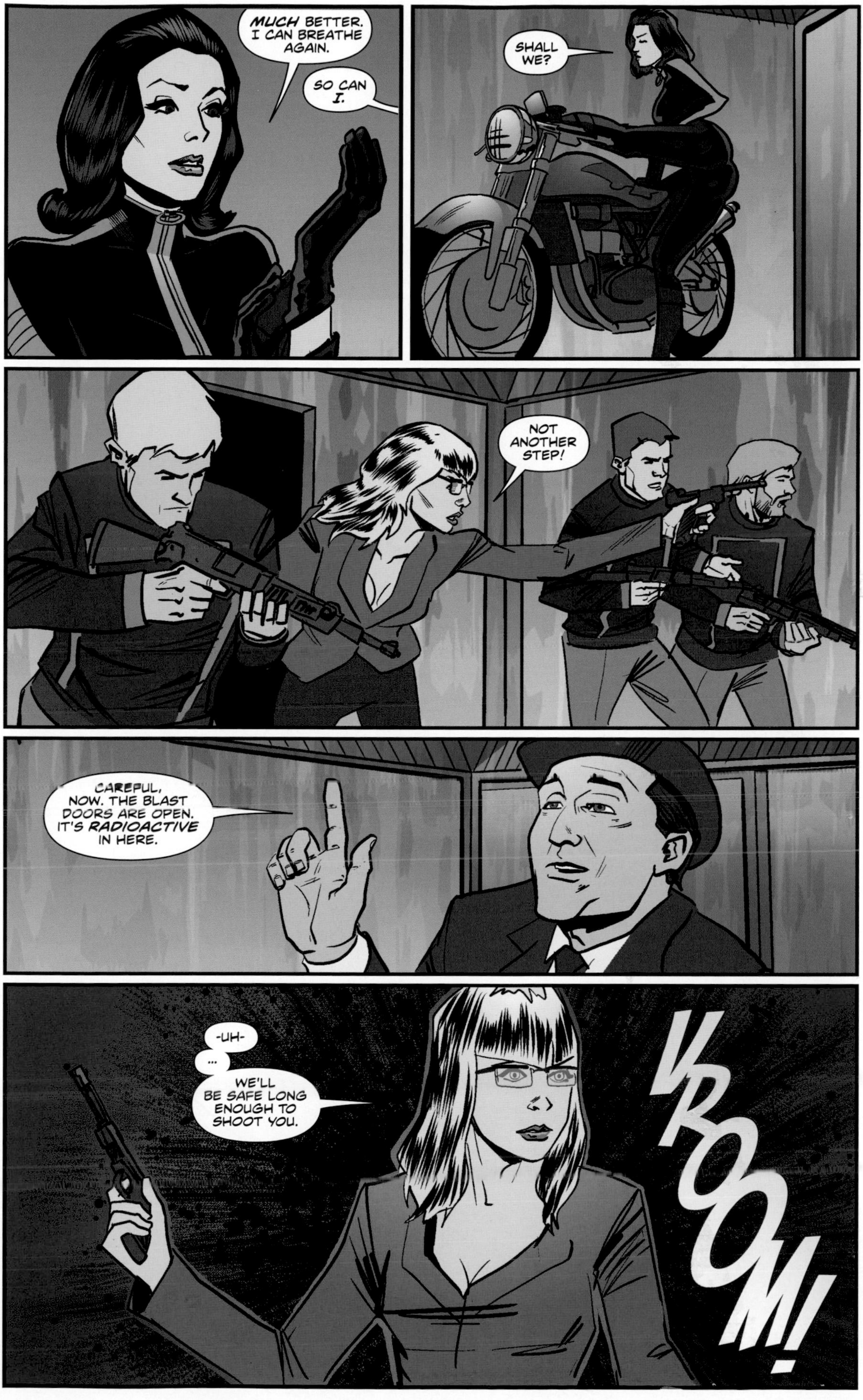
MUCH BETTER. I CAN BREATHE AGAIN.
SO CAN I.
SHALL WE?
NOT ANOTHER STEP!
CAREFUL, NOW. THE BLAST DOORS ARE OPEN. IT'S RADIOACTIVE IN HERE.
-UH-
...
WE'LL BE SAFE LONG ENOUGH TO SHOOT YOU.
VROOM!

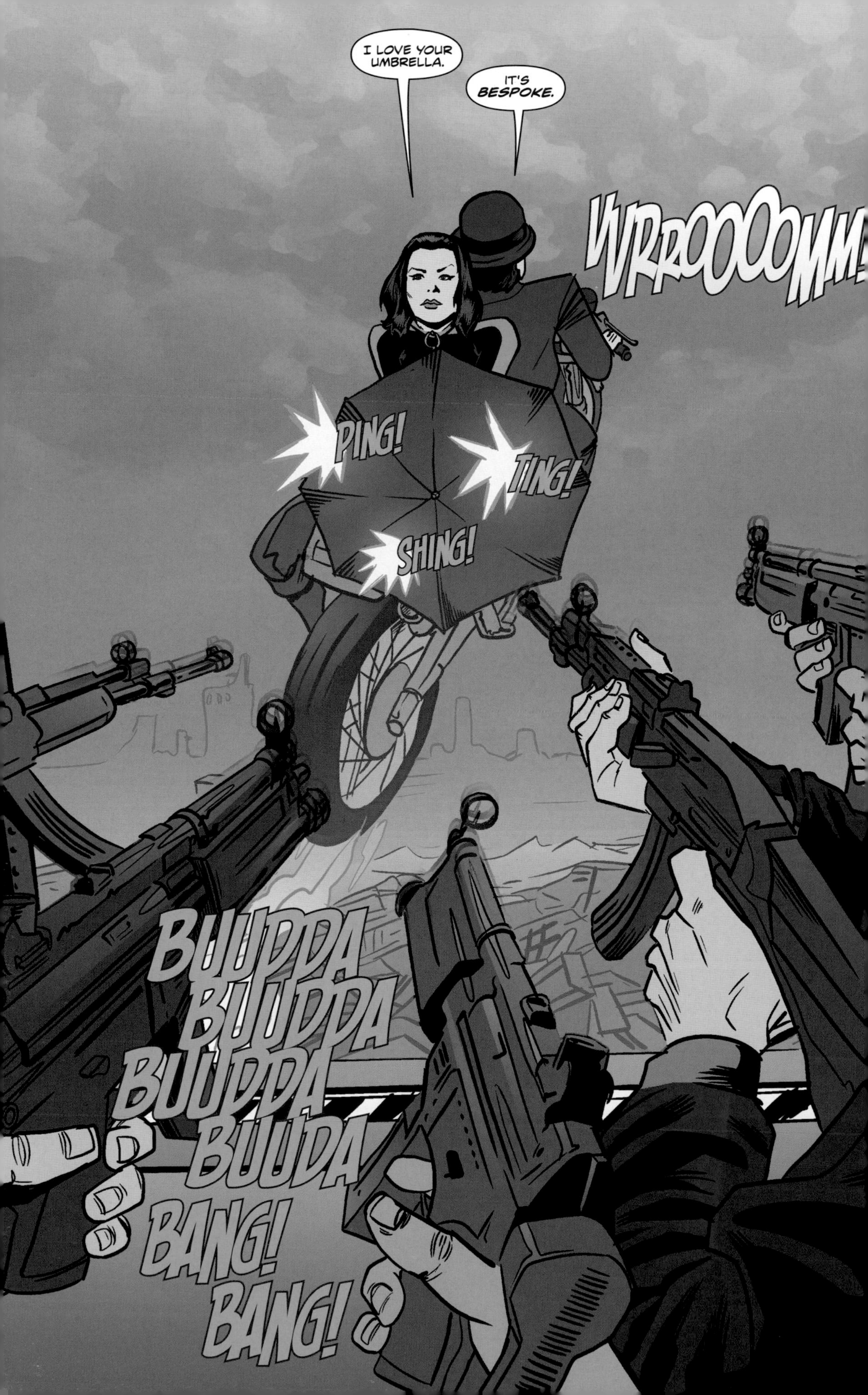
I LOVE YOUR UMBRELLA.
IT'S BESPOKE.
VVRROOOOMM!
PING!
TING!
SHING!
BUUDDA BUUDDA BUUDDA BUUDA BANG! BANG!

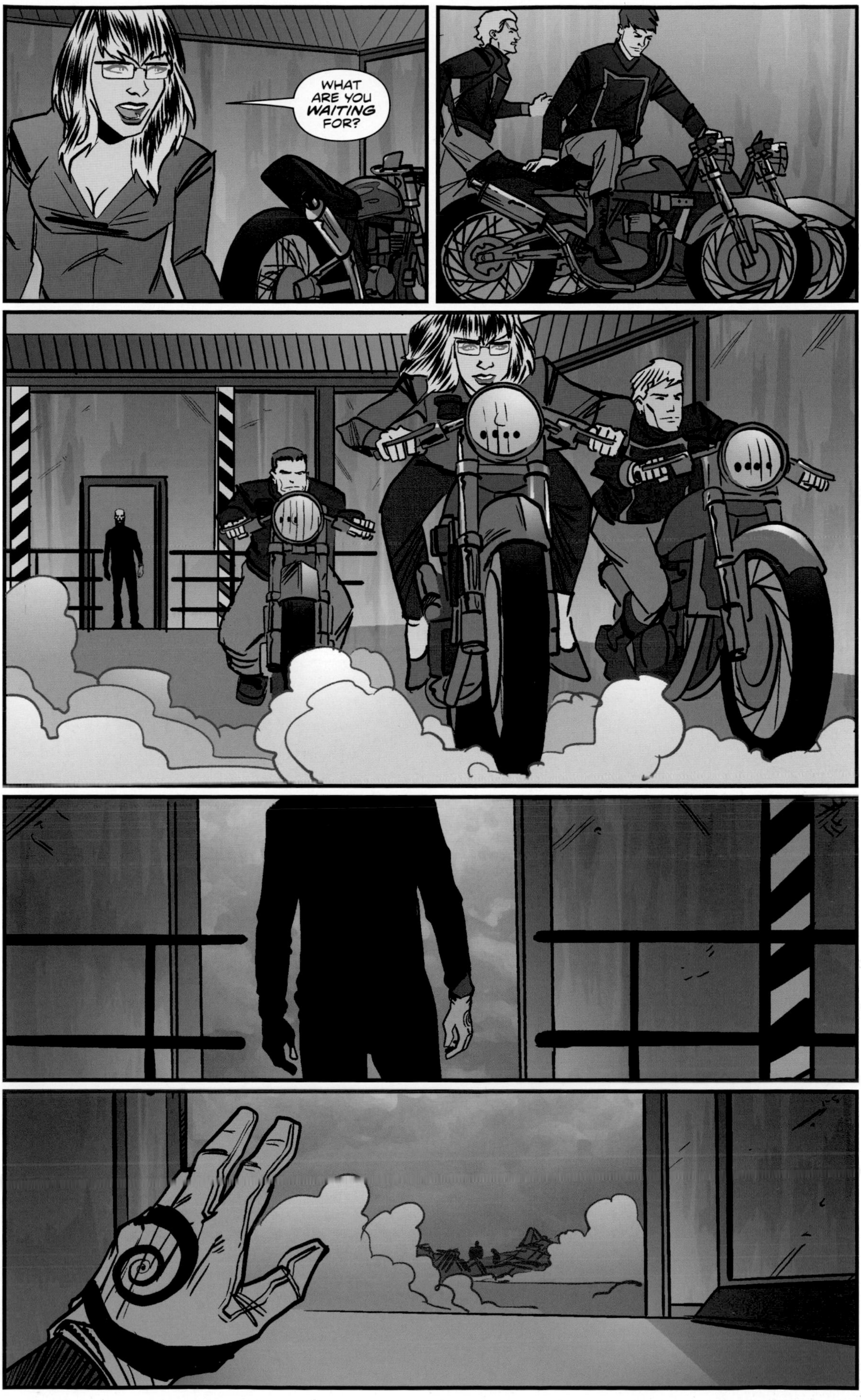
WHAT ARE YOU WAITING FOR?

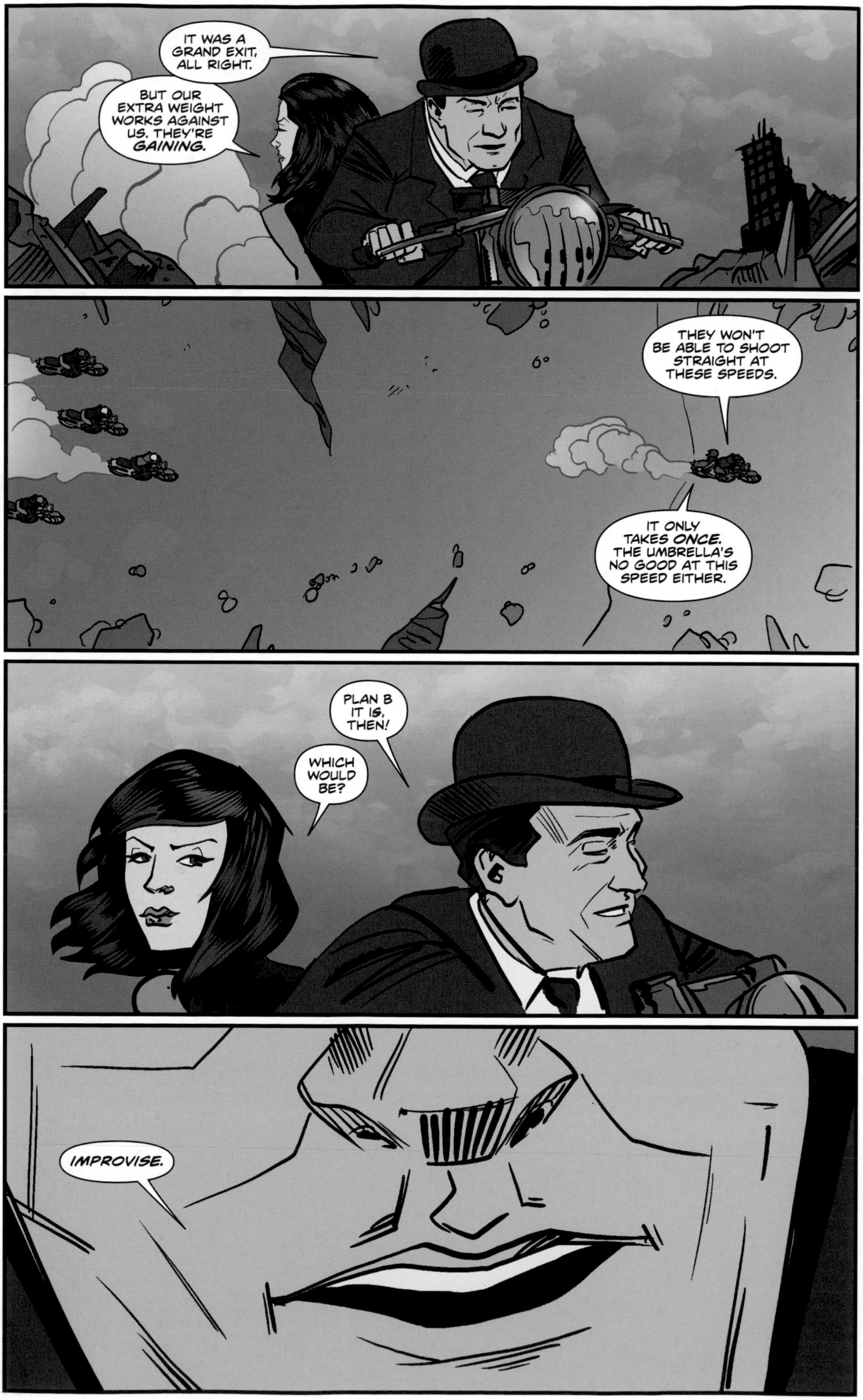
IT WAS A GRAND EXIT, ALL RIGHT.
BUT OUR EXTRA WEIGHT WORKS AGAINST US. THEY'RE *GAINING.*
THEY WON'T BE ABLE TO SHOOT STRAIGHT AT THESE SPEEDS.
IT ONLY TAKES *ONCE.* THE UMBRELLA'S NO GOOD AT THIS SPEED EITHER.
PLAN B IT IS, THEN!
WHICH WOULD BE?
IMPROVISE.

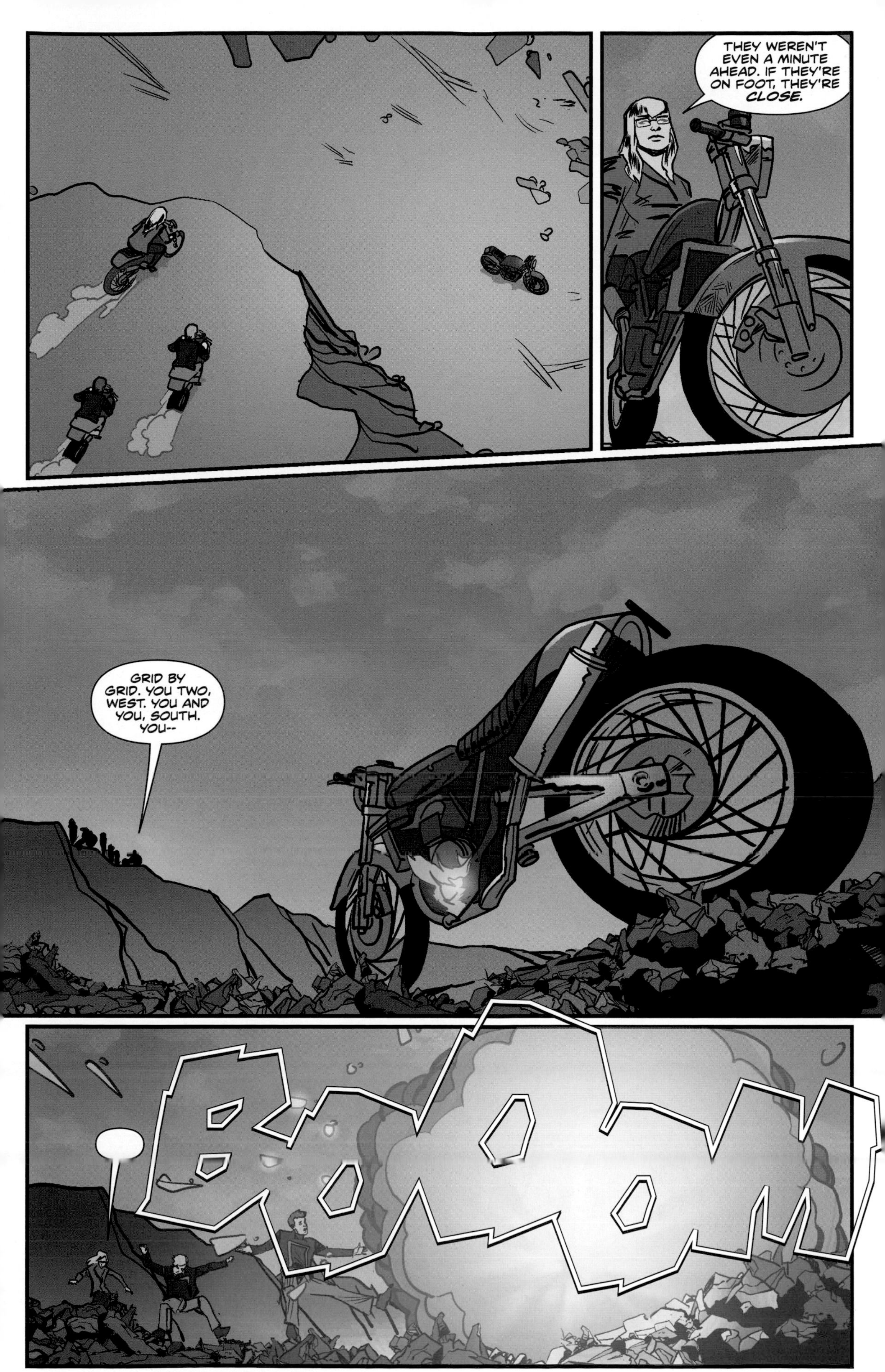
THEY WEREN'T EVEN A MINUTE AHEAD. IF THEY'RE ON FOOT, THEY'RE *CLOSE.*
GRID BY GRID. YOU TWO, WEST. YOU AND YOU, SOUTH. YOU--
BOOOM

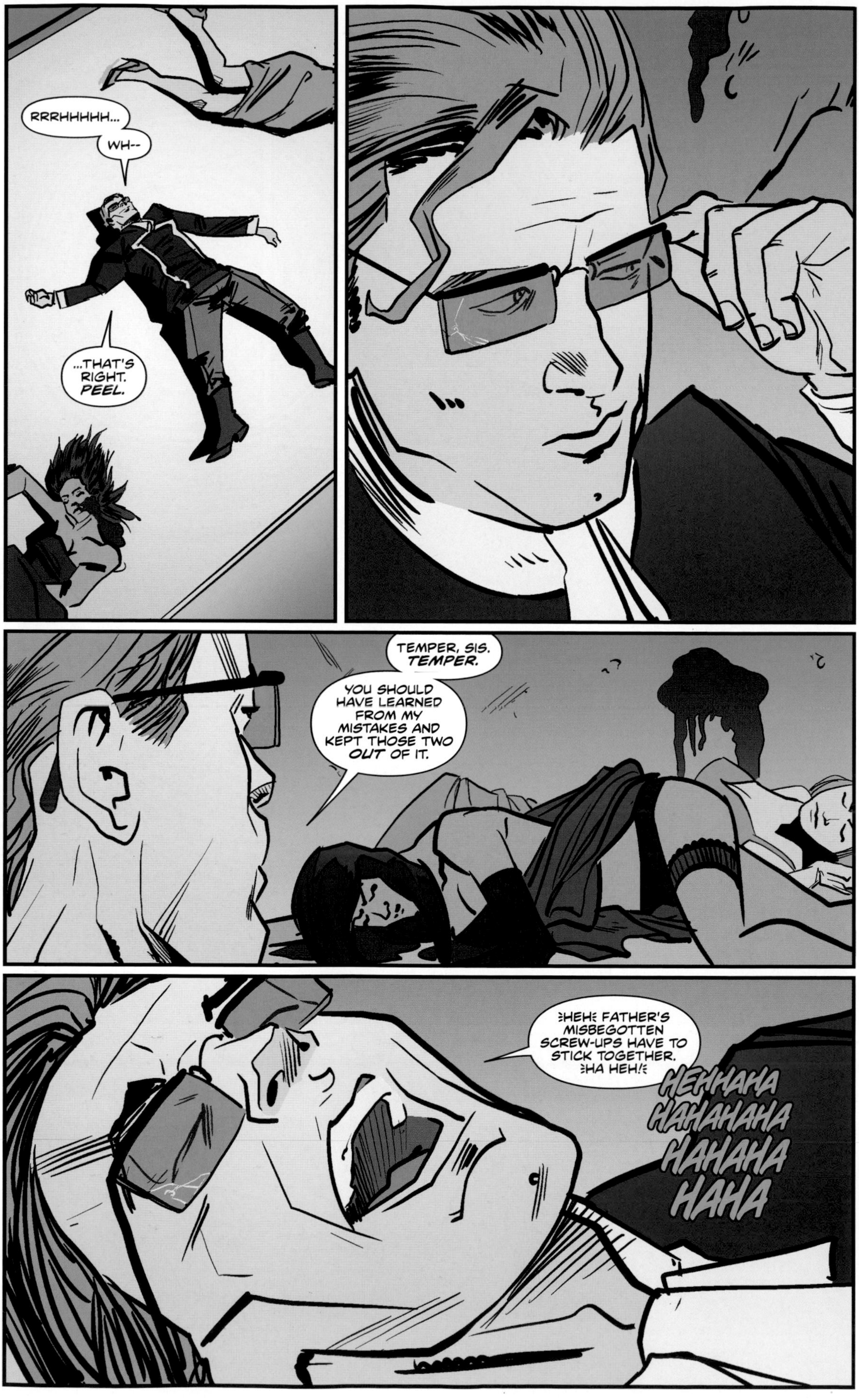
RRRHHHHH...
WH--
...THAT'S RIGHT. PEEL.
TEMPER, SIS. TEMPER.
YOU SHOULD HAVE LEARNED FROM MY MISTAKES AND KEPT THOSE TWO OUT OF IT.
HEH FATHER'S MISBEGOTTEN SCREW-UPS HAVE TO STICK TOGETHER. HA HEH!
HEHHAHA HAHAHAHA HAHAHA HAHA

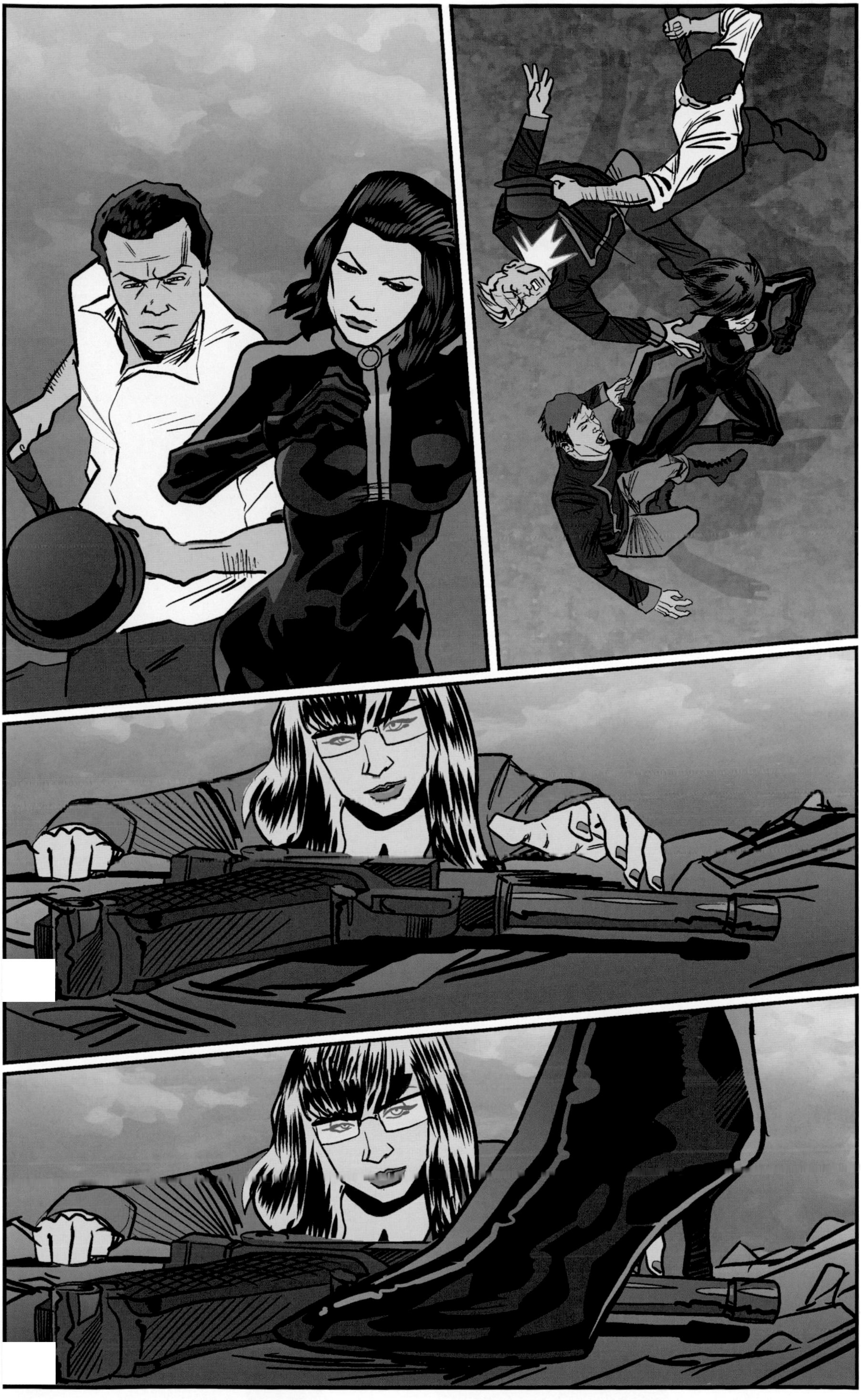

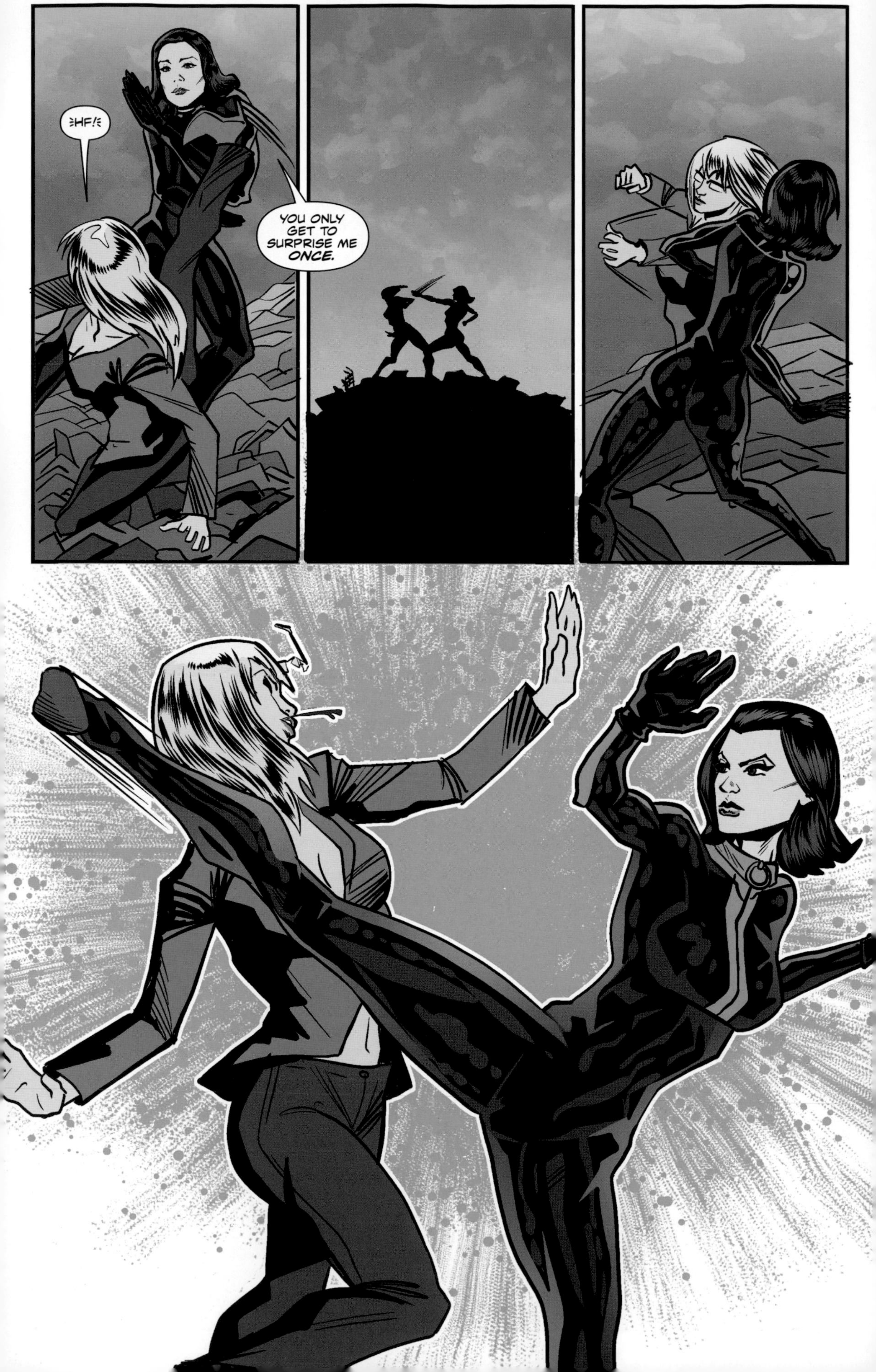
HF!
YOU ONLY GET TO SURPRISE ME ONCE.

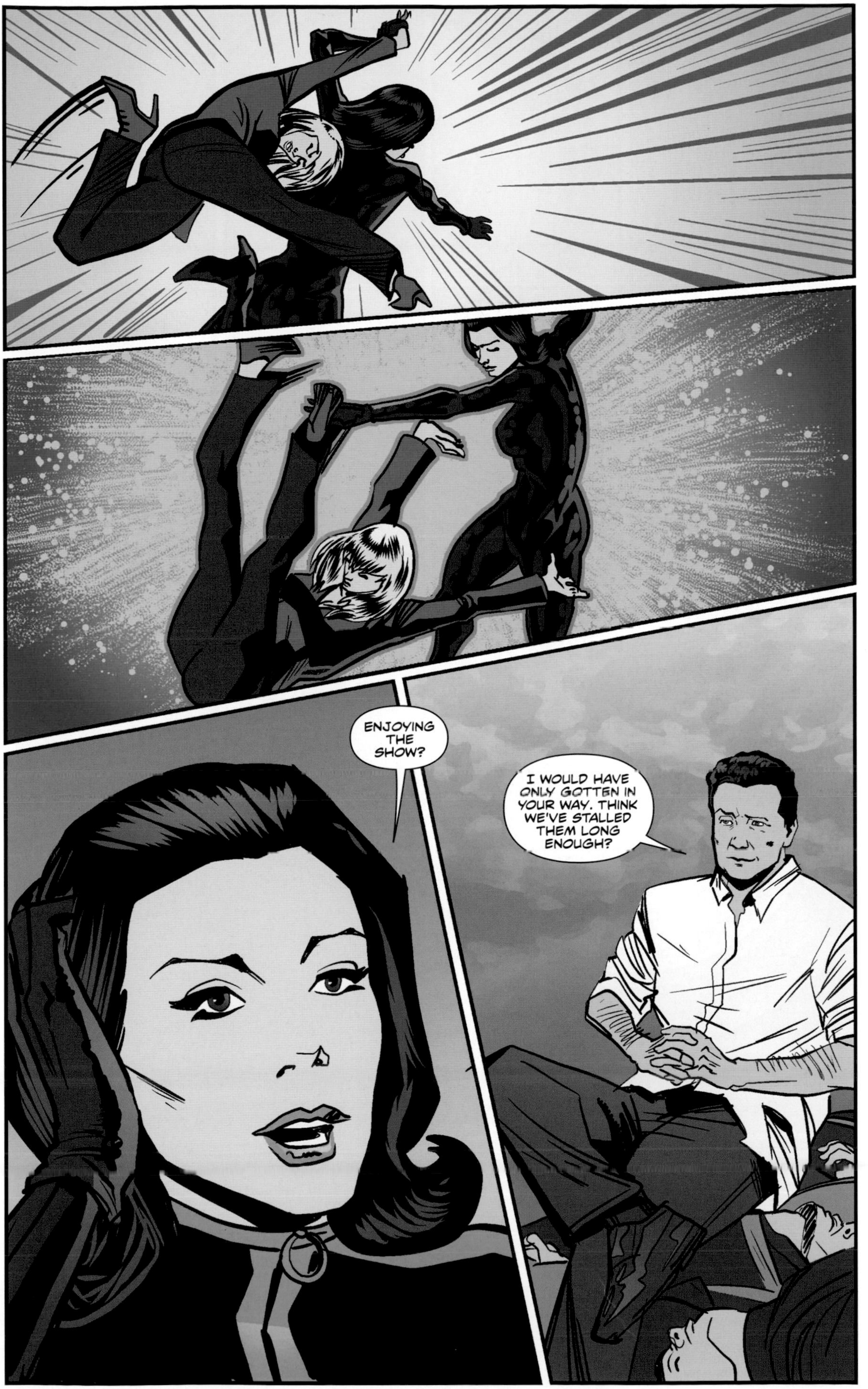
ENJOYING THE SHOW?
I WOULD HAVE ONLY GOTTEN IN YOUR WAY. THINK WE'VE STALLED THEM LONG ENOUGH?

THERE'S ONLY ONE WAY TO FIND OUT.

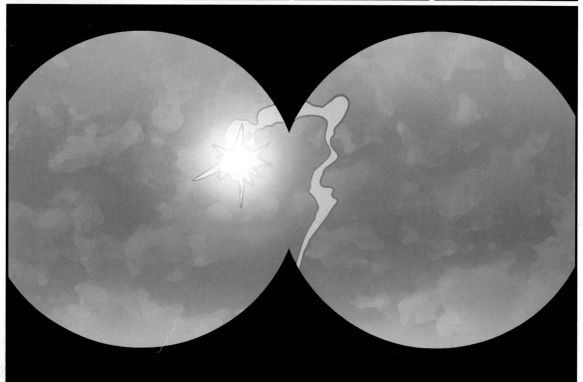

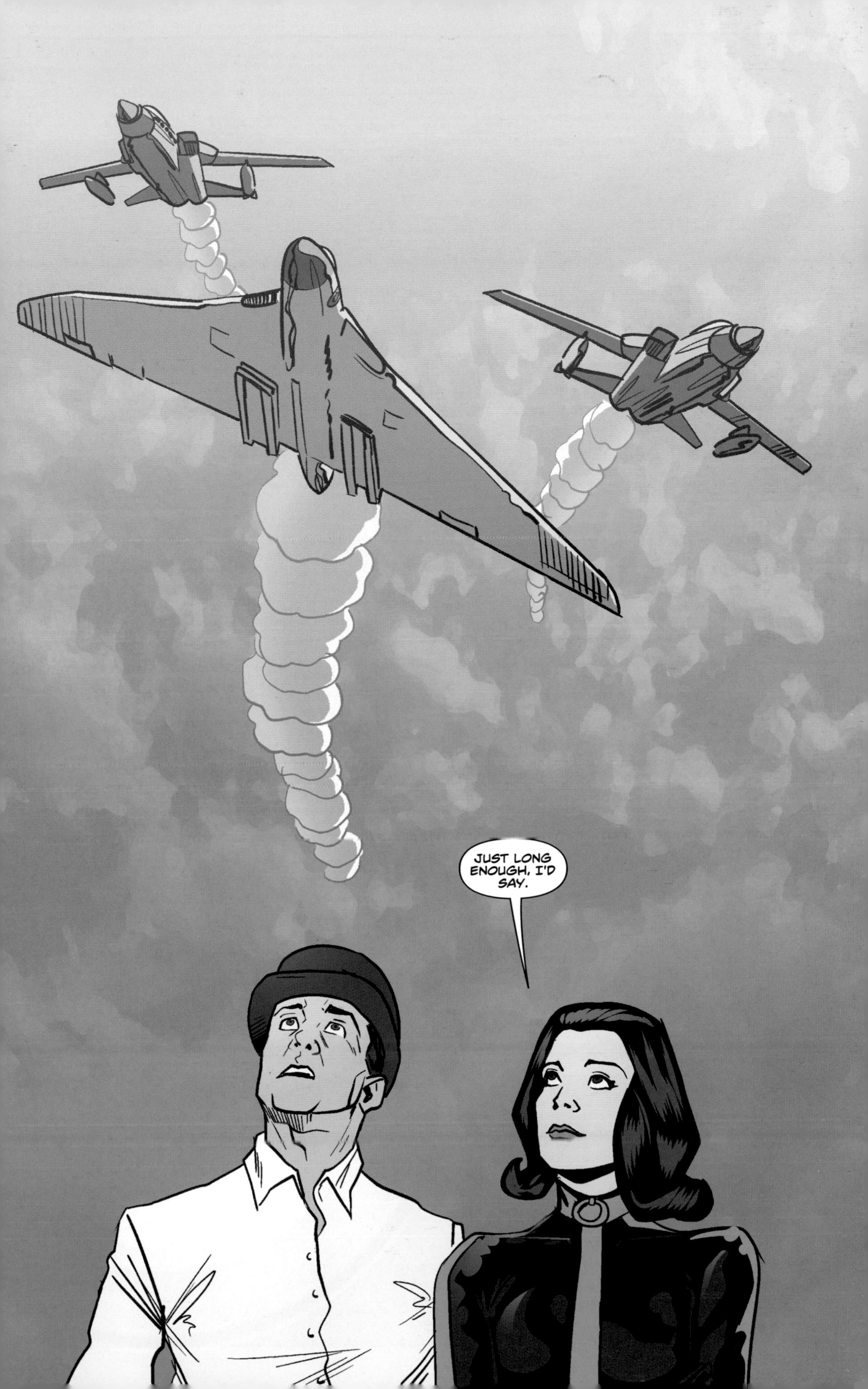
JUST LONG ENOUGH, I'D SAY.

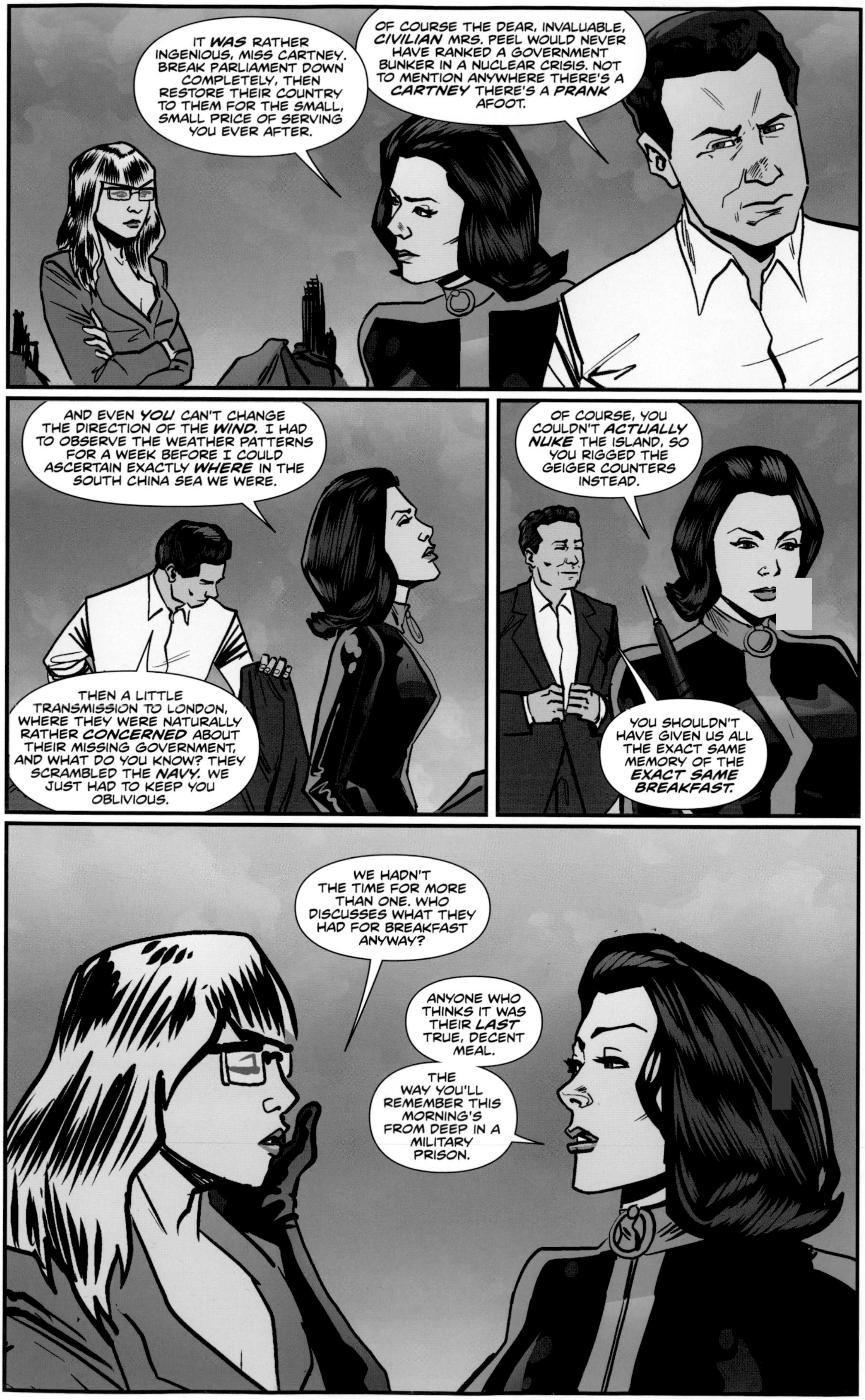
IT WAS RATHER INGENIOUS, MISS CARTNEY. BREAK PARLIAMENT DOWN COMPLETELY, THEN RESTORE THEIR COUNTRY TO THEM FOR THE SMALL, SMALL PRICE OF SERVING YOU EVER AFTER.
OF COURSE THE DEAR, INVALUABLE, CIVILIAN MRS. PEEL WOULD NEVER HAVE RANKED A GOVERNMENT BUNKER IN A NUCLEAR CRISIS. NOT TO MENTION ANYWHERE THERE'S A CARTNEY THERE'S A PRANK AFOOT.
AND EVEN YOU CAN'T CHANGE THE DIRECTION OF THE WIND. I HAD TO OBSERVE THE WEATHER PATTERNS FOR A WEEK BEFORE I COULD ASCERTAIN EXACTLY WHERE IN THE SOUTH CHINA SEA WE WERE.
THEN A LITTLE TRANSMISSION TO LONDON, WHERE THEY WERE NATURALLY RATHER CONCERNED ABOUT THEIR MISSING GOVERNMENT, AND WHAT DO YOU KNOW? THEY SCRAMBLED THE NAVY. WE JUST HAD TO KEEP YOU OBLIVIOUS.
OF COURSE, YOU COULDN'T ACTUALLY NUKE THE ISLAND, SO YOU RIGGED THE GEIGER COUNTERS INSTEAD.
YOU SHOULDN'T HAVE GIVEN US ALL THE EXACT SAME MEMORY OF THE EXACT SAME BREAKFAST.
WE HADN'T THE TIME FOR MORE THAN ONE. WHO DISCUSSES WHAT THEY HAD FOR BREAKFAST ANYWAY?
ANYONE WHO THINKS IT WAS THEIR LAST TRUE, DECENT MEAL.
THE WAY YOU'LL REMEMBER THIS MORNING'S FROM DEEP IN A MILITARY PRISON.

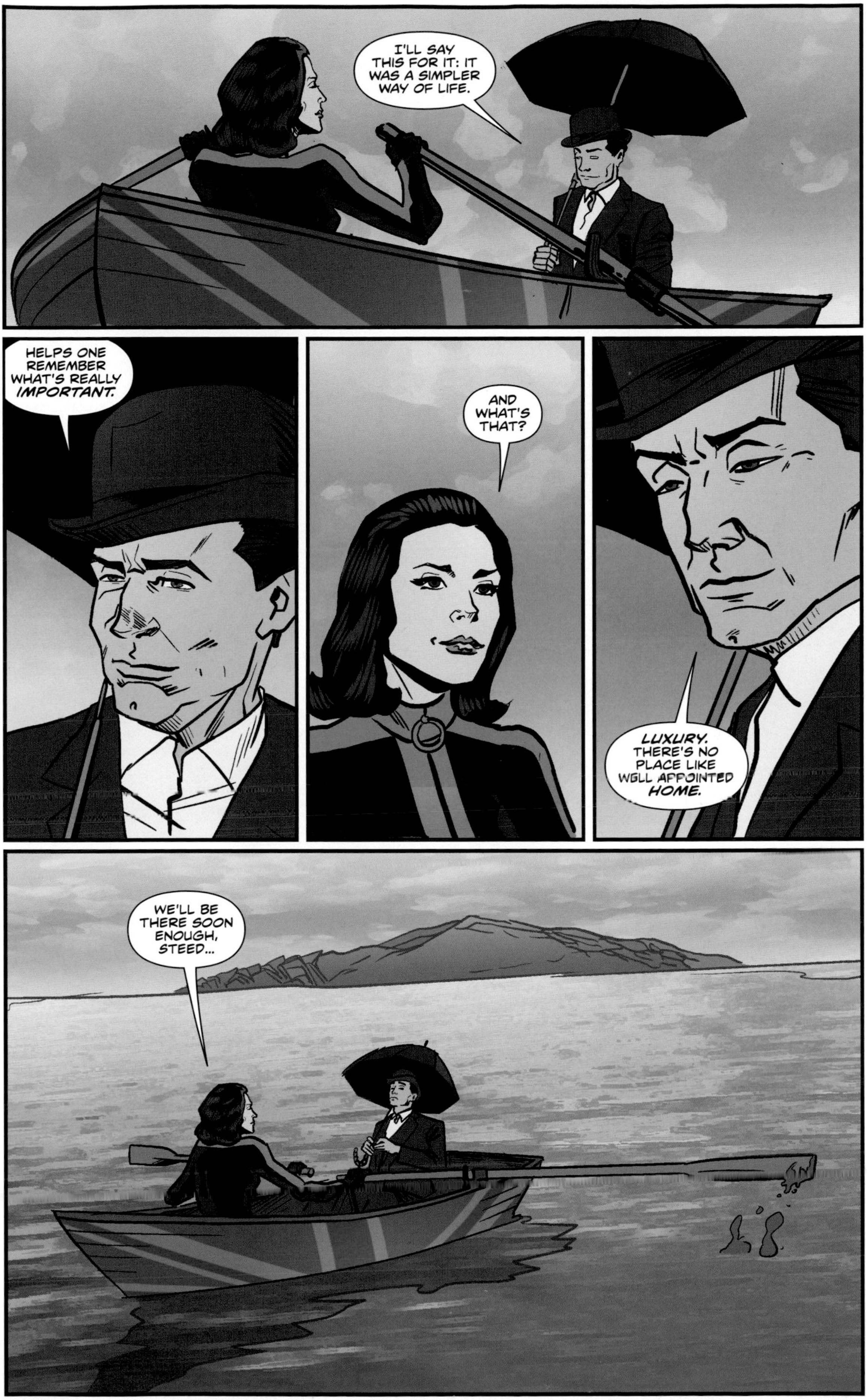
I'LL SAY THIS FOR IT: IT WAS A SIMPLER WAY OF LIFE.
HELPS ONE REMEMBER WHAT'S REALLY *IMPORTANT.*
AND WHAT'S THAT?
LUXURY. THERE'S NO PLACE LIKE WELL APPOINTED *HOME.*
WE'LL BE THERE SOON ENOUGH, STEED...

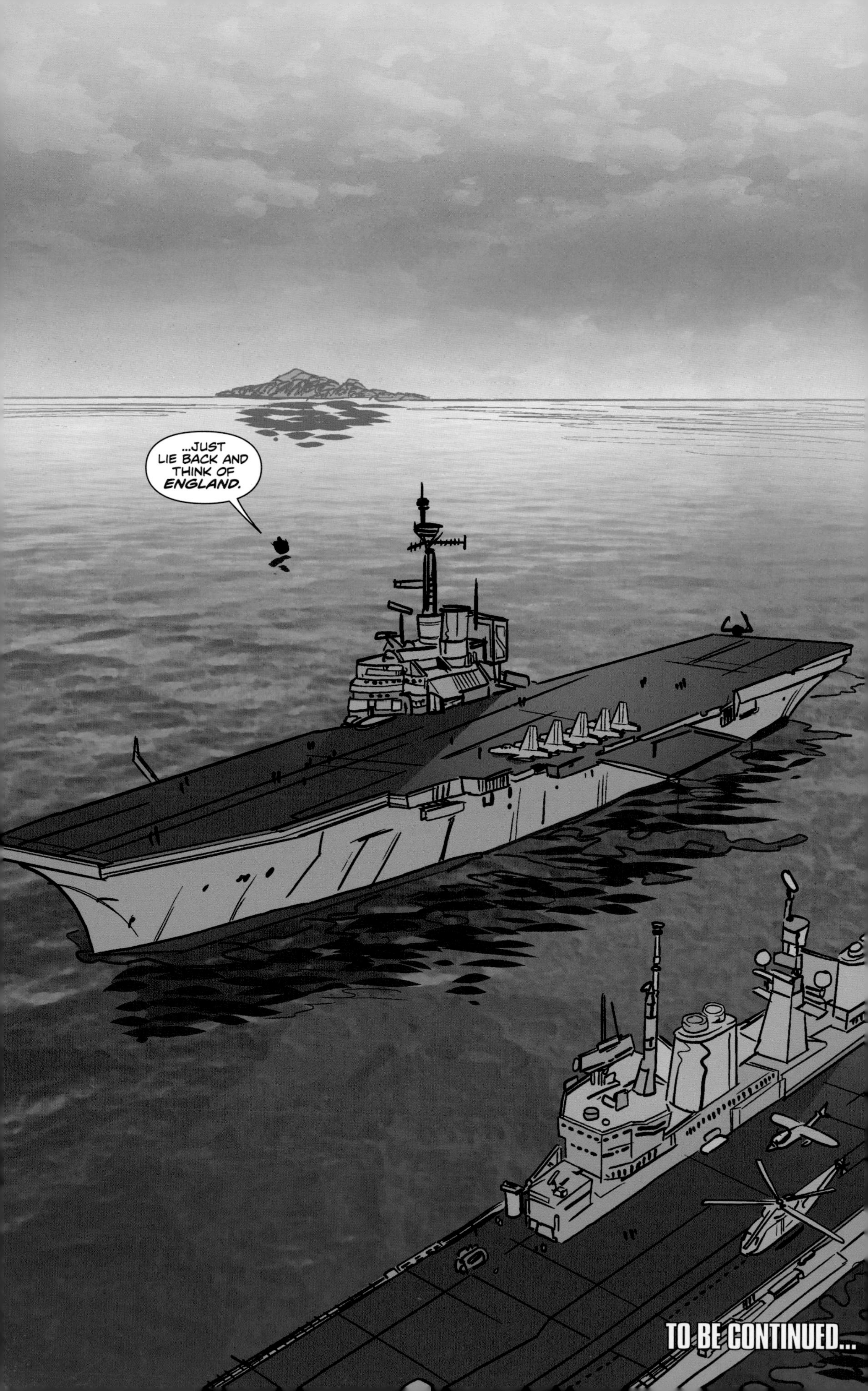
...JUST LIE BACK AND THINK OF *ENGLAND*.
TO BE CONTINUED...

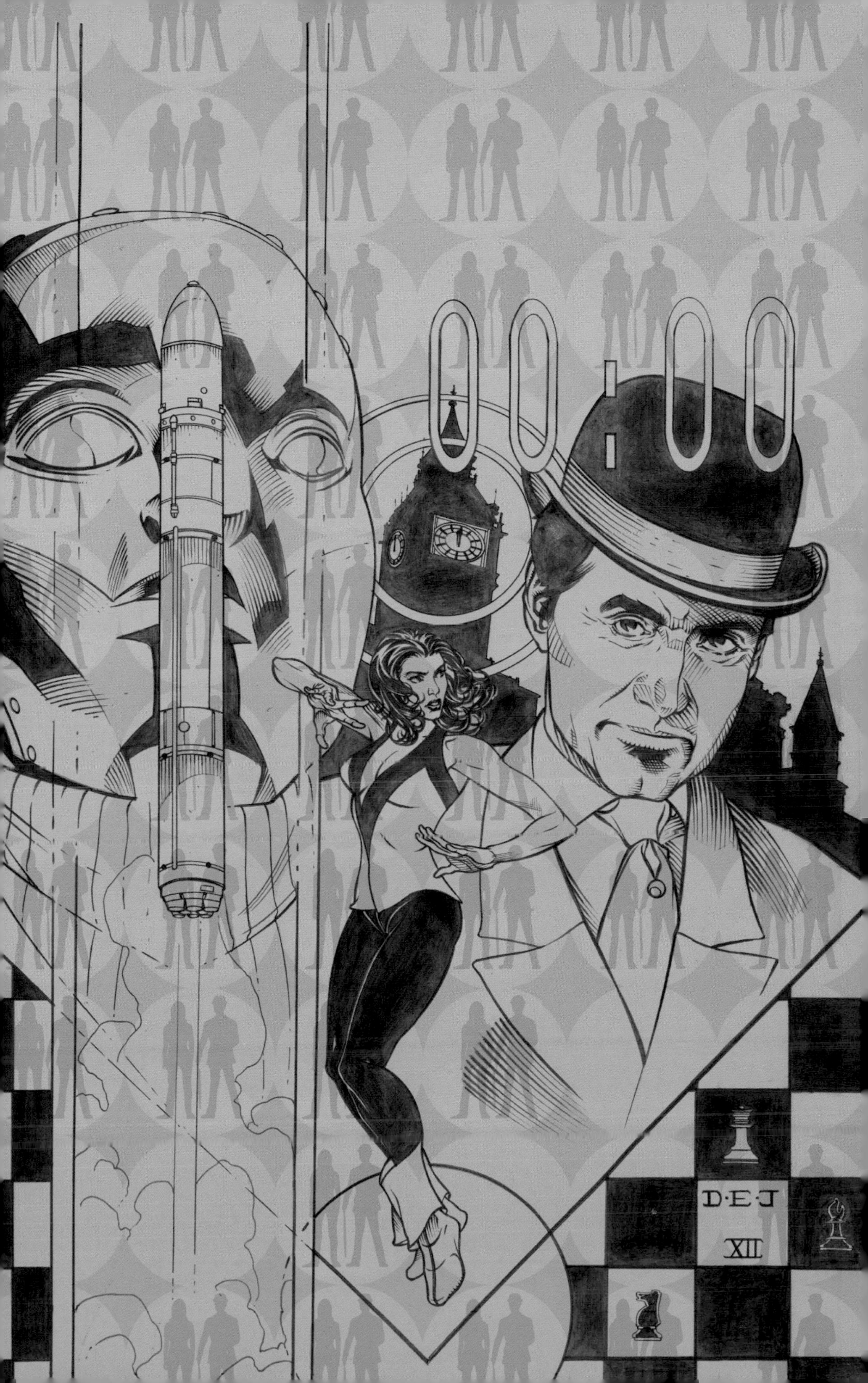
00:00
D·E·J
XII

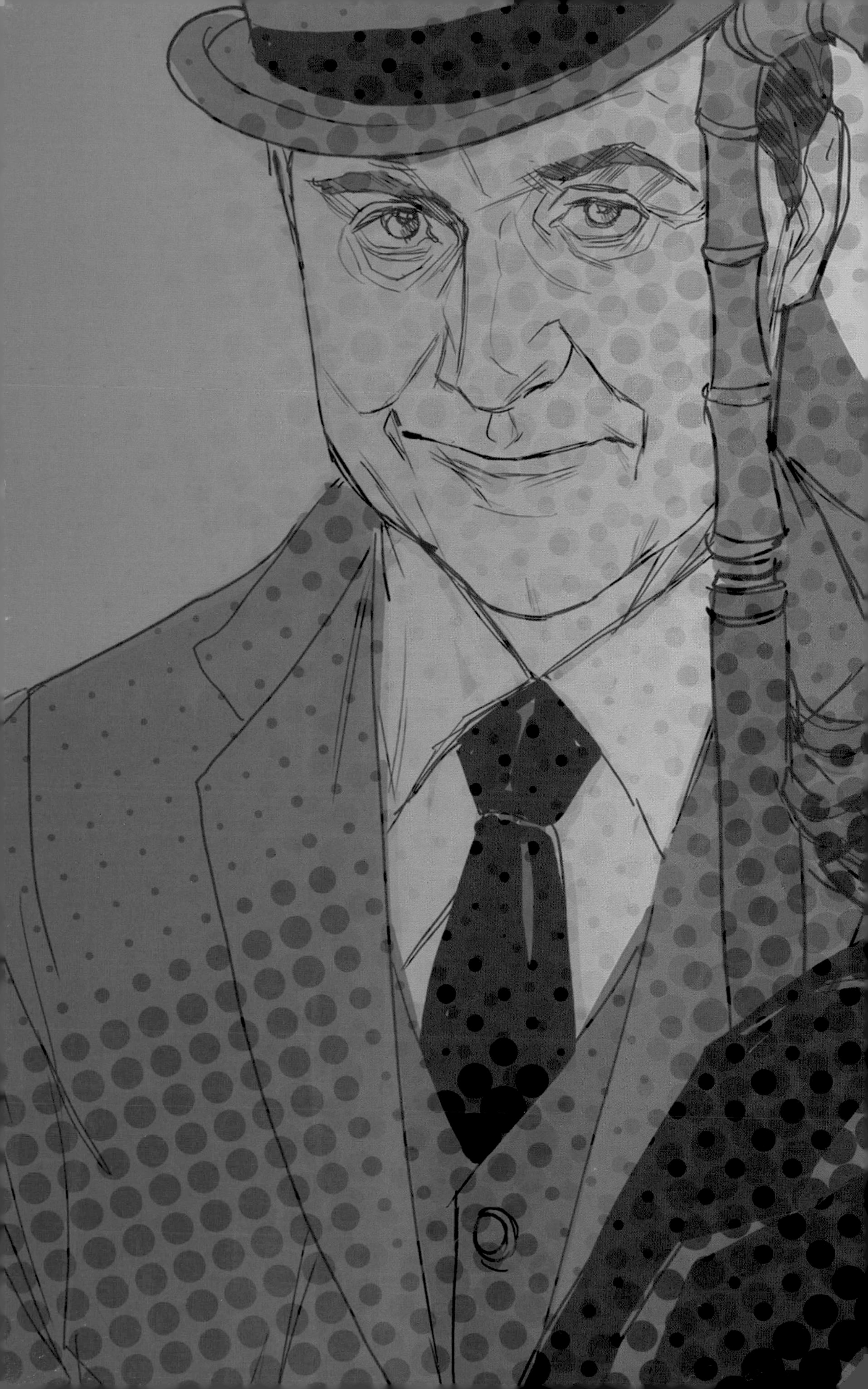

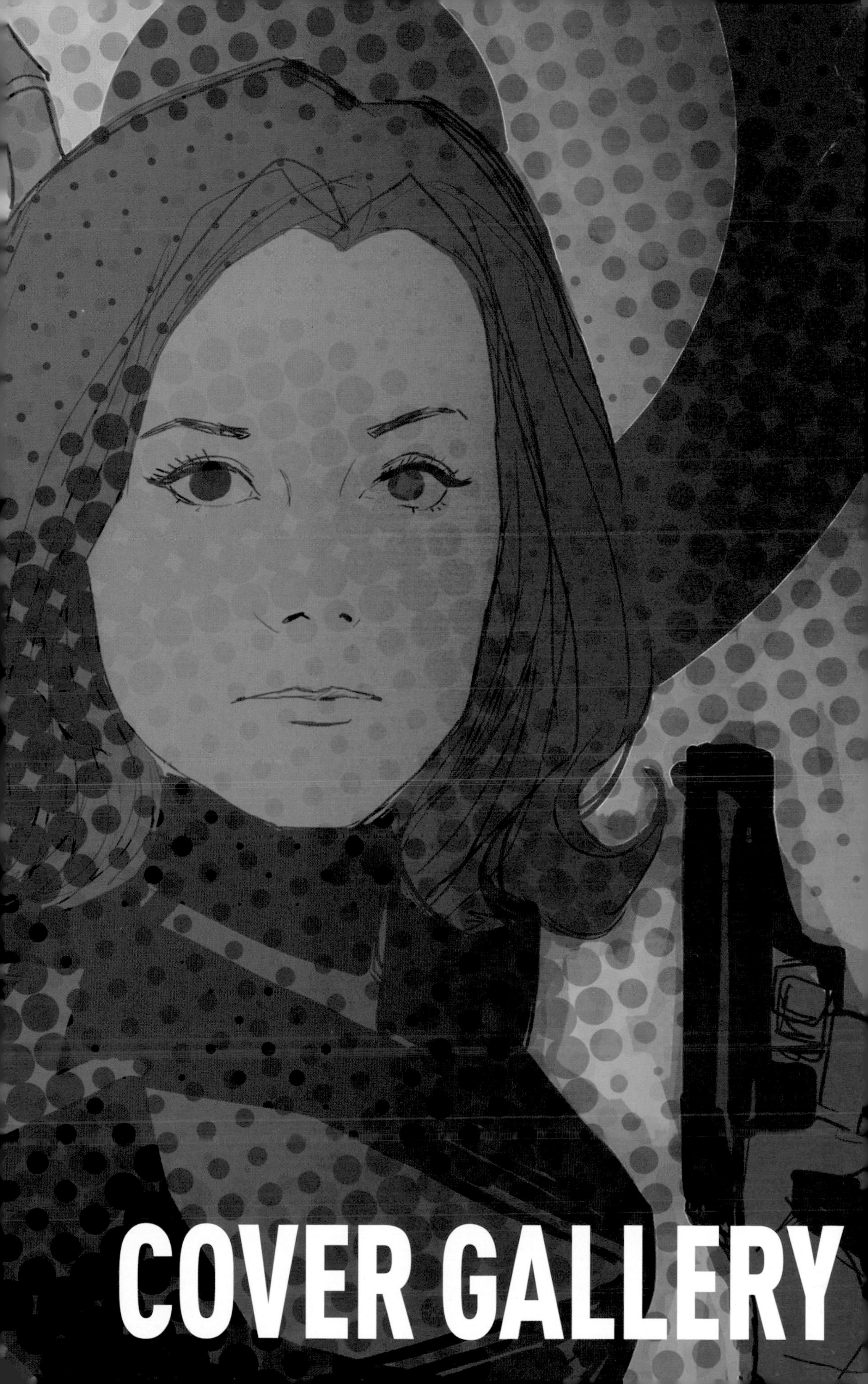

COVER GALLERY

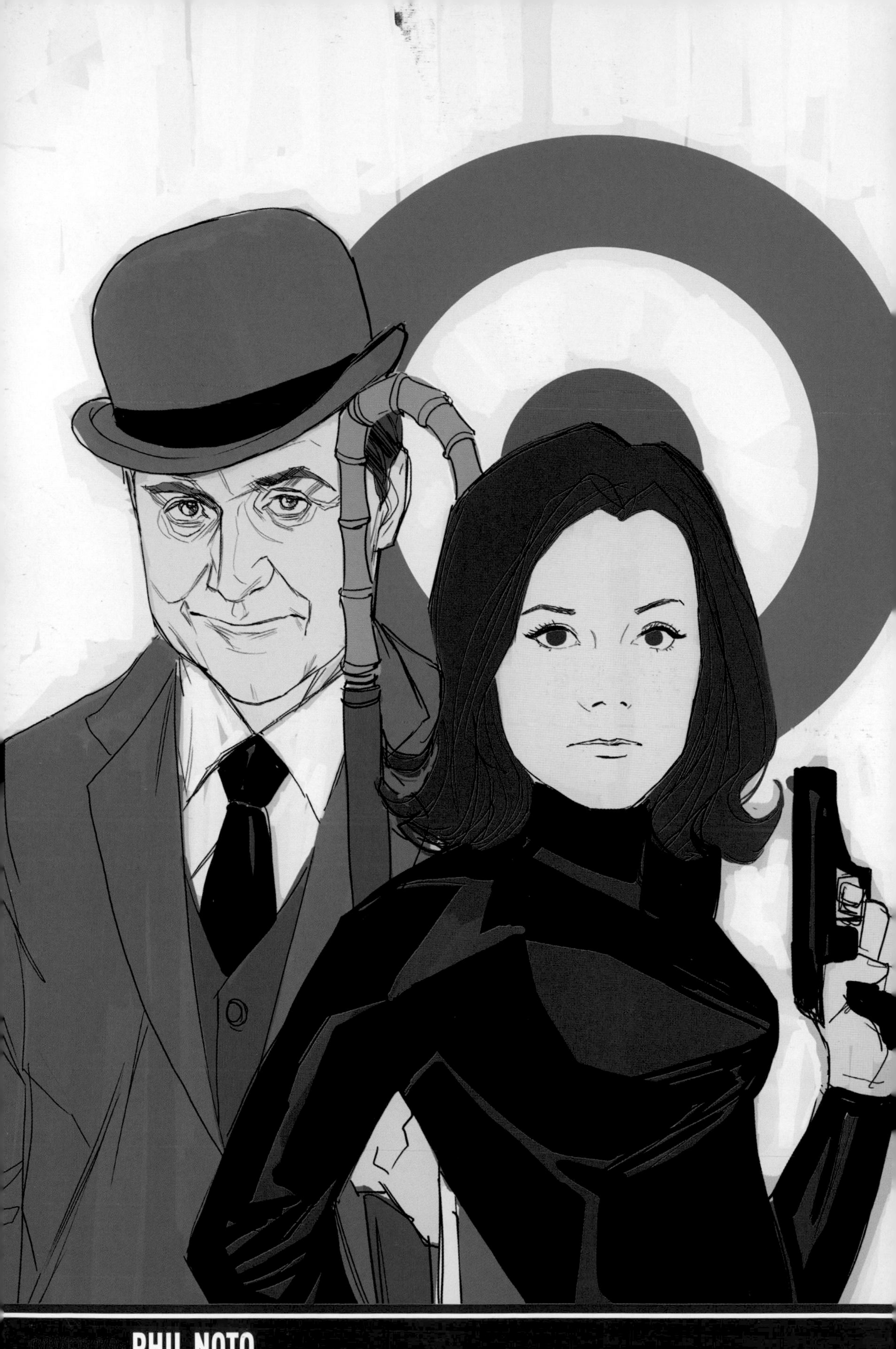

PHIL NOTO

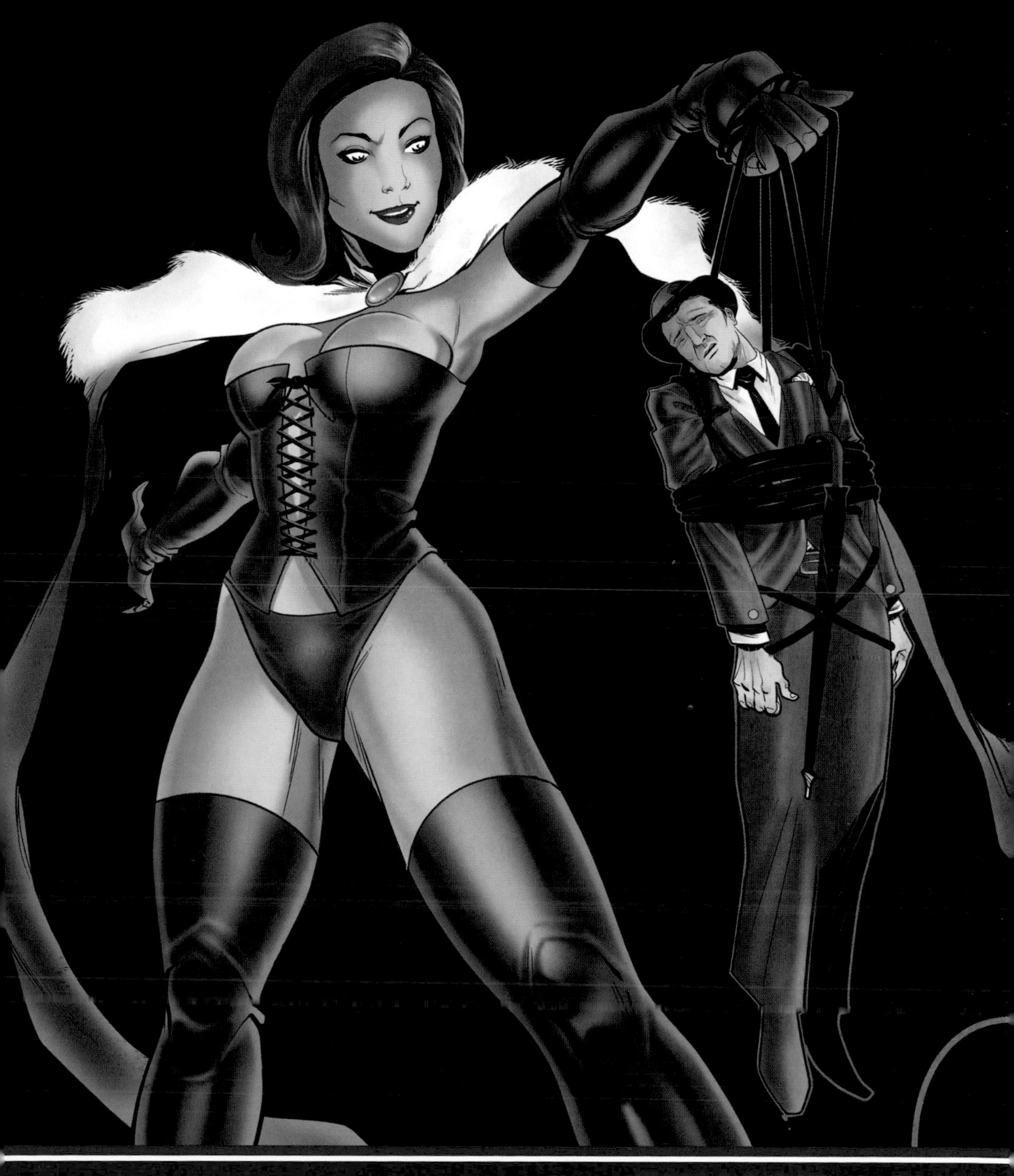

JOSHUA COVEY BLOND

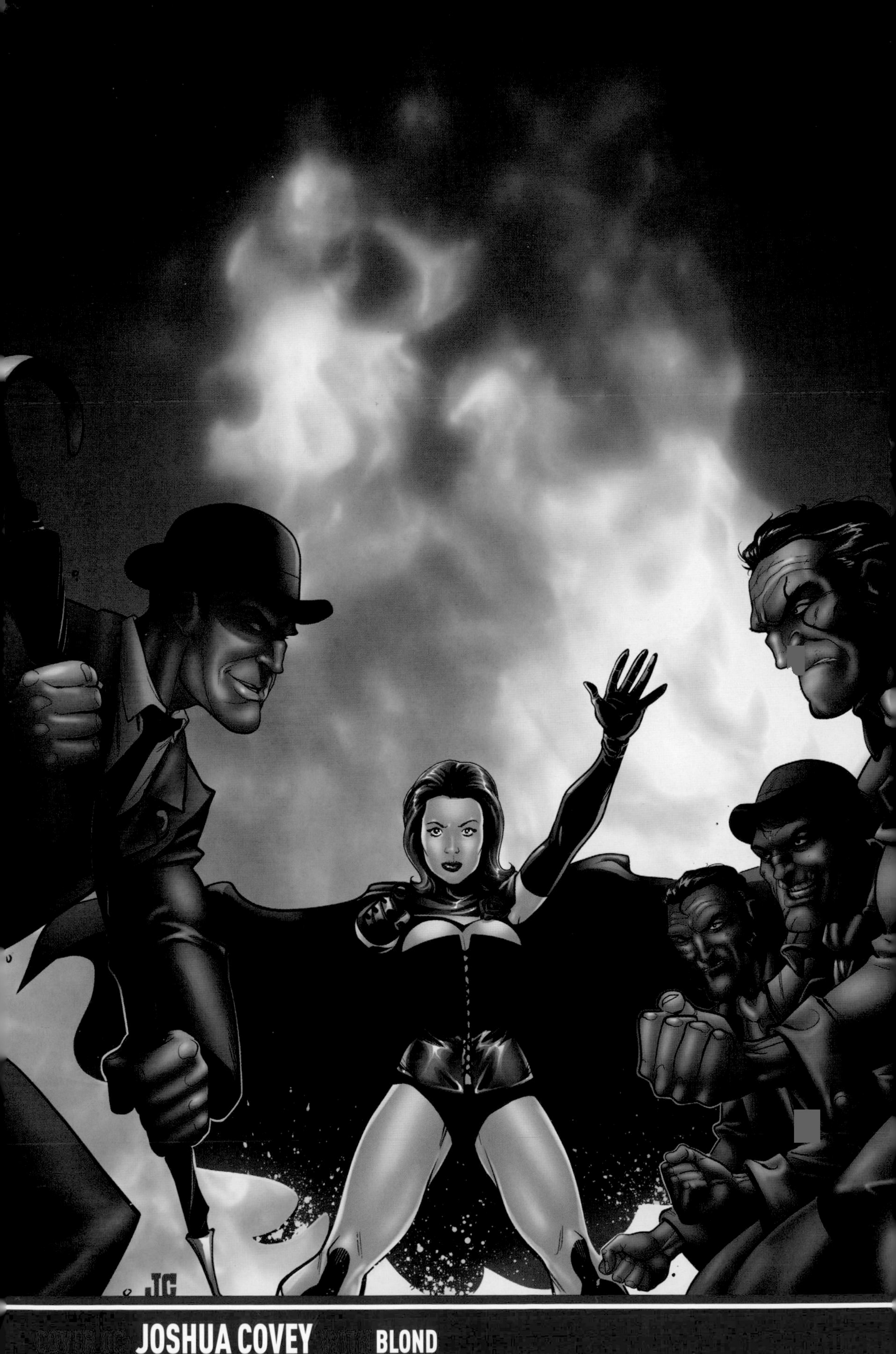

JOSHUA COVEY BLOND

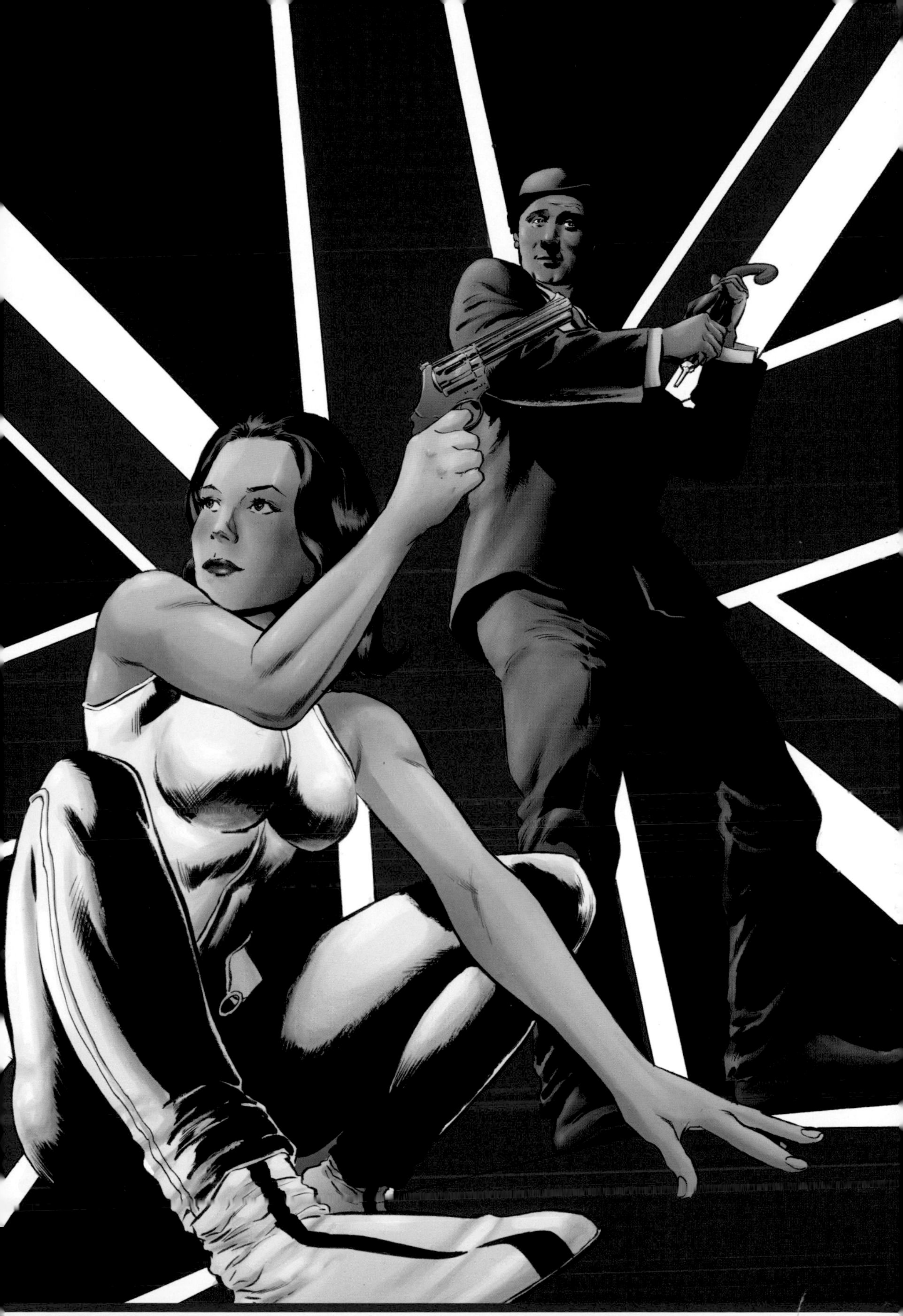

MIKE PERKINS
VLADIMIR POPOV

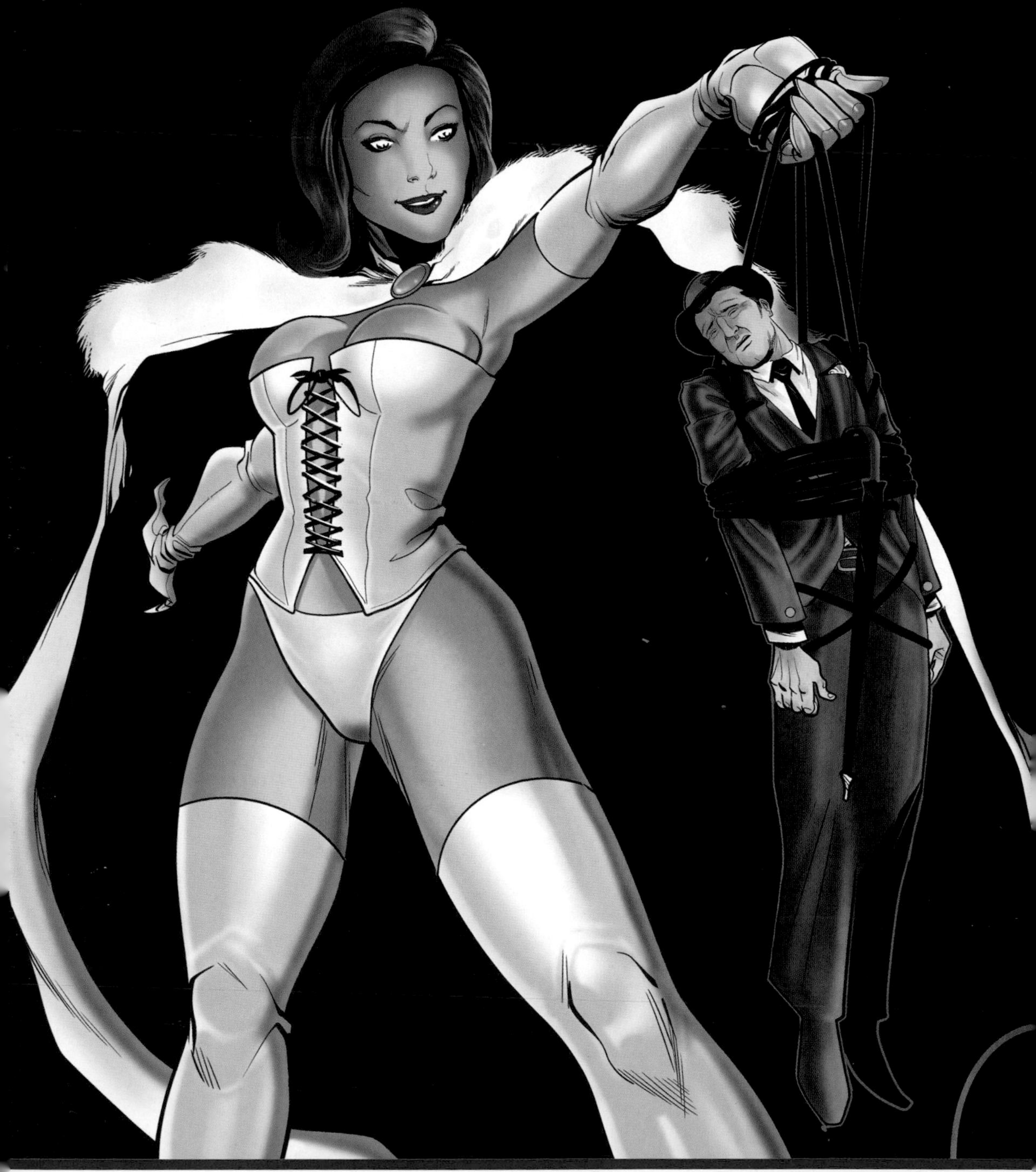

COVER 05 JOSHUA COVEY WITH BLOND

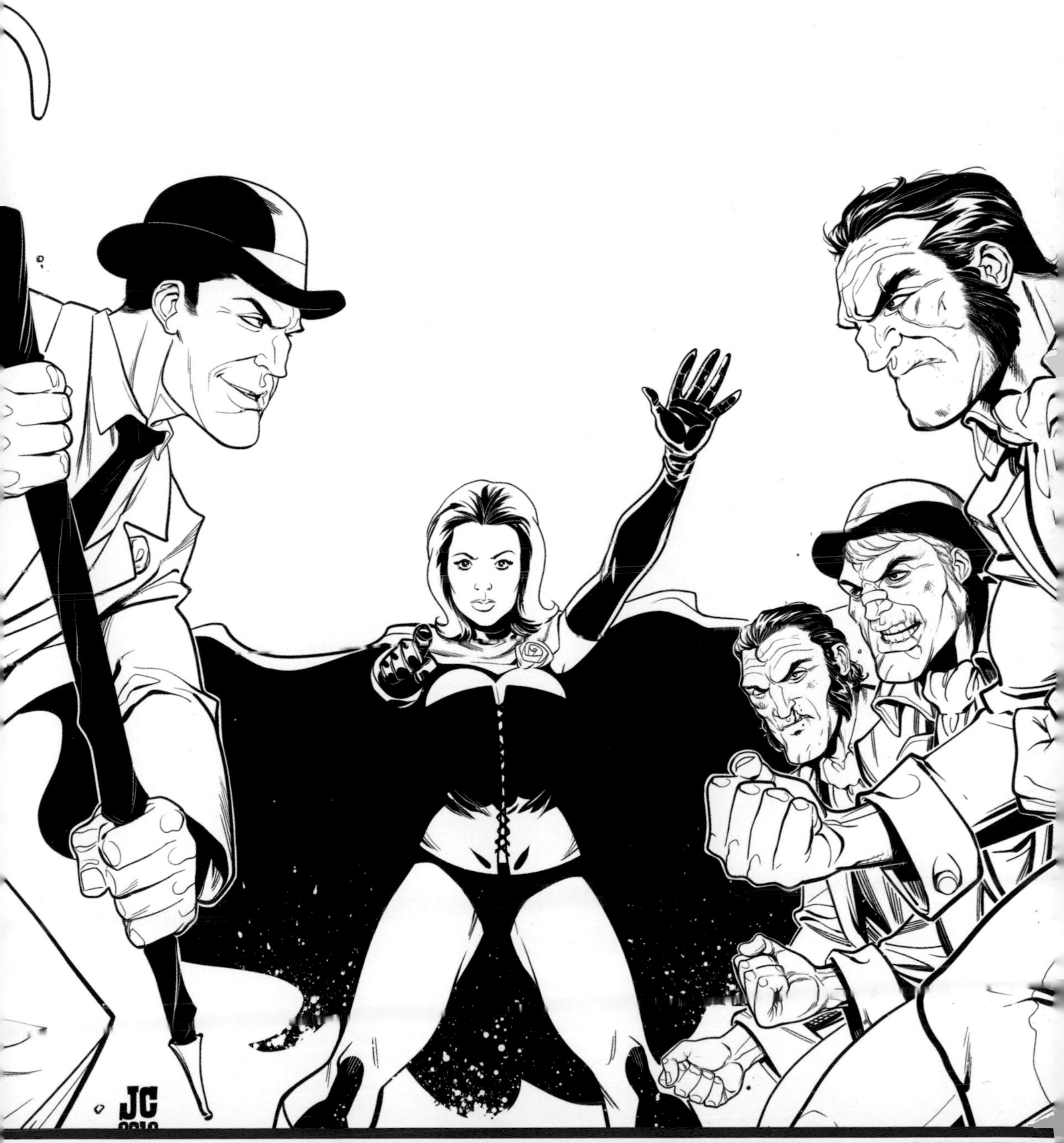

JOSHUA COVEY

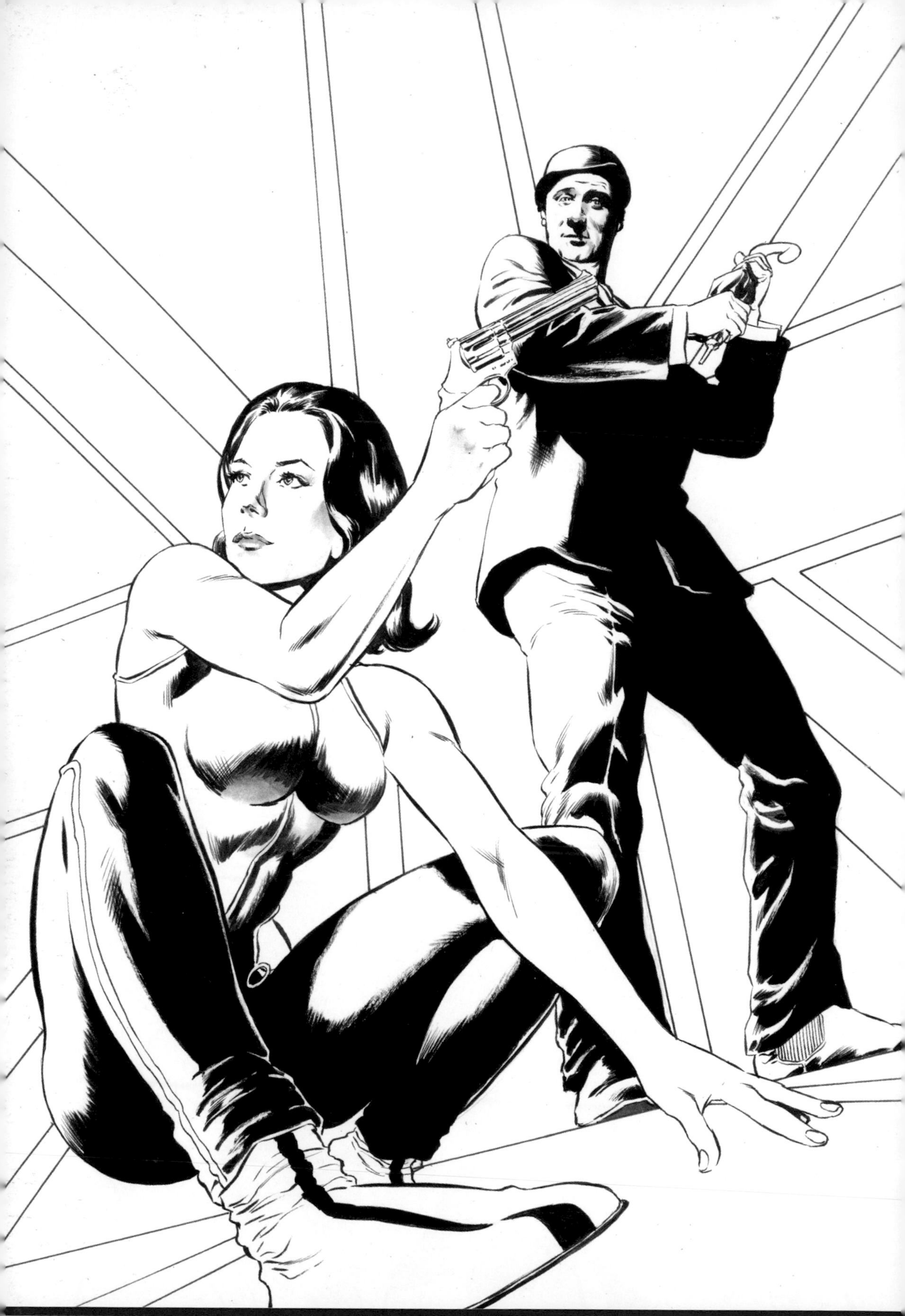

MIKE PERKINS

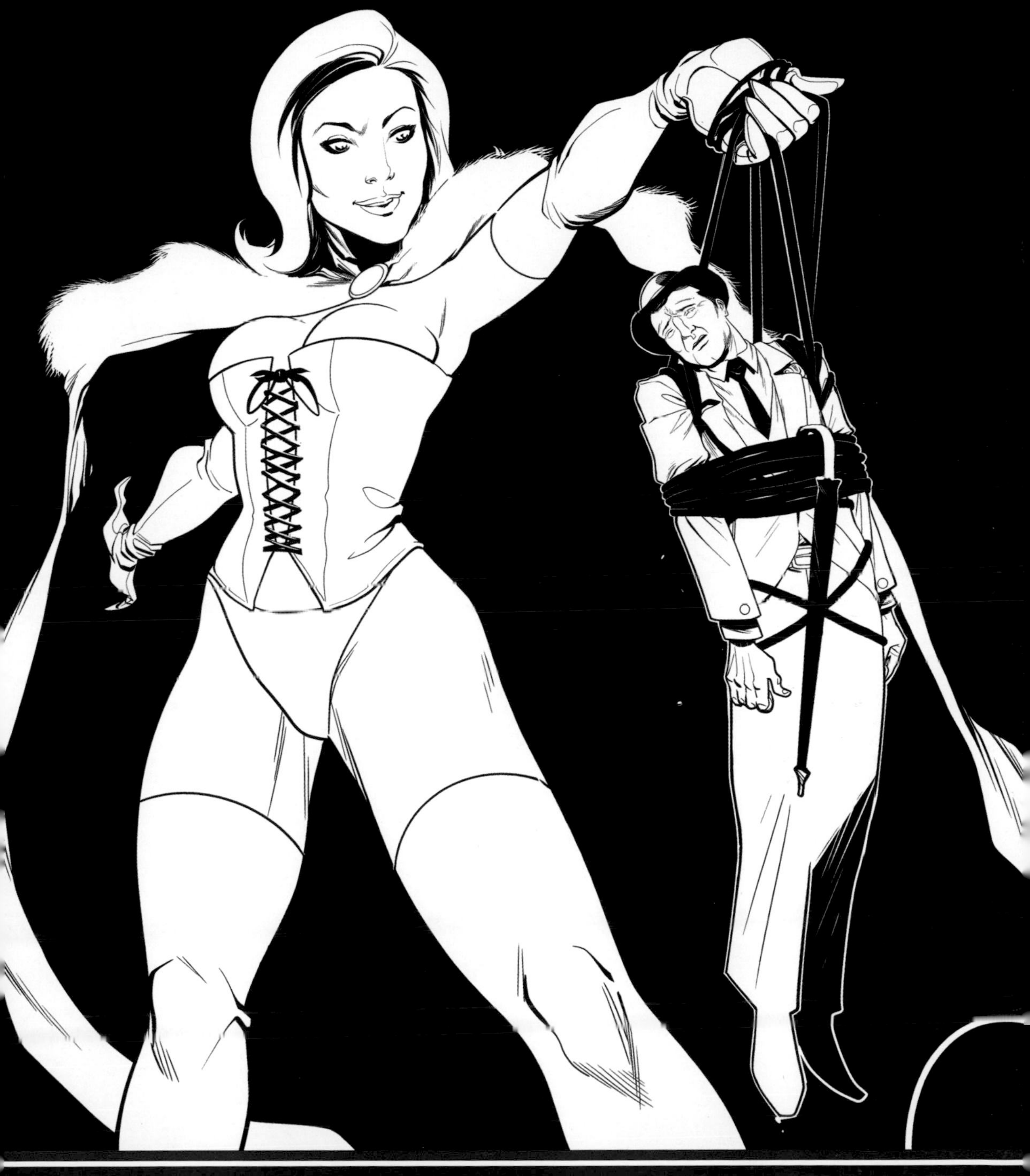

JOSHUA COVEY

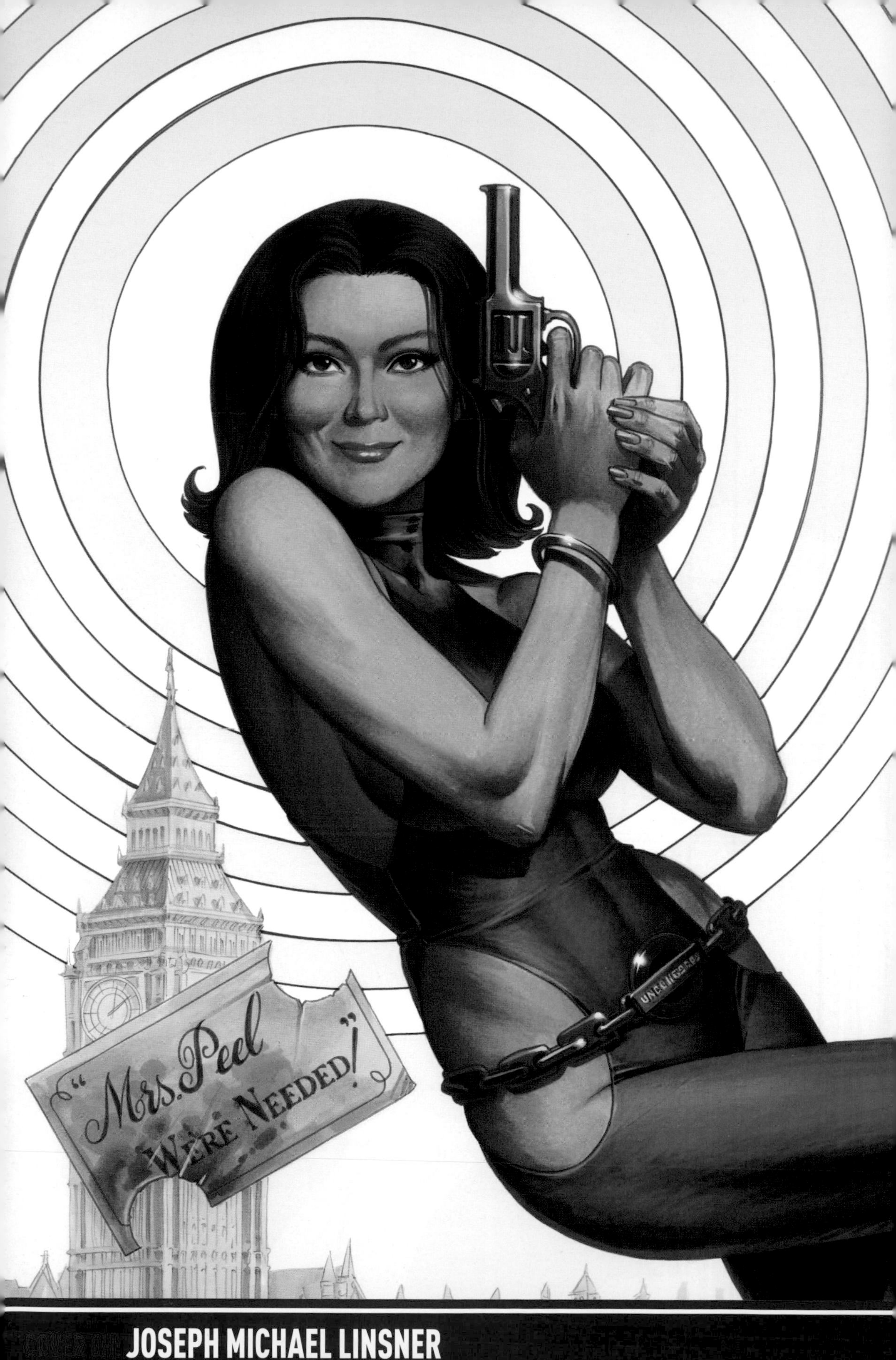
"Mrs. Peel We're Needed!"

COVER BY: JOSEPH MICHAEL LINSNER

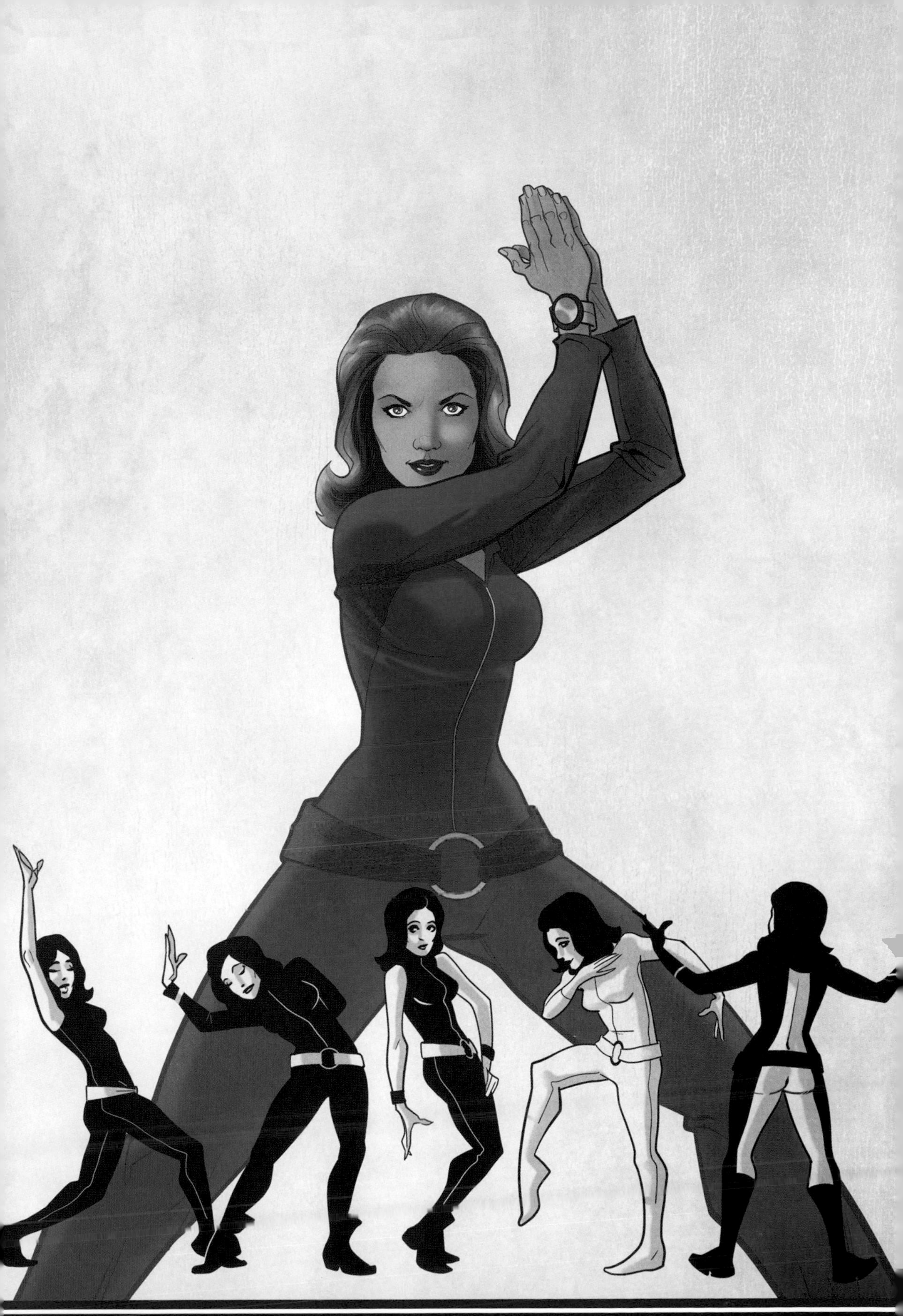

JOSHUA COVEY

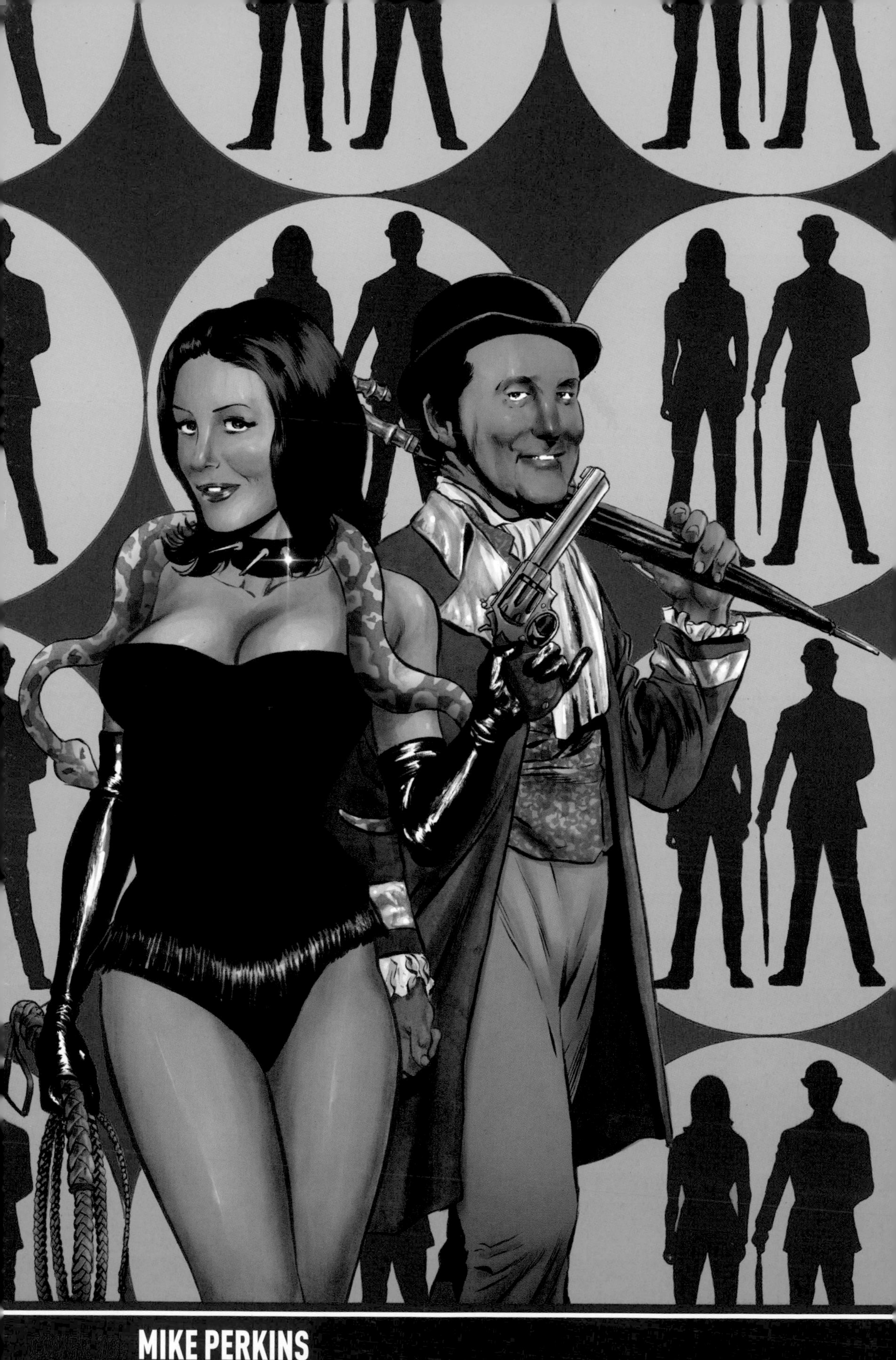

MIKE PERKINS
VLADIMIR POPOV

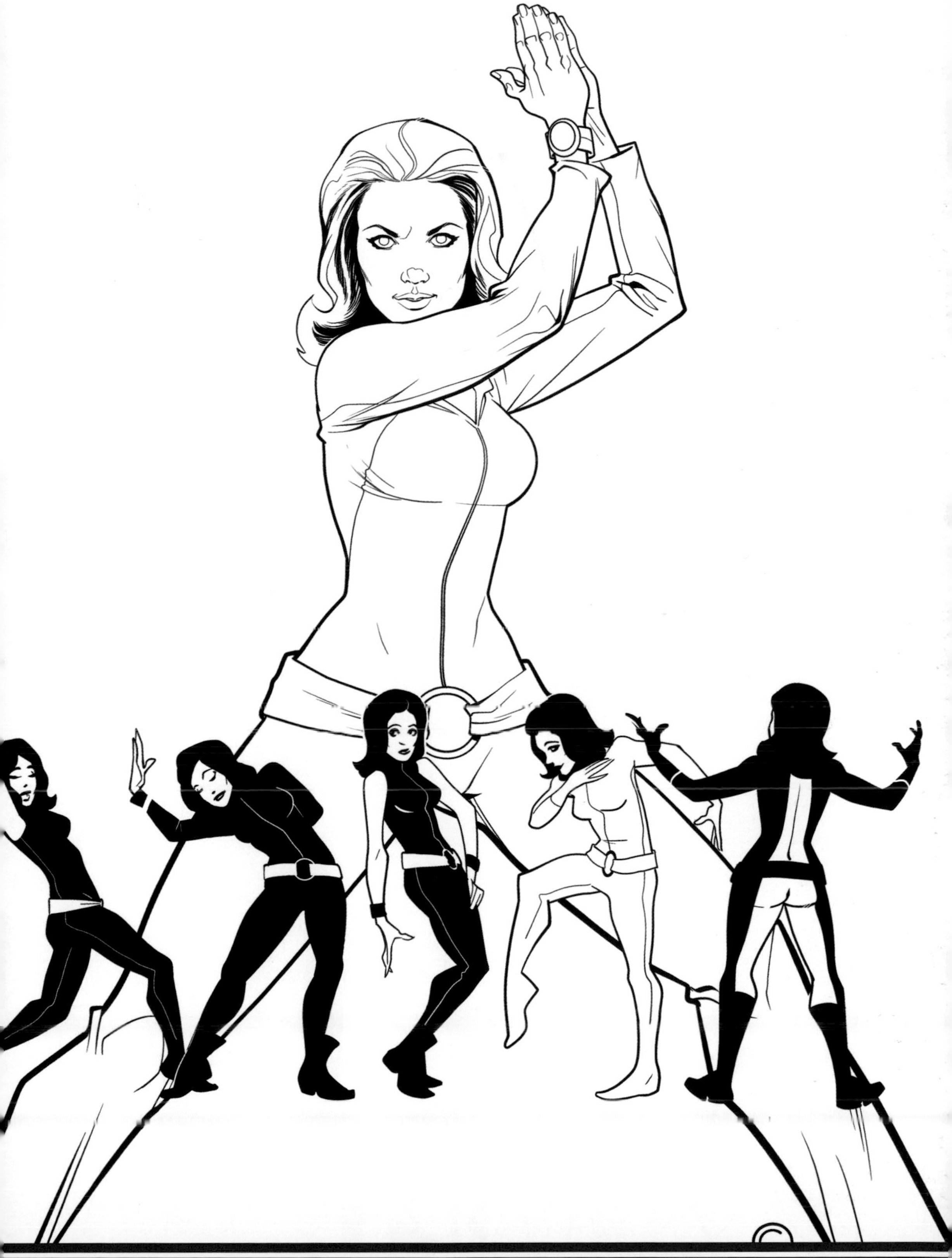

JOSHUA COVEY

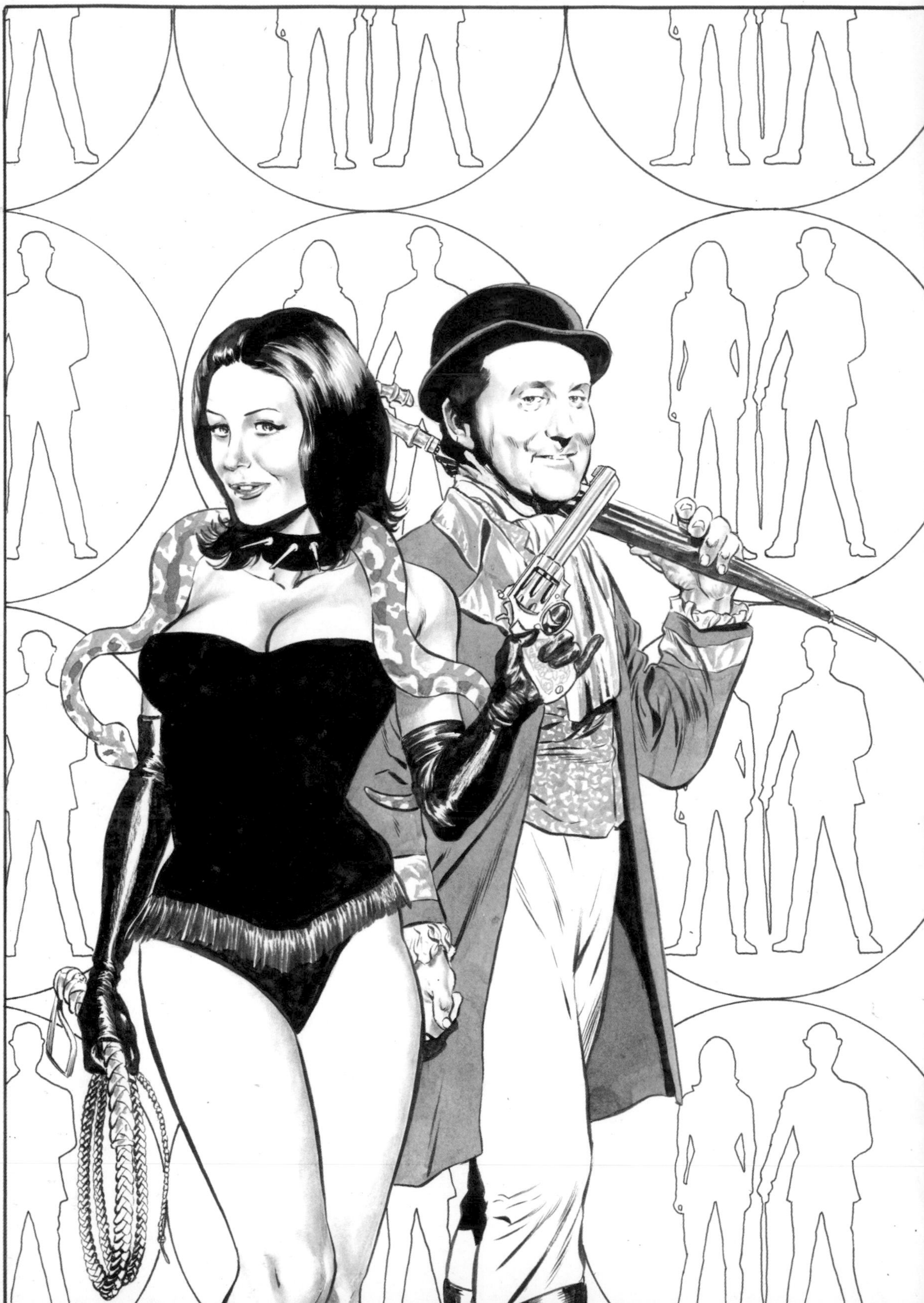

MIKE PERKINS

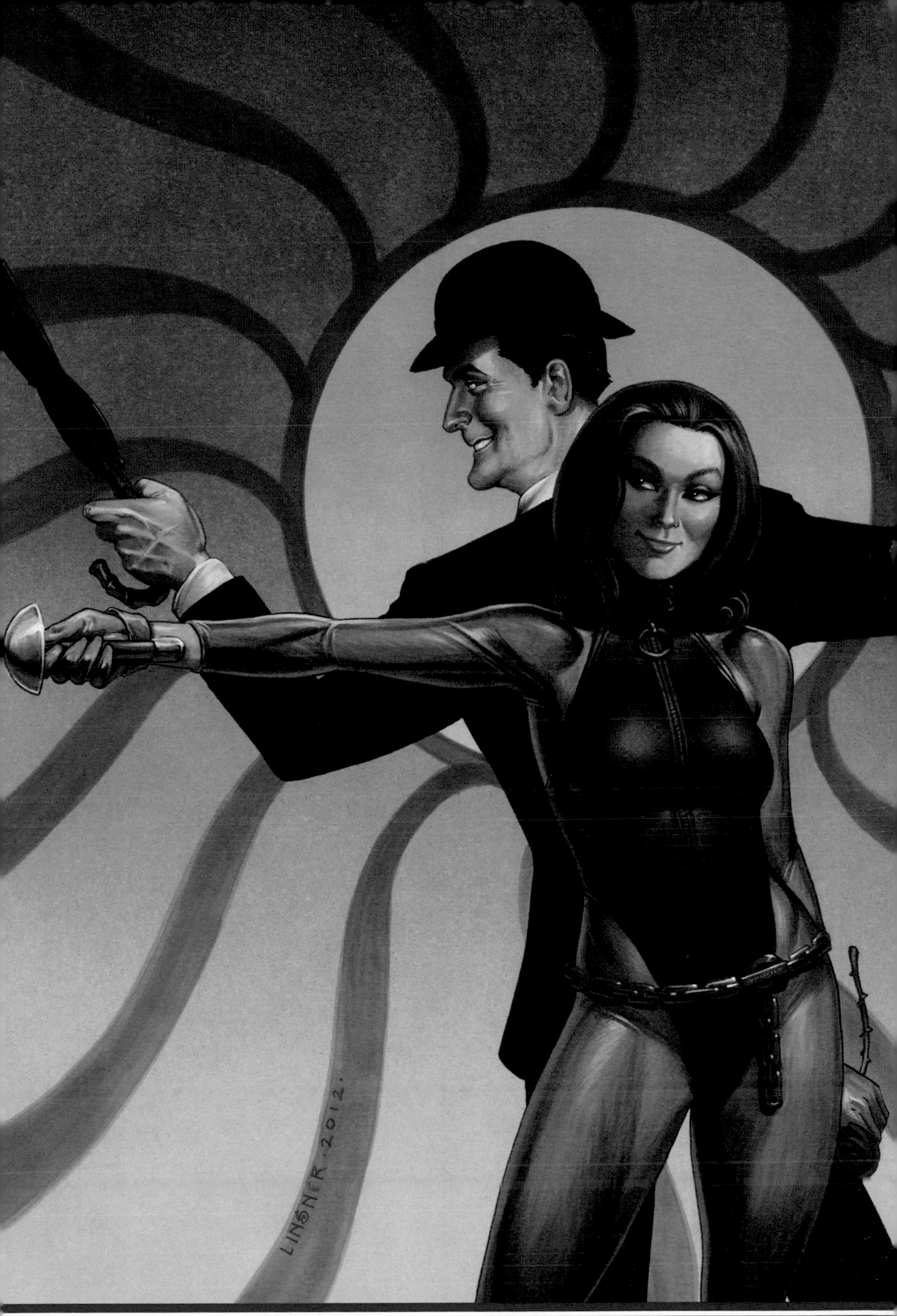
LINSNER 2012.

JOSEPH MICHAEL LINSNER

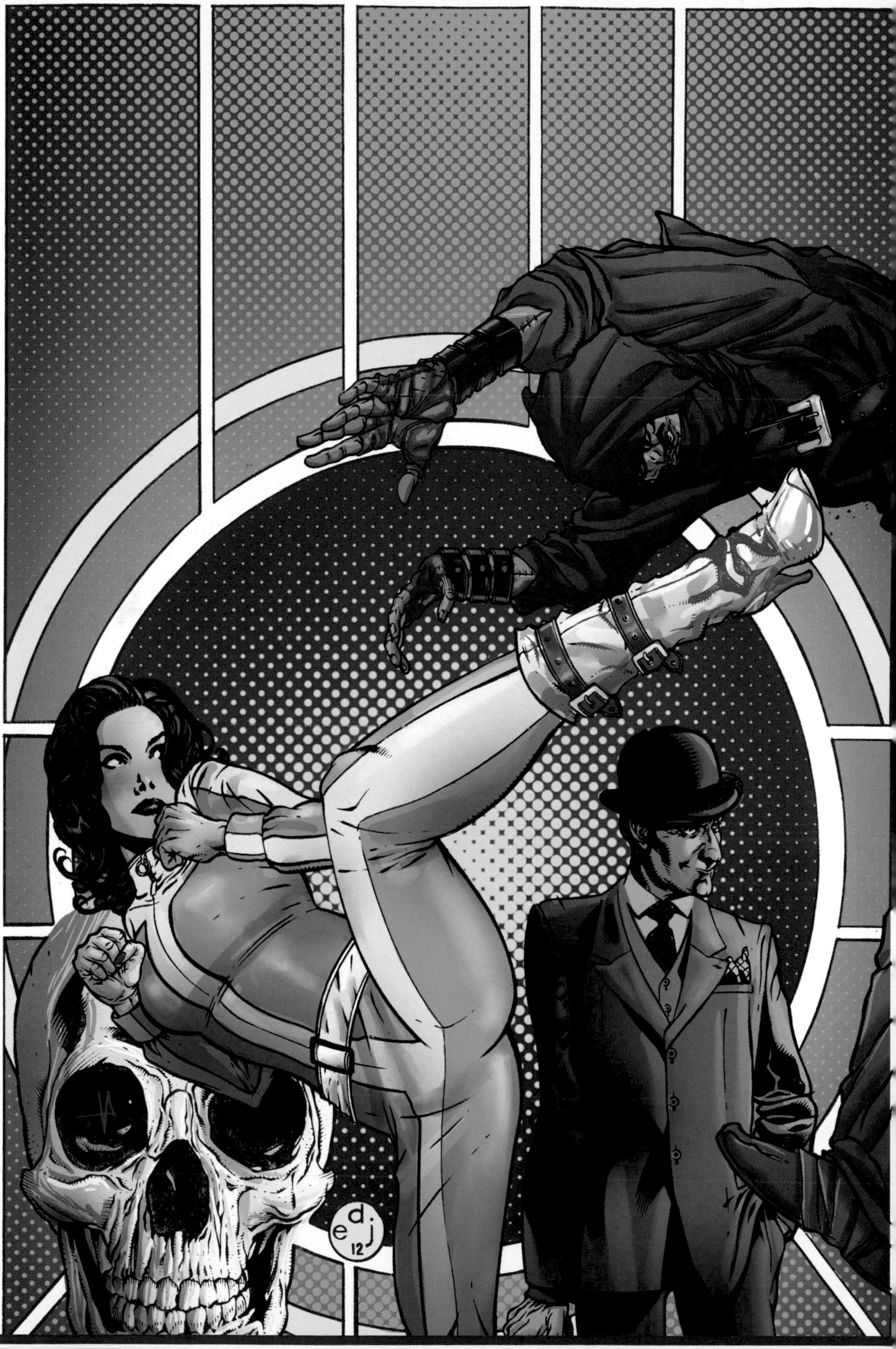

DREW JOHNSON
VLADIMIR POPOV

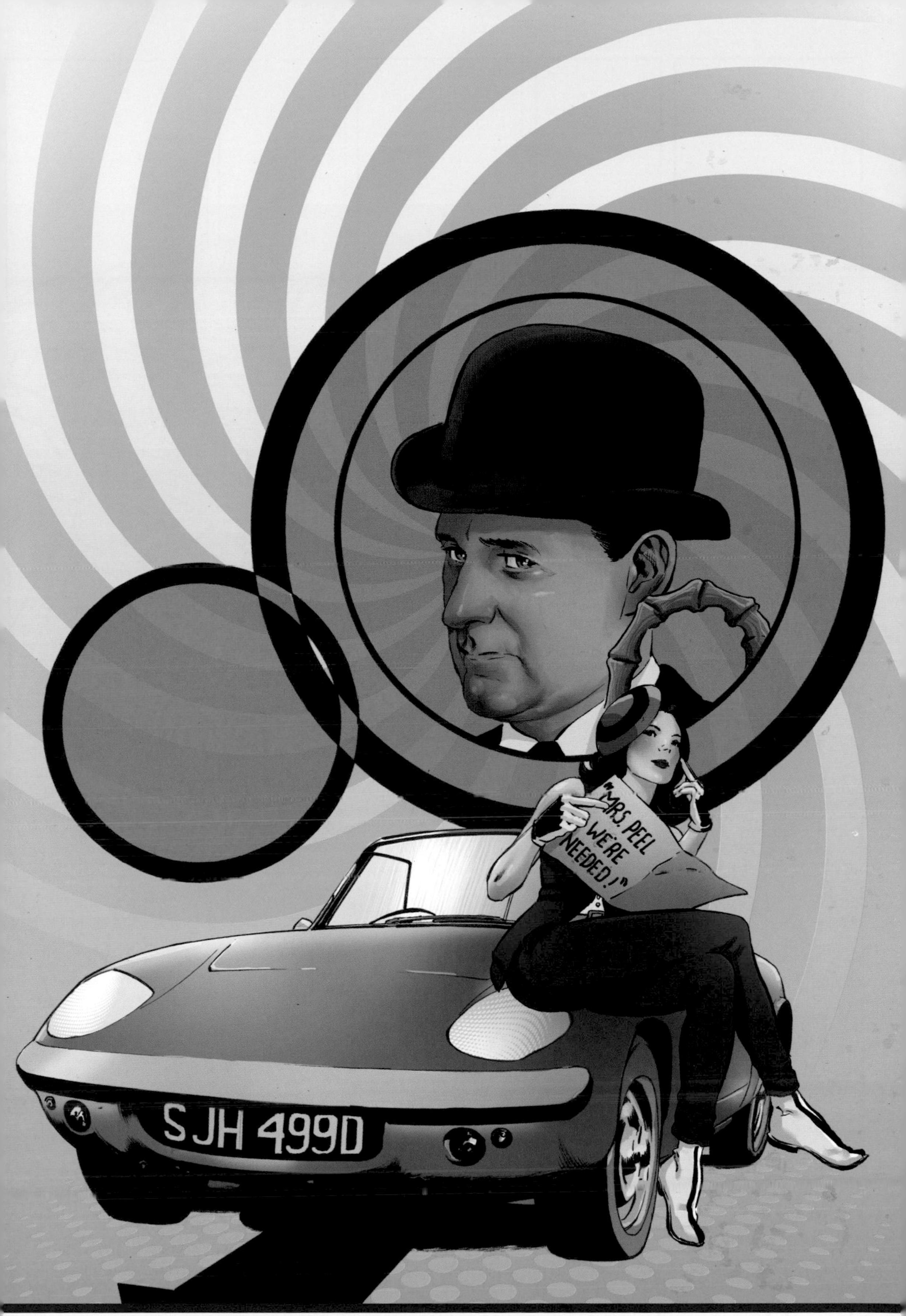
"MRS. PEEL WE'RE NEEDED!"
SJH 499D

MIKE PERKINS
VLADIMIR POPOV

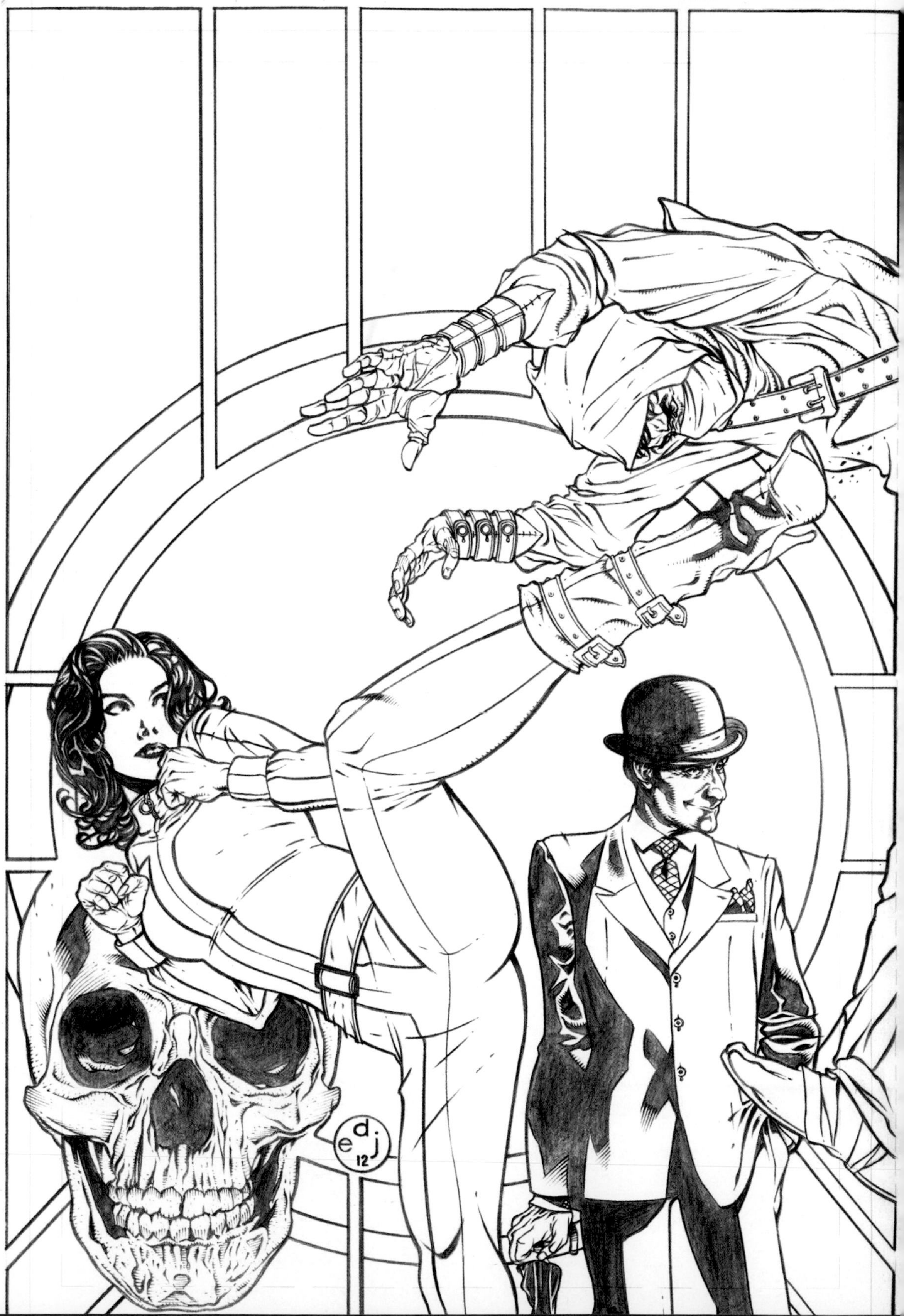

DREW JOHNSON

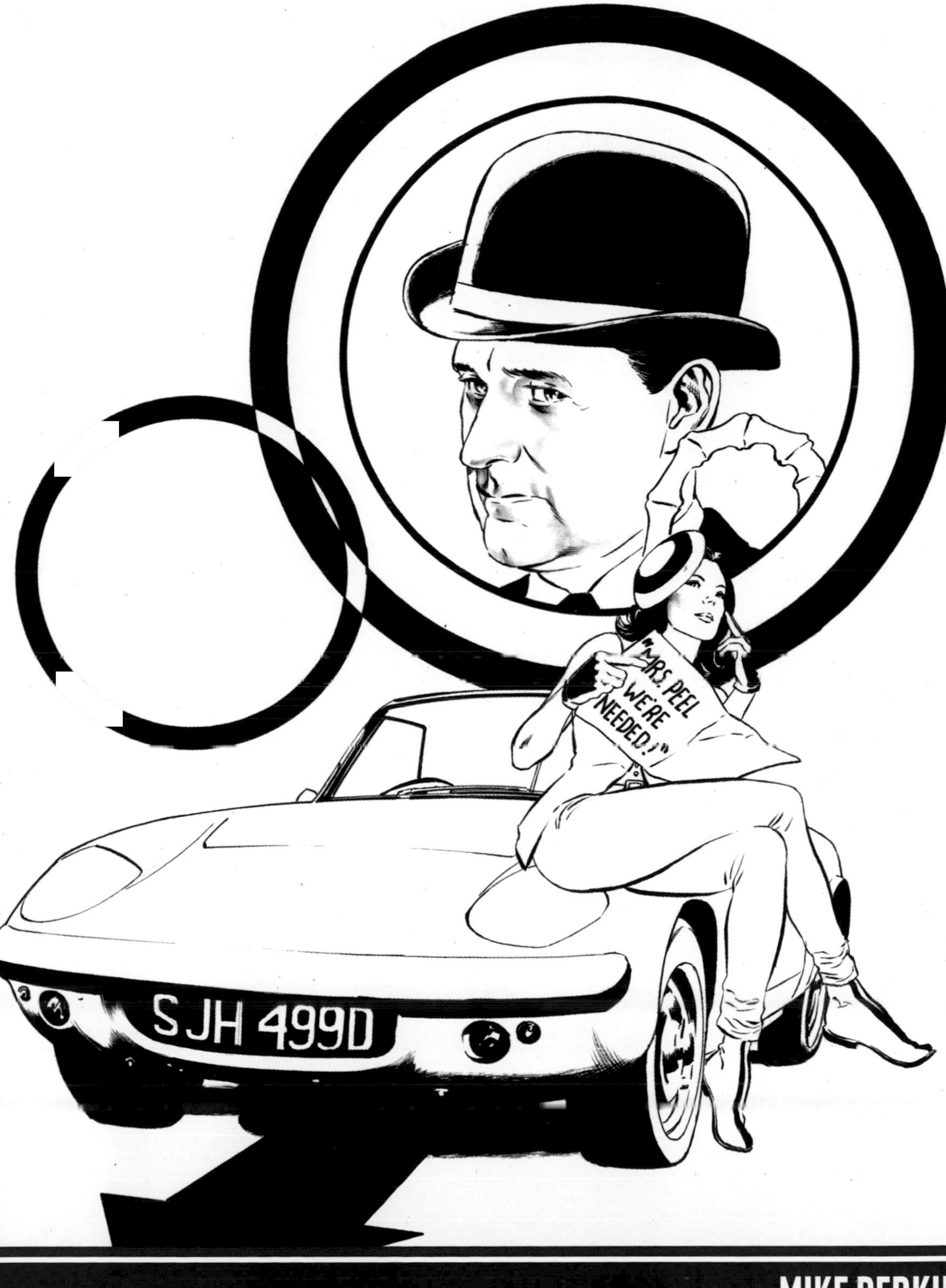
"MRS. PEEL WE'RE NEEDED!"
SJH 499D

MIKE PERKINS

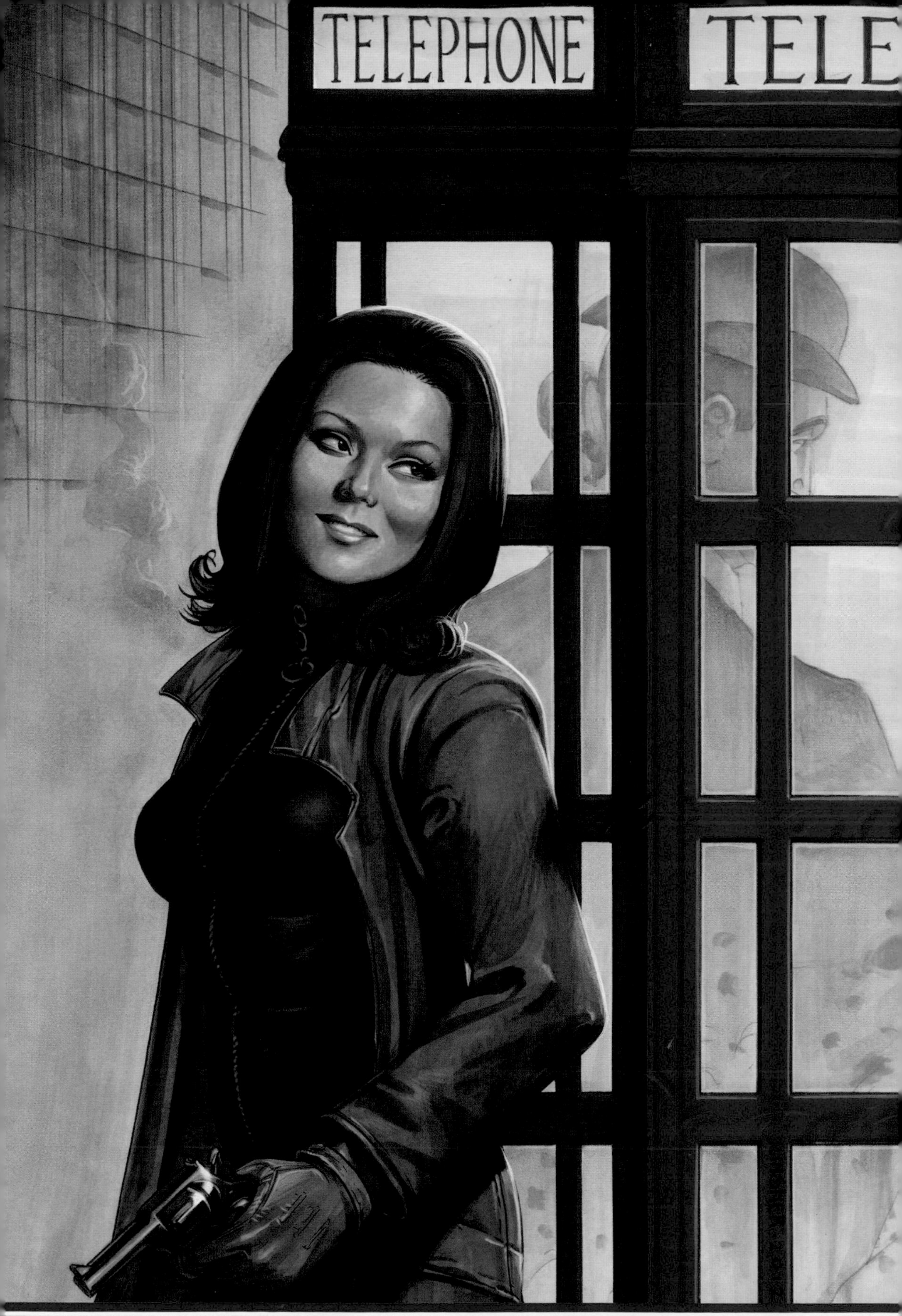
TELEPHONE
TELE

JOSEPH MICHAEL LINSNER

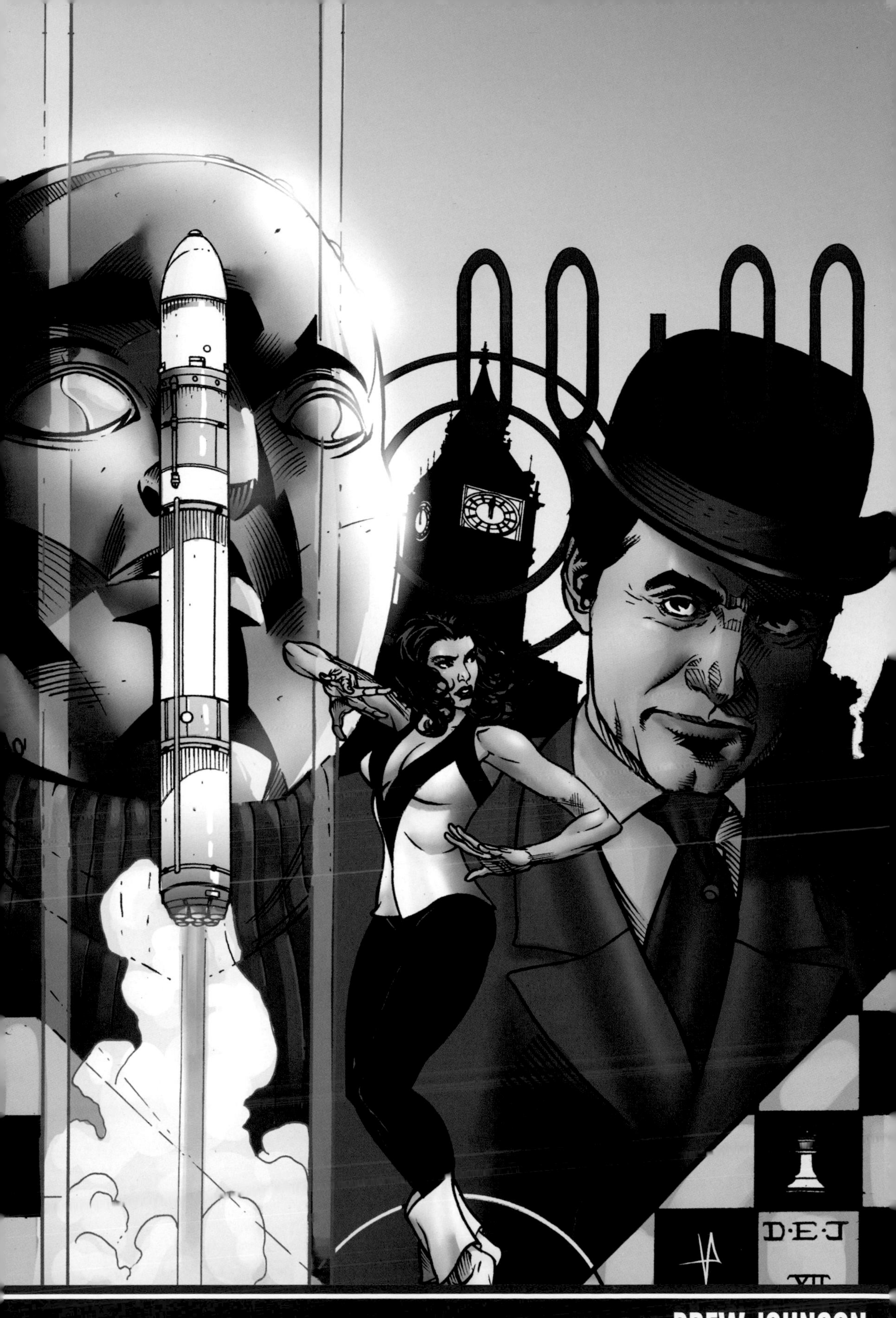
D·E·J

DREW JOHNSON
VLADIMIR POPOV

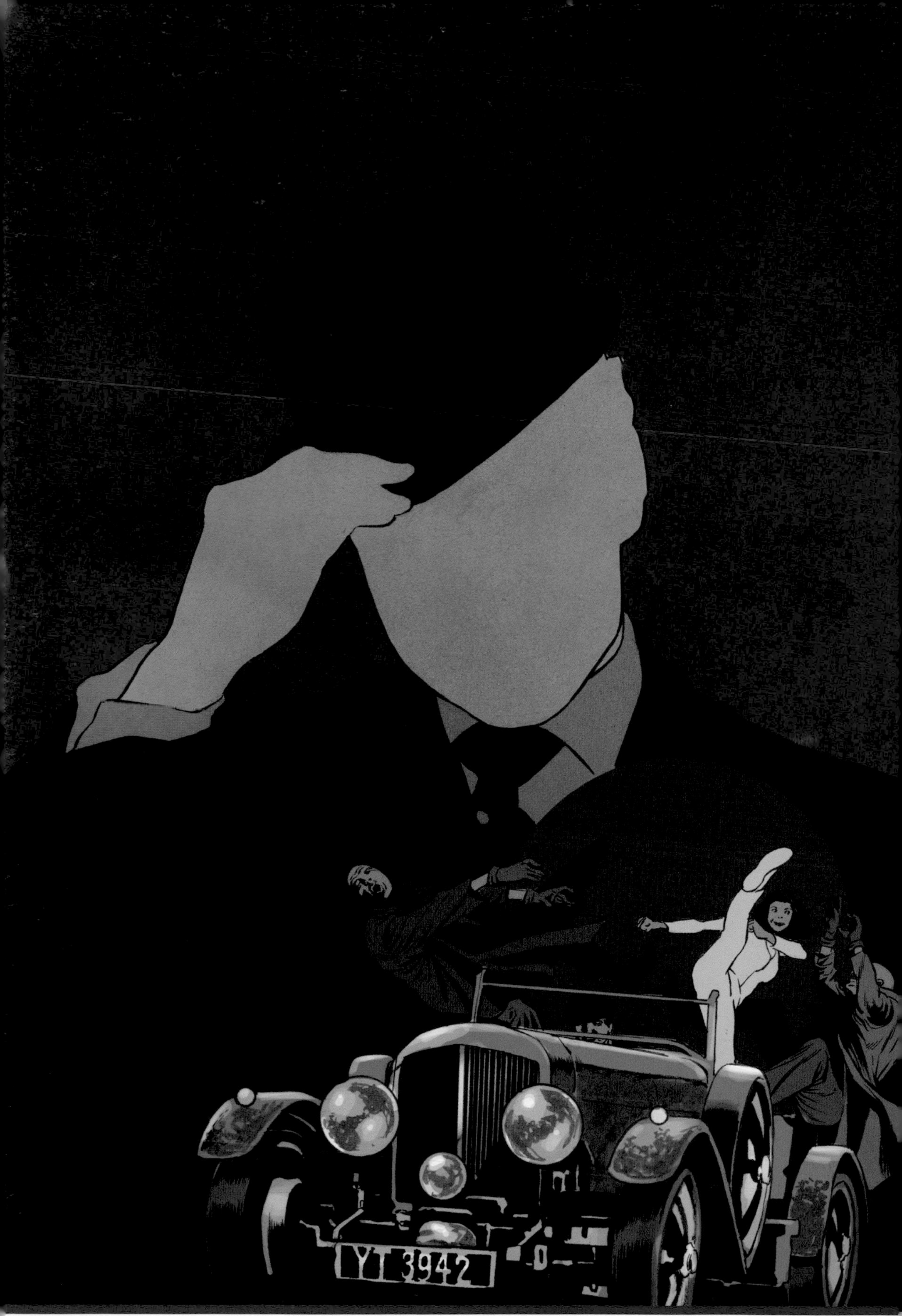

MIKE PERKINS
VLADIMIR POPOV

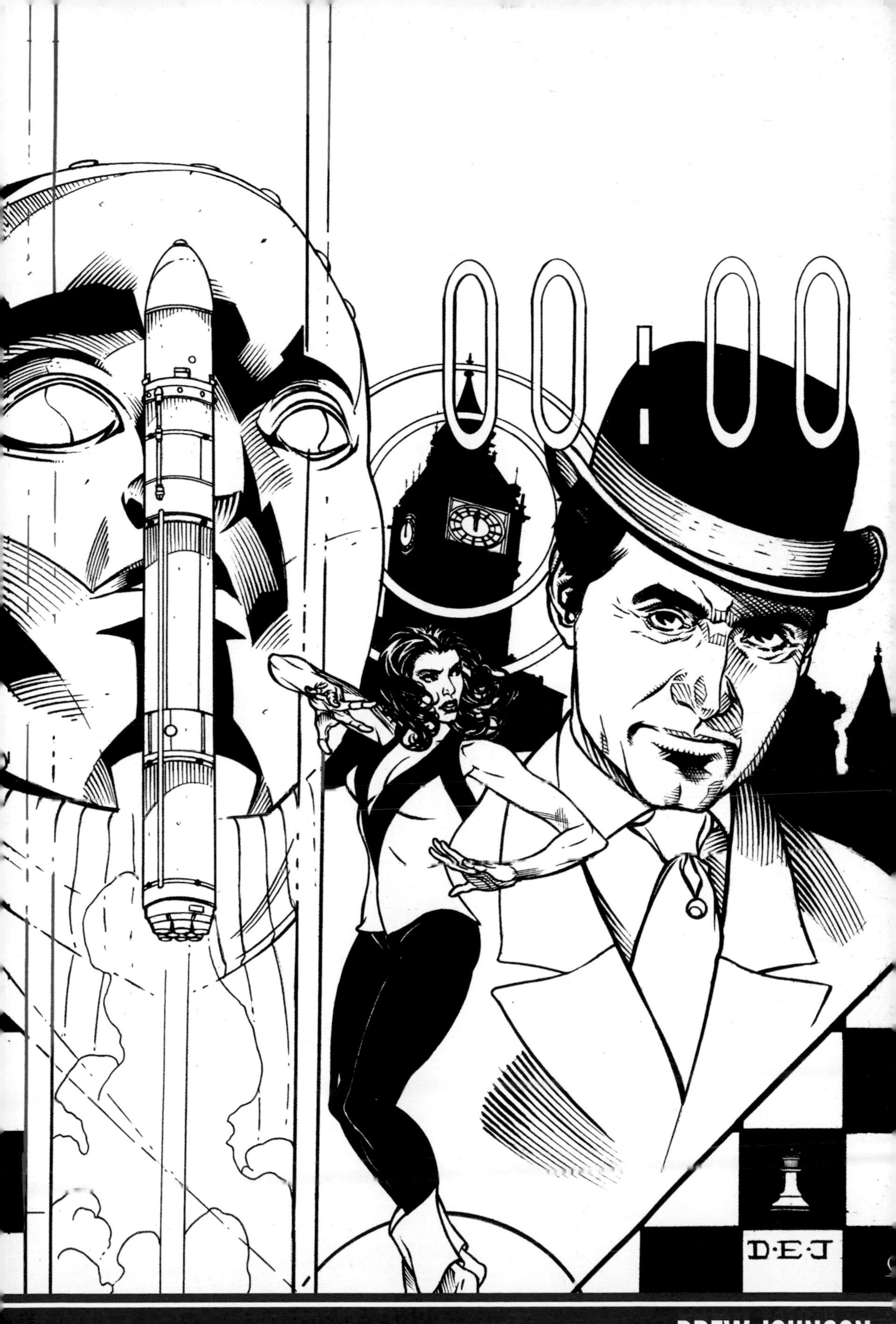
00:00
D·E·J

DREW JOHNSON

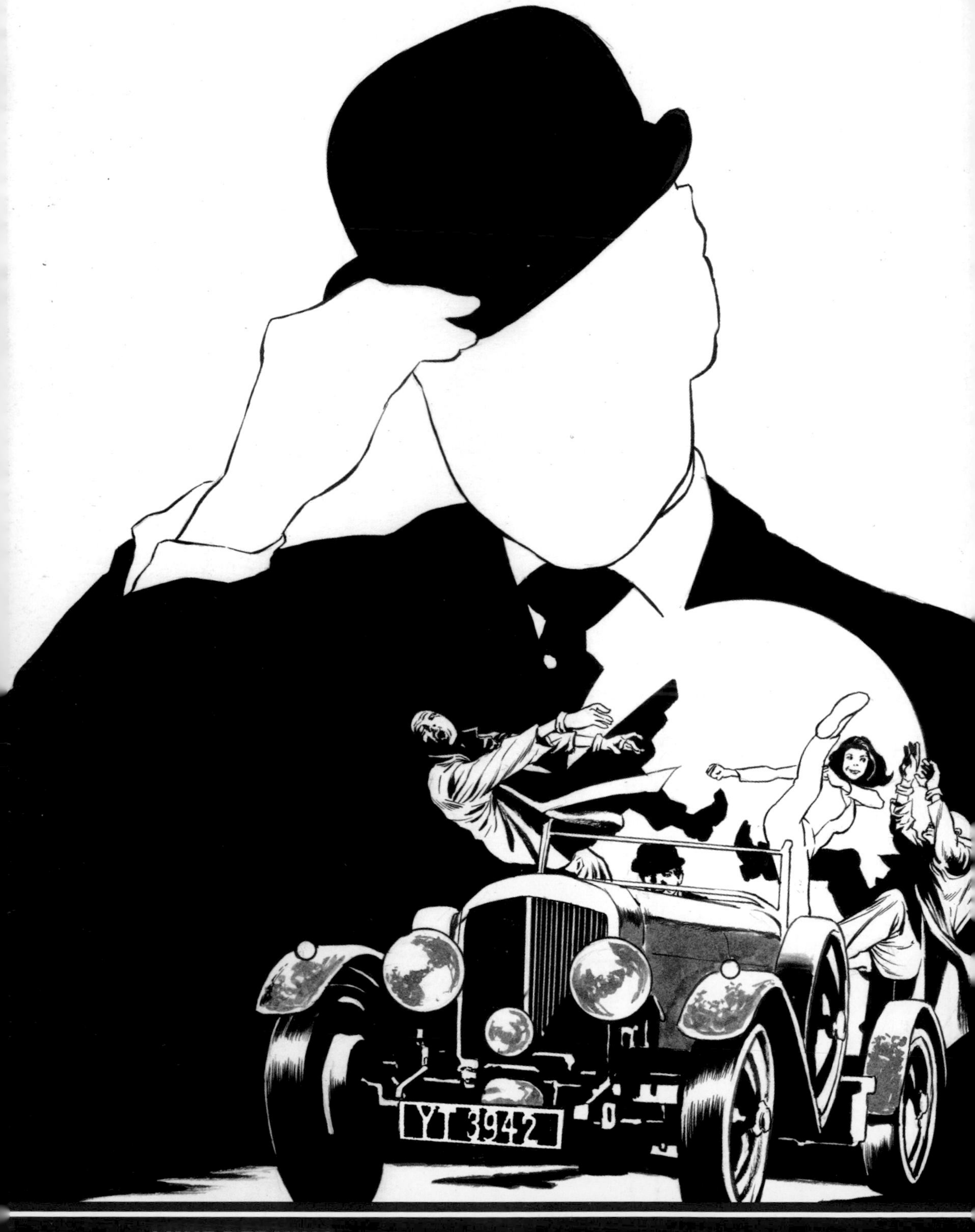
YT 3942

MIKE PERKINS

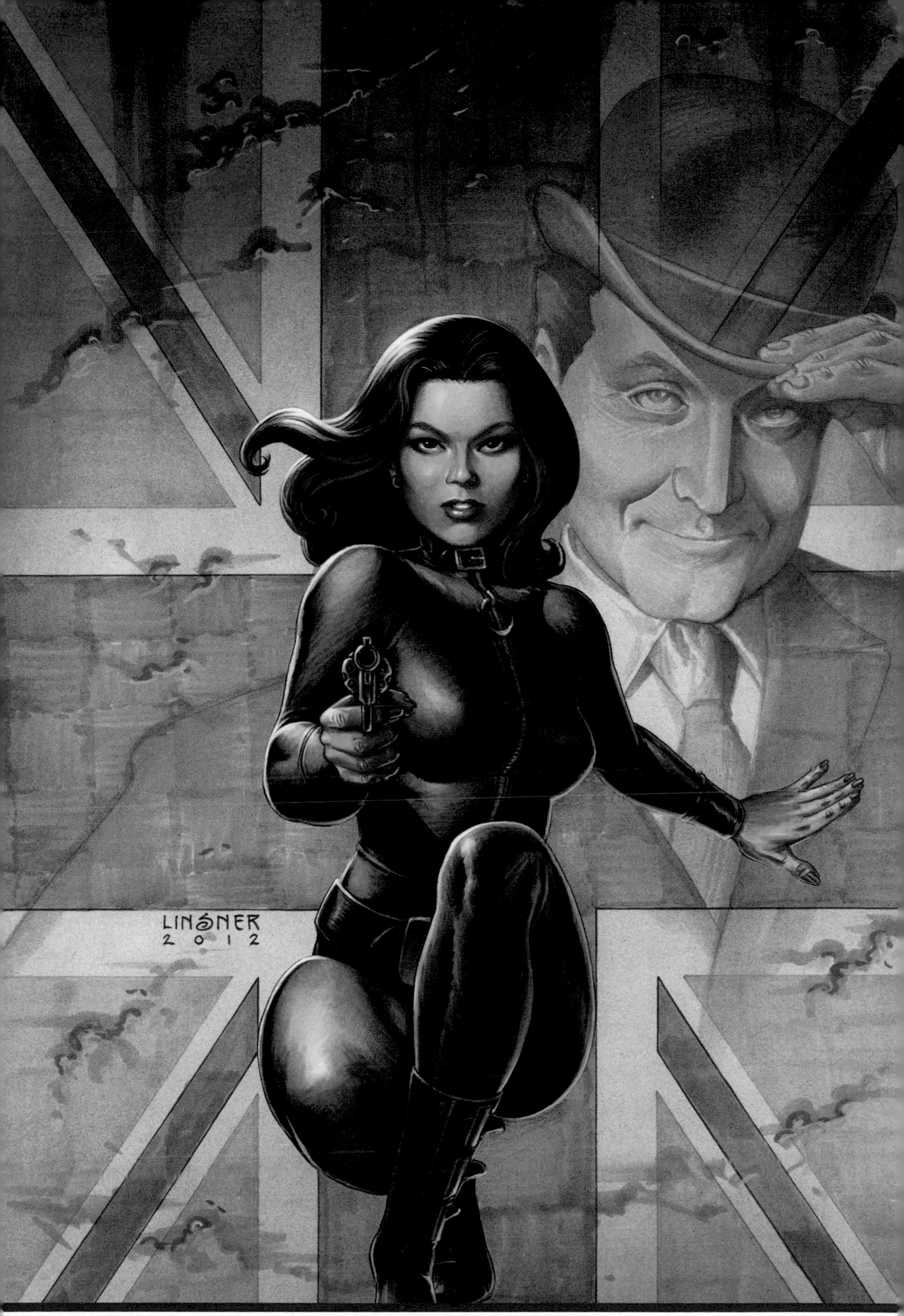
LINSNER
2012

JOSEPH MICHAEL LINSNER

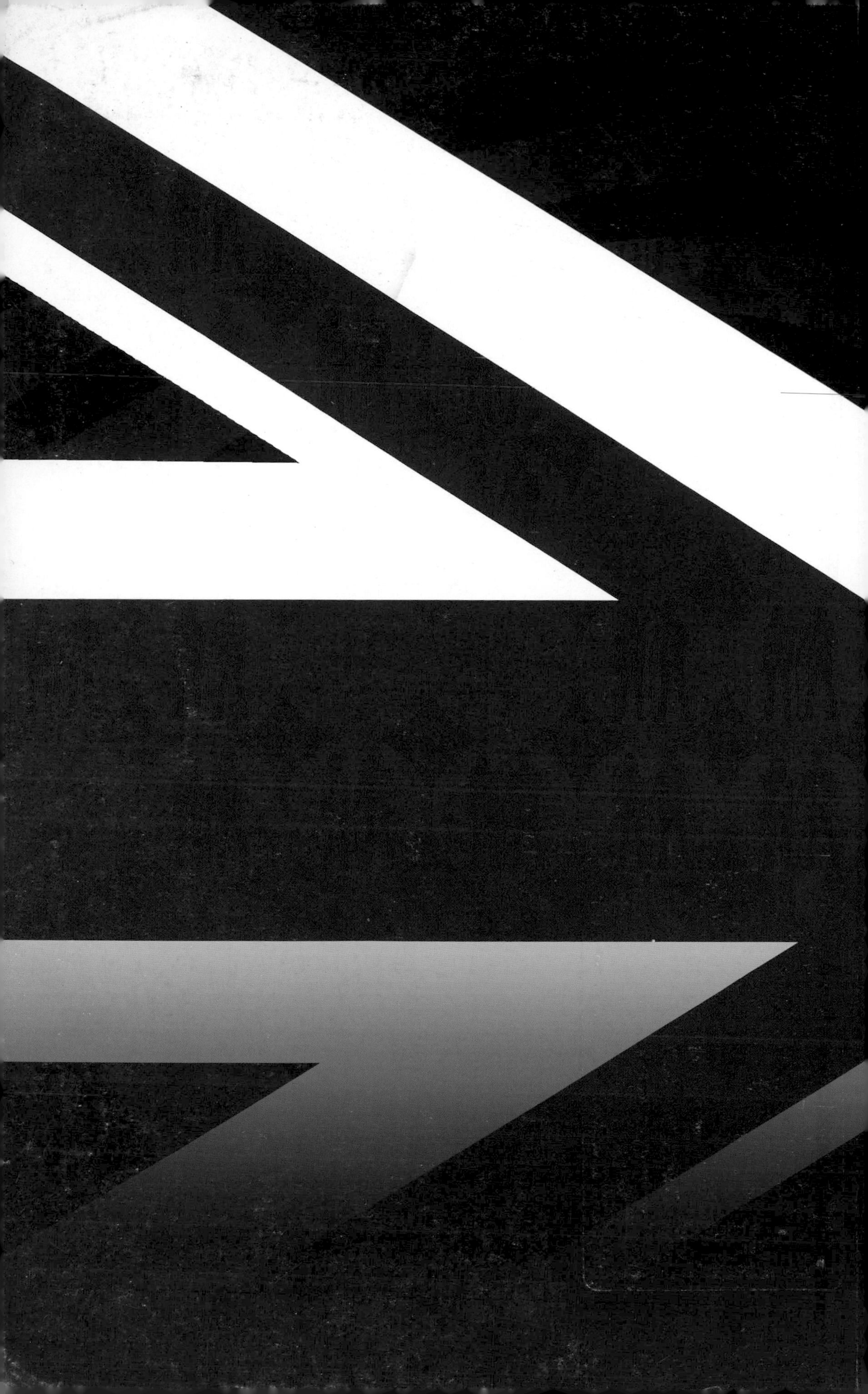